Between Seduction
and Inspiration: Man

Between Seduction and Inspiration: Man

Jean Laplanche

Translated and with an introduction
by Jeffrey Mehlman

New York:
The Unconscious in Translation

Between Seduction and Inspiration: Man was originally published as
Entre séduction et inspiration: l'homme
ISBN 213049945
© Press Universitaires de France, 1999
108, boulevard Saint-Germain, 75006 Paris

Cover art: *David Garrick with his Wife Eva-Maria Veigel*
c. 1757–64
painting by William Hogarth (1697–1764)

ISBN 978-1-942254-05-8
Library of Congress Control Number: 2015939008

CONTENTS

Interpreting [with] Laplanche

On the occasion of the recent publication in English of the volume titled *Dictionary of Untranslatables*,[1] a translation of Barbara Cassin's massive *Vocabulaire européen des philosophies: Dictionnaire des intraduisibles*[2] and a volume saluted on its appearance by Adam Gopnik in the New Yorker as perhaps "the weirdest book the twenty-first century has so far produced,"[3] it was of particular interest that the very first sentence of the American edition's preface should include a telling reference to Laplanche's and Pontalis' *Vocabulaire de la psychanalyse*, identified as a key juncture in the genealogy of the more recent volume.[4] For the reference to the *Vocabulaire* at the threshold of what is arguably the century's "weirdest" book is a reminder of just how strange an accomplishment in the history of reading the Laplanche and Pontalis volume remains. And of how much it has in common with the more recent project. Like the *Dictionary of Untranslatables*, the *Vocabulaire* was, in a word, a multilingual effort, rooted in a sense that French might provide the wherewithal to pry open the distance separating (Freud's) German from itself. And that is the case even as English, and above all American English, would appear (or at least in 1967 *did* appear) to be mobilized in resistance to that very attempt at prying open the German.[5]

---

1 *Dictionary of Untranslatables: A Philosophical Lexicon*, trans. Steven Rendall, Christian Hubert, Jeffrey Mehlman, Nathanael Stein, Michael Syrotinski (Princeton: Princeton University Press, 2014).

2 Barbara Cassin, *Vocabulaire européen des philosophies: Dictionnaire des intraduisibles* (Paris: Seuil and Dictionnaires Robert, 2004).

3 Adam Gopnik, "Word Magic" in *The New Yorker,* May 26, 2014, p. 36.

4 *Vocabulaire de la psychanalyse* (Paris: P.U.F., 1967). Translated by D. Nicholson-Smith, *The Language of Psychoanalysis* (New York: Norton, 1974).

5 The entire sequence resembles a parody of de Gaulle's reading of World War II: it would have fallen to the French to split the German citadel in two were it not for the Anglo-American pact to ensure that such a defeat (of the Germans by the French) not take place. De Gaulle's reaction to the American invasion of North Africa in 1942, which took place without French participation, was to voice the hope that Vichy would drive America back into the Mediterranean. See Stacy Schiff, *Saint-Exupéry: A Biography* (New York: Knopf, 1994), pp. 389-390.

Now one reason we know all this is that Laplanche himself culled the most important lessons to be gleaned from the *Vocabulaire* in a separate volume titled *Life and Death in Psychoanalysis*.[6] Here is how that reading worked. For each of a series of key terms in Freud, Laplanche succeeded in demonstrating that there were two apparently incompatible concepts at work. Moreover, if one were to string together the first of those meanings for each doubly inscribed term, one would arrive at an interpretative scheme which we may call Scheme A. And if one were to string together the second meaning for each of those terms, one would arrive at a second interpretative scheme, which we may call Scheme B.

We are thus left with two interpretative schemes, A and B, battling it out to invest a single terminological apparatus.[7] But this is only the beginning. For the most important phase of Laplanche's reading, which he never made as explicit as he might have, is that whereas one scheme, say: B, seemed to exist in total ignorance or innocence of the other (scheme A), what A turned out to mediate was nothing so much as a theory of the inevitability of the error constituted by the second scheme (B). Put in other terms: if Freud's ultimate subject were a certain irreducibility of repression, then his theory of repression itself would be subject to being repressed—whence the inevitability of the error about psychoanalysis or repression itself constituted by what we have called Scheme B, a different interpretation of the very same words that had been used to elaborate the theory of repression in the first place.

---

6 *Vie et mort en psychanalyse* (Paris: Flammarion, 1970). English translation by J. Mehlman, *Life and Death in Psychoanalysis* (Baltimore: Johns Hopkins University Press, 1976).

7 The two interpretive schemes were identifiable early on as either quintessentially French (structuralist) or American (ego psychological). (See *French Freud: Structural Readings in Psychoanalysis*, ed. J. Mehlman, *Yale French Studies*, p. 48, 1972.) Eventually Laplanche would categorize them as either "Copernican" (A) or "Ptolemaic" (B). That opposition is maintained in the current volume.

Such was the Laplanchian lesson to be derived from a systematic reading of the *Vocabulaire de la psychanalyse*: psychoanalysis as a kind of self-consuming artifact. And the structure of that reading was that of a criss-cross or chiasmus.

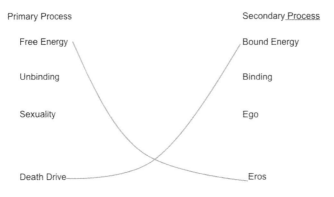

Jean Laplanche, *Life and Death in Psychoanalysis*: Chiasmus informing the evolution of Freud's thought.

At a certain point, the "pleasure principle," the soul of libidinal circulation in the unconscious, becomes the name of the nourishing principle of Eros, as it builds larger and larger libidinal units, i.e., as it ultimately comes to figure the narcissistically constituted ego, which is on the side of repression rather than on the side of what is repressed…

In summary: the unconscious is a structure that tends to play havoc with every deliberate speech act, and the shape of that structure is a chiasmus.

And then, as Laplanche began to consolidate his theory, it seemed to some of us–who saw in *Life and Death in Psychoanalysis* a touchstone or *nec plus ultra* of readerly complexity– the model changed. Consider the following: one of the more exquisite moments in Laplanche's reading of Freud coincided with the implicit realization that the movement whereby the drive, *leaning* or *propped* on the instinct, attained autonomy was inseparable from a residual form of "seduction" whereby the adult unconscious succeeded in virtually "seducing" or displacing or peeling off the drive, become a kind of "new foundation" for whatever might be at stake in psychoanalysis, from the instinct. The genesis from within of the drive, "leaning" or "propped" on the instinct, would be ultimately inseparable from the genesis from without by seduction, and that no matter how complicated the deferred or split temporality of the process.[8]

And then, in a book called *Nouveaux fondements pour la psychanalyse*, everything changed.[9] The "new foundation" was to be the seduction theory itself and it would assume its new importance at the expense of the very "propping" of what was after all the "new foundation" of the drive. The very term "new foundation" in Laplanche seemed to participate in a logic of double inscription of the sort that Laplanche had identified in Freud. The result was less the shimmering, differential beauty of what has always seemed to me one of the great acts of reading of the twentieth century than a will to assert the fundamental anthropological truth of the human condition, which is that a variety of seduction, the basis of the unconscious, was the ontological ground of our humanity.

And what was seduction as newly construed by Laplanche? Not, as Freud developed and later, in his September 1897 letter to Wilhelm Fliess, famously abandoned, a hypothesis of sexual assault, but

---

8The split temporality of the trauma is the focus of Chapter II of *Life and Death*. My translation of *Anlehnung* (or *étayage*) as "propping" was never fully accepted by Laplanche, who preferred "leaning-on." On the other hand, "propping," I am told by Cathy Caruth, was received by the critic Harold Bloom as a master stroke because of its resonance with Wordsworth's characterization of the maternal breasts in Book II of *The Prelude* as "the props of my affections." Meanwhile, John Fletcher, a major scholar and translator of Laplanche's work, has suggested, in a move that deserves to be included in Cassin's *Dictionary of Untranslatables*, that "propping" is indeed the right translation for the French term *étayage*, but that *étayage* is inadequate as a translation for the original *Anlehnung*. On Bloom and "propping," see Cathy Caruth, *Empirical Truths and Critical Fictions: Locke, Wordsworth, Kant, Freud*, pp. 44-45 ((Baltimore,: Johns Hopkins University Press, 2009).
9*Nouveaux fondements pour la psychanalyse* (Paris: P.U.F., 1987). English translation by David Macey, *New Foundations for Psychoanalysis* (London: Blackwell. 1989).

nothing that might be considered as essentially structural either.

No, the "new foundation," the very core of the unconscious, was to be a speech act of sorts, contaminated by unconscious sexuality on the adult's part and which the child or infant spends a lifetime misinterpreting over and again in an attempt to figure out what the aim of that speech act might have been. Think of it rather as the "*confuses paroles*" of Baudelaire's signature poem "Correspondances," the confused words emitted by the "*vivants piliers*," the animate pillars or strangely insensitive parents, stony in their impassiveness. Or rather: the unconscious per se would be composed of the failures and residues of such acts of interpretation or translation (of those "*confuses paroles*"), precisely what resists translation, which, it may be recalled, was Robert Frost's definition of poetry.

Above all, the unconscious, in Laplanche's new dispensation (and to the extent that it was the precipitate of a perverse speech act of sorts), was not to be understood in terms of structure. In Laplanche's terms: "Has there ever been anything less sexual than Sophocles' tragedy?"[10] The Oedipus complex, to the extent that its function was structural, was on the side of repression and not, as the Lacanians (but also Freud) would have it, on the side of the repressed.

	Structure	Speech Act
Laplanche I *(Life and Death)*	Unconscious	Ego
Laplanche II *(New Foundations)*	Ego	Unconscious

Chiasmus informing the evolution of Laplanche's thought

---

10 Chapter 11 in this volume.

In sum, in the fullness of its evolution, Laplanche's work assumed the shape of a chiasmus as much as Laplanche's reading suggested Freud's did. An original configuration which saw a structural unconscious potentially playing havoc with every speech act, the province of the ego, gave way to an unconscious elicited by a speech act and which might only be (further) repressed by anything smacking of the structural, said to be the province of the ego.

Consider now an exemplary case of the genesis of the unconscious as it surfaces in the first chapter of Laplanche's *Entre séduction et inspiration : l'homme*, which dates from 1992.[11] It takes us from seduction (in the familiar sense) to revelation (of a religious sort) by way of persecution (as exemplified by what Laplanche regarded as Freud's most probing text on religion, the analysis of the Schreber case). Throughout, Laplanche's focus is to shore up the claims for a kind of primal address emanating from the other and quite distinct from any projection of fantasy allowing one to pull the rabbit of otherness solipsistically out of the hat of selfhood.

Now on the subject of religious revelation, Laplanche is quite idiosyncratic. He calls on the German idealist philosopher J. G. Fichte, patron saint of German nationalism at its most fanatical, but precisely from a period in his career that preceded his "delusional" idealism, an idealism no less delusional, we are told, than that period of Freud's thought in which he too was intent on generating an outside solely on the basis of an imagined interiority. For before the delusional idealism, Laplanche tells us, Fichte had published a highly original text on religion titled *Attempt at a Critique of All Revelation*.[12] And it is this pre-idealist text of Fichte that corresponds, in Laplanche's mind, to the period of Freud's thought when the seduction hypothesis, in however crude a manner, was still available as an option for Freud.

---

11 Chapter 1 in this volume.
12 Translated by G. Green (Cambridge: Cambridge University Press, 2010).

Specifically, what interests Fichte is the dimension of address in which every act of revelation seems rooted. Revelation is inseparable from the enigma of whatever the revealer *intends* by what it is that he reveals. Laplanche is much taken with this idea and particularly with the German term used by Fichte: *Bekanntmachung* or "making known." Now no sooner does Laplanche attend to this word than he seems to relinquish the possibility of translating it, telling us that *Bekanntmachung*, was the heading on notices plastered to the walls during the German occupation, which, out of derision, or perhaps through the influence of surrealism, "we" had deformed into *"bécane machin."* Such is an example in a nominally theoretical text on the unconscious of what Laplanche calls the "refuse (*déchet*) of translation."

Now the phrase *"becane machin"* in French has been translated by Philip Slotkin in Britain as the "thingummy contraption," which, of course, nicely captures the "anything goes," "n'importe quoi," or "floating signifier" aspect of the unconscious.[13] (Years earlier, I had reached the conclusion that what was uncanny about the Freudian concept of the uncanny was that absolutely anything might become uncanny.)[14]

At the same time, how bizarre that the signage of the Nazi occupation (with its proclamation of *Bekanntmachung*) should provide a model, however twisted, of the unconscious… More curious still when one realizes that Laplanche offers in a footnote in the same text as an example of seduction per se, executed indirectly by German soldiers in the only French available to them, the words: *"Promenade, mademoiselle?"*

So: of the three categories investigated in his text—seduction, persecution, and revelation—both revelation (*Bekanntmachung*) and seduction (*"Promenade, mademoiselle?"*) brought him and me, his reader, back to World War II and the German occupation. Not so for persecution, which is illustrated by a speculative reading of the

---

13 J. Laplanche, *Essays on Otherness* (London: Routledge, 1999), p. 184.
14 See J. Mehlman, *"Poe pourri*: Lacan's Seminar on 'The Purloined Letter'" in *Aesthetics Today*, ed. M. Philipson and P. Gudel, (New York: Meridian, 1980), p. 425.

Schreber case—without apparent reference to the war.[15] But then the connection between persecution and the occupation was so direct as to make it only minimally available to investment by the unconscious. And then, I was taken aback by an echo provoked in me, but perhaps in Laplanche as well, by the very model of the enigmatic message as he conceived it. The focus is a kind of exclusion of the recipient: "Je te montre…quelque chose que, par définition, tu ne peux comprendre…"[16] The words were a virtual transcription of a sentence once addressed to me in a restaurant in the Place des Vosges by Jacques Lacan: "Je vais vous dire quelque chose que vous n'allez pas comprendre…" I had asked his opinion of the recently published *Anti-Oedipe*, an anti-Freudian collaboration between Gilles Deleuze and Félix Guattari. His answer was that to appreciate his thoughts on Deleuze and Guattari's book I would have to read him (Lacan) on Dr. Schreber, the very figure who would be the focus of Laplanche's development on "persecution" in the text under consideration.

If there were such a thing as a "convergence of unconsciouses" (Laplanche's?, my own?), I seemed to be heading there.

Let us return to the *Bekanntmachung* (let it be known) or *bécane machin* (thingummy contraption) culled from Fichte, in a text originally published by Fichte anonymously in 1792 and widely attributed to Kant, Fichte having, so to speak, *be-Kanted* himself. Now in the course of retranslating the volume in which the *Bekanntmachung* comments of Laplanche appear and wishing to come up with something more acceptable to American ears than the "thingummy contraption" of British provenance, I discovered that the primary meaning of *bécane* in French is in fact a "machine." For better or worse, I came up with "whatchamacallit" for *machin* and thus for the entire phrase the "whatchamacallit machine." This meant, of course, that the lexi-

---

15 Chapter 1 in this volume, see page 40 ff..
16 "I will show you…something which, by definition, you are not going to understand."

cal match was not between "machine" and *machin*, but chiastically, between "machine" and *bécane*.

I remain enough of a Laplanchian to want to say that this was what he, in *Life and Death*, would term a "call to order," to chiastic order, coming from the unconscious. It will be recalled that chiasmus was the figure structuring Freud's metapsychology in *Life and Death*, but also the figure structuring the relation between speech act and structure in the transition from *Life and Death* to *New Foundations*. So the chiastic switch or swerve from English "machine" away from French "*machin*" was, as it were, a call back to chiasmus and the beauties of *Life and Death*, a book that had transfixed me.

But I sensed there was something deeper. About thirty years ago, in a text I called "Writing and Deference: The Politics of Literary Adulation" (a title for which Derrida never forgave me), I found myself attending to a series of texts by Jean Paulhan and particularly to speculations related to what he called a linguistic "principle of counteridentity," centered on the role played by homophonic antonyms.[17] The example that most intrigued me involved the reversal at the core of the apparent transcription of German *Sauerkraut* into French *choucroute*. For what most intrigued Paulhan was that despite appearances, *Kraut* was translated not by *croute* but by *croute*'s diacritical other, *chou*.

Switch now to Laplanche (as he now reappears in English) and the case of *Bekanntmachung* or *bécane machin*. What is most interesting in English "whatchamacallit machine" is that English "machine," despite appearances, does not translate *machin*, but its chiastic other, "*bécane*."

But things can be taken further. In *De la paille et du grain* ("The

---

17See J. Mehlman, "Writing and Deference: The Politics of Literary Adulation" in *Genealogies of the Text: Literature, Psychoanalysis, and Politics in Modern France* (Cambridge: Cambridge University Press, 1995), p. 105. Laplanche, in this volume, observes that the word *Rückbildung*, which might be translated as "deconstruction," would have been an entirely appropriate name for psychoanalysis as Laplanche views it, were it not for the fact that an "alien" philosophical tradition had laid claim to it," p. 252.

Wheat and the Chaff"), the text of 1947 in which Paulhan offered his excursus on linguistic "counteridentity," he presented a political coefficient to the very structure of counteridentity we have been discussing. After the war, Paulhan, who was a hero of the Resistance, claimed that there was no basis for the Comité national des écrivains (CNE), organ of the Resistance, to claim the moral high ground since its members, before the war, had nursed dreams of collaborating… with Moscow. Even as the wartime collaborationists had been preparing their French-patriotic resistance to just such a collaboration before the war. Such would be the chiastic principle of counteridentity as it worked its way through French politics before, during, and after the war, and such would be the basis of the amnesty for acts of collaboration–*and resistance*–that Paulhan, himself a hero in the Resistance, would call for. *Résistants* with the souls of collaborators; collaborators with the souls of *résistants*. *Bonnet blanc et blanc bonnet*, as Paulhan put it in 1947 in a political context. Or: *Sauerkraut* and *choucroute* in a linguistic one. To which we may add, thanks to Laplanche, *Bekanntmachung /"bécane machin"* in a psychoanalytic context that is not without political reverberations.[18]

But by now the reader will have perceived the extent to which questions of translation, which Laplanche placed at the heart of psychoanalysis, have led me to unconscious concerns that may be as much my own as Laplanche's.[19] I have never been psychoanalyzed or at least I felt I had never been psychoanalyzed until my last visit with Laplanche at the Chateau de Pommard. He was connected to his oxygen tank and would die not long after. He had read my memoir, *Adventures in the French Trade*, commenting, to my bemusement:

---

18 "*Bécane machin*," the reverse repetition of *Bekanntmachung*, is a phrase used to refer to a second-hand bicycle. I have the distinct recollection of Laplanche telling me that when in the Resistance, his task was to convey secret messages concealed in the tire or handle-bar of his bike. The relation between the call to collaboration (*Bekanntmachung*) and the act of resistance it was made to conceal (in a *bécane machin*) is a model whose pertinence would appear to be both psychoanalytical and political.
19 See below p. 11.

"J'y ai bien reconnu tes amours anti-sémites."[20] The implication was that any subject of ongoing fascination can only be sustained by a libidinal investment. (And French anti-semitism, as a glance at my bibliography made clear, had long since become a subject of fascination for me.[21]) For better or worse I felt that afternoon that I had been analyzed by Jean Laplanche.

And if I had missed his point, it was as though he had repeated it at the end of the text on seduction, persecution, and revelation. For the principal example of the kind of address he associated with revelation (i.e., the *Bekanntmachung* and all the freight it bears with it) is the very essence of the Jewish faith and the enigmatic message at its core: "*Shema Yisrael*: Hear O Israel!" The entire Bible is said to be an expansion of that imperative and its call to translate.

But where does that leave us? Or rather, since psychoanalysis, if it is to have any validity, must be highly individualized, where did that leave me? The answer, at its most succinct, is that it left me in a world stretched taut between *Bekanntmachung* (or the Nazi occupation of France) and *Shema Yisrael* (or the epitome of Judaism). It was a world of life and death, *vie et mort*, and it was the world into which, at the beginning of 1944, but in the United States, I was born.

And there, via Laplanche, lay the opening of a world in which I experienced a certain revelation almost fifty years ago, bearing the name of *Vie et mort en psychanalyse*. For I have spent a considerable part of my life as a reader attempting to rediscover the kind of complexity that Laplanche had revealed in Freud, but displaced onto—or infused into—other texts.

And such would be the *transfert en creux*, the "hollowed out transference" to which Laplanche would direct me, allowing its

---

20 "I did indeed recognize your anti-semitic loves in it." See *Adventures in the French Trade: Fragments Toward a Life* (Stanford: Stanford University Press, 2010).

21 The most pertinent text in this context would be my *Legacies of Anti-Semitism in France* (Minneapolis: University of Minnesota Press, 1983).

wound to stay open in the enigma of the several words he addressed to me and which I have ever since found it difficult to transcribe without a tremor: "*J'y ai bien reconnu tes amours antisémites.*"[22]

Jeffrey Mehlman
November, 2014

***

Several of the essays in this book have been translated before. I have benefited in particular from consulting the careful work of Philip Slotkin ("Seduction, Persecution, Revelation" in Laplanche: *Essays on Otherness*, ed. J. Fletcher, London: Routledge, 1999); Luke Thurston ("Psychoanalysis as Anti-Hermeneutics" in Radical Philosophy, 79, September-October 1996); and John Fletcher ("Narrativity and Hermeneutics" and "Sublimation and/or Inspiration," both in New Formations, 48, Winter 2002-3).

—J. M.

---

22 For my own premonition of what Laplanche had intuited, see my introduction to *Genealogies of the Text*, pp. 1-6.

Editorial note

Decisions about translating Laplanche's writing into English have largely been left to each translator. The translations however have been reviewed for terminological consistency and to some degree for some consistency of style. We have taken account of the fact that some of Laplanche's published texts appear to be transcriptions of lectures and that the copy editing of published texts is sometimes less than perfect.

 With Laplanche's encouragement, UIT decided to publish the English translations of his work in more or less reverse chronological order. *Sexual: La sexualité élargie au sens freudien*, containing his major work from 2000 to 2006, was the last volume to be published in his lifetime. Laplanche was eager to be involved in the translation of his work, generous with his time, and gracious in his assistance. The English translation–"Freud and the *Sexual*"–benefited directly from his guidance. With one important exception, the decisions made for that volume have been carried forward to rest of the UIT series. The note below addresses some issues we faced and offers brief explanations of the decisions made.

Jonathan House
General Editor

Âme/animique – soul/psychical/mental

Laplanche argued that the German *Seele* has the same religious philosophical resonances as does the French *âme* and so *âme* and *animique* should be used for *Seele* and *seelisch* etc. We think the situation is different for 'soul' not only because its use in the sense of 'mind' or 'psyche' is less common in English than is the case for *âme* and *Seele* in French and German, but because adjectival forms 'soulical' and 'soulish', while they exist, are so rare that their use in these texts would be distracting, if not confusing. So, except in rare instances, such as 'apparatus of the soul', we have used 'mind' or 'psyche' and their derivatives.

Après-coup – **après-coup**

Freud's used the word *Nachträglichkeit* which is an unusual substantive form of the everyday German adjective *nachträglich* (afterwards). Laplanche suggested that the neologism 'afterwardsness' be used as the English translation of the term. We have decided otherwise.

Laplanche said more than once that Lacan had the merit of being the first to recognize the conceptual importance of the notion. It was, however, Laplanche and Pontalis in "The Language of Psychoanalysis" who first theorized the concept and it was Laplanche who later developed the theorization more fully. If concepts have nationality, après-coup is French. In the years since Laplanche first advocated 'afterwardsness', the word 'après-coup' has become common in Anglophone psychoanalytic discourse. For that reason, starting with the present volume, we have decided to use après-coup as the English term for the concept.

Drive/Instinct

All quotations from the Standard Edition in which the word 'instinct' is used to render *Trieb* in the original German have been modified to replace 'instinct' with 'drive'.

Étayage – **leaning-on**

Étayage is the French translation of the German word *Anlehnung* which Stratchey, in the Standard Edition, renders as 'anaclisis' – a cognate of the Greek *anaklinein* (ἀνακλίνω - *leaning on*). In translating Laplanche's work there is a long standing debate about the relative merits of translating *étayage* by 'leaning-on' or by 'propping'. In Jeffrey Mehlman's translation of *Life and Death*, he used 'propping' often in the reflexive form. Laplanche preferred 'leaning-on' to emphasize the activity of the drive leaning-on the instinct, an activity which tends to be obscured. For this series, we have chosen to use 'leaning-on'.

Étrangèreté – **strangerness**

Étrangèreté is a neologism combining the meanings of *étrange*, 'strange', and *étranger*, 'foreigner'. We render it with the neologism "strangerness" which we hope conveys the same meaning and evokes more or less the same associations.

Théorie de la séduction généralisée – **General Theory of Seduction**

Some translators have rendered the phrase 'theory of generalized seduction' which is a reasonable choice but loses the echo of the distinction between Einstein's general and restricted theories of relativity. The restricted theory of seduction is Freud's theory of seduction, and it is specific in the sense that it explains the origins of specific psychopathologic entities: hysteria and other neuroses of defense. The General Theory of Seduction is concerned with the origin of the human subject.

Between Seduction
and Inspiration: Man

Introduction

This volume assembles my principal writings of recent years (1992–1998). The reader, moving from text to text, will occasionally encounter what may appear to be recurrences. These are but the reflection of a theme whose persistence justifies the title of the collection, an overriding motif that might be characterized as that of the "fundamental anthropological situation."

To the extent that contemporary psychoanalysis is bent on inquiring into its very foundations, it is traversed by major oppositions: those between "biology" and "psychogenesis"; "nature" and "culture"; and, more urgently, to the extent that it is more closely related to our practice, that between a classical view, in which childhood is considered to be what determines the adult's fate, and a "hermeneutic" option, which makes of the adult the grand master of interpretation who alone confers a meaning on the data of childhood.

It should be noted that these three types of opposition are far from overlapping. In particular, viewing childhood, "nature" (indeed animality), and the biological as coinciding may lead to the most serious conceptual confusions. To take but two examples, the notorious Freudian "bedrock of the biological" turns out to be initially linked not to actual biology but to the perception, itself broadly humanized, of the morphological difference of the sexes. Similarly, there is every reason to think that, within the development of the human individual, biological or instinctual sexuality appears not before but *after* a drive-based infantile sexuality, which is linked to fantasy and altogether informed by the interhuman relation.

But let us return to the apparently less debatable opposition, that between a before and an after, between the child and the adult. It was to little avail that, on this subject, Freud introduced the prophetic term *Nachträglichkeit* (après-coup*), for it remains indefinitely riven between two apparently irreconcilable interpretations: a delayed determinism of the present by the past or, inversely, a sovereign retroactive attribution of meaning, the casting into hermeneutical narrative form of the past by the present.

Without claiming to invalidate the opposition between determinism and hermeneutics, I attempt, on the contrary, to mobilize and displace it, recalling in the register of psychoanalysis proper something that we keep forgetting: before and after, the adult and the *infans*, "before" succeeding each other, are "initially" coexistent realities joined in a primal act of communication. "Initially" or "from the outset"? Let us risk a strange formula. There is a "first case" of the "before-after" opposition; there is an "initial impulse" that sets the opposition "before/après-coup" into motion.

In the "fundamental anthropological situation" confronting adult and *infans*, the dissymmetry is structural. It is not, in essence, the distinction between parent and child since even in the absence of parents it can exist between a child and a specific "succoring" adult (Freud). It is not reducible to a difference in age, experience, or knowledge. The difference, which even psychoanalysts have a tendency to forget, is quite simply that one of the parties does not yet have a sexual unconscious and the other one does.

The theory of seduction can *hold* against its abandonment or eclipse only if one takes fully into account, within the original situation, on the one hand the factor of communication and on the other the insinuation of the adult's unconscious in his own message.

The *other* at stake here is a concrete other inhabited by some-

* [See Editorial Note on terminology pages xix–xxi]

thing "unknown to itself" and not an "instance" or "agency" (such as a Lacanian A or *a*, concerning which one would be hard-pressed to say if either one has an unconscious).

Post-Freudian thought seems to have assigned itself the task of effecting a reduction of the Freudian unconscious, which is individual and real, the "psychical reality" whose existence is, moreover, endlessly imposed on us by the analytic situation. For such is the true "bedrock" that—without being in any way biological or animal—is no less "resistant."

The primacy of the other and its enigma is not necessarily "closed down" when the concrete adult-child relation disappears. It constitutes the very heart of the analytic situation as well as of what one might attempt to describe as an opening onto—and by way of—*inspiration*.

I

Seduction, Persecution, Revelation

To Jean-Pierre Maïdani-Gérard

I will not conceal my strategy. It consists in three propositions:

(1) I say "seduction," and the response is, "Of course, a fantasy of seduction."

(2) The psychotic says "persecution," and the response is, "Of course, a delusion of persecution."

(3) The religious individual says "revelation," and the response is, "Of course, a myth of revelation."

"Of course," is uttered in the three cases. "Of course" is a dismissal of the idea that the neurotic, the psychotic, and the religious individual must "in some sense be right." That phrase comes from Freud, but when he assumes this point of view it is in reference to the *content* of the symptom. And it should be stated that when it comes to the content of fantasies, delusions, and beliefs, there are a plethora of interpretations. But here I would like to proceed a good deal further, uncovering a "rightness" to be found in the very *form* of the assertion: seducing, persecuting, and revealing, after all, are active verbs, and it is that activity of the other that I intend to examine.

The one who replies "of course" is Freud—and everyone else. That is if it is indeed true that the tendency of the human being is to deny and reincorporate alterity and true that Freud's theoretical ten-

Presented at the Journées de l'Association psychanalytique de France, December 12, 1992. *Psychanalyse à l'Université* 18, no. 72 (1993): 3–34.

dency reproduces this closure and process of recentering.

Is it paradoxical that the most radical discovery of alterity, the discovery by psychoanalysis of that "other thing" in me, and of the connecting of that other thing to the other person, should end up—by way of its various reformulations—in an ever tidier recentering?

That repetitive motion of closure in Freud is not, however, linear and unidirectional. There are various paths leading, for example, from seduction to a fantasy of seduction, then from that fantasy to the biological, or even, at a different level, from drive (*Trieb*) to instinct (*Instinkt*). In reading attentively a late text, such as the *Moses*, one perceives that the return to the term "instinct" is far more insistent and extensive than had been suspected.[1]

Preliminary to this analysis, and before embarking on my three themes, the three cases of decentering and recentering, I would like to situate it as echoing the thoughts of Guy Rosolato, particularly his recent paper on "primal fantasies and their corresponding myths."[2]

Such echoes simultaneously entail resonances and harmonics, which run deep, but also divergences, concerning which Rosolato alone can determine whether they are minor or significant.

Seduction

My first theme, then, will be the opposition between *seduction* and *fantasy of seduction*, in which I accord priority to seduction over fantasy. For which reason I will appear to some to be a gentle or—depending on the context—fearsome lunatic. Don't we all know where every unitary perspective leads? Doesn't psychoanalysis teach us plural-

---

1 For example: "We find that in a number of important relations our children react, not in a manner corresponding to their own experience, but instinctively, like animals, in a manner that is only explicable as a phylogenetic acquisition." Sigmund Freud, *Standard Edition of the Complete Psychological Works of Sigmund Freud* (1939), 23:132–33. Further references to the *Standard Edition*, ed. James Strachey (London: Hogarth, 1956–1974), appear in the text as SE, followed by volume and page number.
2 "Les fantasmes originaires et leurs mythes correspondants," in *La Nouvelle revue de psychanalyse*, 46 Fall (1992): 223–46.

ism, plurality, and even juxtaposition—the very kind of juxtaposition that prevails in the unconscious where everything persists side by side without any need for synthesis. "Alongside" seduction, it will be objected with an obstinacy no less forceful than my own, are there not "also" other scenarios that are no less important or "primal?" What could be more primal than the primal scene? More fundamental than castration? And more primordial than a return to the womb?

Why then accord a privilege to seduction among the three or four principal scenarios? Why not, moreover—an additional bit of stubbornness—accept the little word that would reconcile us all: "fantasy *of?*" After all, isn't psychoanalysis centered on fantasies? Does not the practice of analysis postulate fantasy as the sole realm in which—from beginning to end—it functions?[3]

The two objections I receive are, finally, only one: forgetting

---

3 I will play the devil's advocate here, but a devil who wins a majority of the votes. Initially, in analytic treatment, the fundamental rule would entail a reduction to the subjective level; and the latter, in turn, a situating of all contents on the same level. "There is no index of reality in the unconscious," Freud recalls when explaining the abandonment of his theory in 1897. But Freud, without precaution, extends that absence of an index of reality to the treatment itself; no doubt because of the fact that treatment, to a certain extent, is intent on staying as close to the unconscious as possible. To say everything and to do nothing but "say" things implies, to be sure, a growing unreality of what is "said," and does so to the benefit of the imagination. But, starting from there, every confusion becomes possible: pretending that the psychological reality of treatment is the psychical reality of the unconscious; pretending that the discourse of treatment succeeds in abolishing the referential dimension of every utterance, etc. I have discussed at length the modalities of this reduction of the analytic situation to illusion in *Problématiques V: Le baquet. Transcendance du transfert* (Paris: PUF, 1987), pp. 88–134.

As for the purpose of treatment, it appears to be the consensus—and, as it were, the lowest common denominator—that its aim is to fully assume the position of the person who says "I." The grammatical quibbles over "Wo Es war, soll Ich werden" are interesting, to be sure, but whether Freud's *Ich* is an ego and/or an I, ultimately what "must come to be" is always a recentering; cf. Jean Laplanche, *La Révolution copernicienne inachevée* (Paris: Aubier, 1992), pp. 32–35. This is also frequently the case for Lacan: more than one of his formulations brings us to the ideal of a "full utterance," that is, finally, an utterance centered on itself. We will see, however, that his contribution extends further than that.

that seduction is a fantasy and erroneously attributing to it priority over other factors that are no less primal. If seduction is only a fantasy, it has no right to precedence over the other productions of *my* fantasy life. Primal scene and castration are among imaginings that are equivalent as scenarios created by me under pressure of drive or desire.

On the other hand, to maintain the *reality of seduction* is to affirm its priority or primacy in relation to other "primal" scenarios.

Is *seduction* more real than the observation of the primal scene? In the name of what experimental or statistical confirmation might I sustain such an absurdity? Similarly, one might very well challenge me to prove that children are masturbated by an adult any more often than they are threatened with castration by that adult. And that is because the entire matter lies with the term *reality*, the kind of reality involved. What is at stake is knowing whether or not psychoanalysis has contributed anything new in this realm, whether or not it has succeeded in affirming the existence of a *third register of reality*.[4]

"Psychical reality": I have on more than one occasion insisted on the fact that Freud posited this term as the *index* of an entirely distinct realm in the psyche, but also that he failed to maintain any consistency in its definition as, precisely, different from the reality of the psychological realm in general. The *psychological* reality is the fact that, in any event, it is *I who think* "seduction," that the seduction cannot be anything other than my way of apprehending it. In relation to the psychological, *material* reality can be distinguished easily: it consists of the observable sexual gestures. But as soon as one stops to think about it, the "observable" dimension very quickly becomes debatable. Observable if we are dealing with a genital conception of sexuality: touching the child's penis can undoubtedly be considered an actual seduction. But touching the lips or touching the anus? Shall

---

4 As it happens, my first stammering communication to the analytic community, many years ago, was delivered to the Société française de la psychanalyse on the theme of "reality in neurosis and psychosis." "La réalité dans la névrose et la psychose" (Paris: Société française de psychanalyse, 1961).

we say that there is seduction because these are preformed erogenous zones? But, despite appearances, such a conception remains pre-Freudian once one is prepared to admit along with Freud that the entirety of the body is, at the outset, a potentially erogenous zone. Starting from that basic postulate, what is the status of the gesture of touching the child's big toe? Is it a case of seduction or not? On what condition does it become a seduction? What kind of *reality* is in play? What are the "indices" of that reality?

The solution that suggests itself is the presence of a sexual fantasy *in the adult*. But here a distinction must be made: either one postulates an immaterial communication from unconscious to unconscious, fantasy to fantasy, which would be to postulate in an altogether unjustified way the prior existence of fantasy and an unconscious in the baby. Or one begins to entertain the idea that there exists a *tertiary domain of reality*, which is neither the pure materiality of the gesture (assuming it is capable of being isolated) nor the pure psychology of the protagonists(s).

Reality of the message, irreducibility of the fact of communication. What psychoanalysis adds to the mix emerges from its experience, namely the fact that the message is frequently compromised——at once bungled and successful.[5] Opaque to whoever receives it, and opaque as well to whoever emits it. Put simply, seduction is neither more nor less real than a parapraxis or slip. The reality of a slip is not reducible to its materiality. A slip is neither more nor less real materially than a correctly pronounced word. But neither is a slip reducible to the fantasies forged in relation to it by each of its interlocutors, fantasies that are often quite poor and reductive. It conveys a message that is detectable, observable, and partially interpretable by psychoanalysis. It is as a function of this *tertiary domain of reality* and not as a function of material reality that I persist in saying

---

5 It is noteworthy that the *Introductory Lectures on Psychoanalysis* introduce the development of Freud's ideas not with dreams but with parapraxes, which are phenomena of communication.

"seduction," and not "fantasy of seduction."

As for the *priority* that I give it, it consists in the fact that the other principal scenarios invoked as primal or originary have a seduction at their core, in that they too convey a single or several messages from the other, always initially moving from adult to child.

I shall leave aside the return to the mother's breast and its correlative: a new birth. Freud, in a moment of great lucidity, demonstrates that it is far from being as fundamental as Jung claims. It takes root in the primal scene and is supported by the wishes issuing from it, specifically that of being sexually penetrated by the father.[6]

What interests me here is the extent to which there is *seduction, that is, an unconscious message, in the primal scene and in castration.* Insofar as the first is concerned, there is something of an exercise of force on Freud's part, which consists of wanting to construct it on the basis of only two ingredients: perceptual reality, on the one hand, and the child's fantasy, on the other, with an endless variation of proportions between them. Such is the familiar story of the Wolf Man, which I will not dwell on here. But what is never questioned is the reality that is neither purely material nor purely subjective: the adult *offering* the scene to be seen or overheard; suggesting, through a bit of behavior, a gesture, even a conjugal kiss. Is not allowing something to be seen quite often offering it up for observation? There are more explicit ways than allowing something to be seen out of negligence. When the Wolf Man's father takes his child to see animals copulating, how can one suppose that we are dealing with an innocent walk without any further intention?[7]

The primal scene conveys messages. It is traumatizing only because it proposes, indeed imposes its enigmas, which compro-

---

6 In "From the History of an Infantile Neurosis," the case history of the Wolf Man, in *SE* 17:100.

7 What could be less innocent than a stroll? I recall that, during the period of the German Occupation, the few French words known to German soldiers were "Promenade, mademoiselle?" A sexual invitation, coded as such.

mise the spectacle addressed to the child. Far be it from me to want to offer an inventory of such messages. In my view, in fact, there are no objective enigmas: the only enigmas are those that are proposed, duplicated in one way or another in the relation between the sender of the message and his own unconscious. The messages of the primal scene are quite often of violence, savagery, castration, and anality. A message of exclusion is virtually inherent in the very circumstance: I am showing you—or letting you see—something that, by definition, you cannot understand and in which you cannot participate; something defined by Melanie Klein as the "combined parent" designates precisely such an enigmatic node as a double bind.

Pontalis and I, in a slightly rhetorical passage devoted to fantasies of origin, advanced the following: "In the primal scene, it is the origin of the individual that is depicted."[8] I will posit *a posteriori* the extent of my skepticism regarding that statement and would like to be clear on the subject. We can begin by eliminating at the outset the idea of an "objective" enigma. On what basis can one in fact think that the spectacle of parental intercourse—for the little investigator who the child is—might open onto the question of fertilization and, further on, childbirth? As I maintained a moment ago, there is an enigma— as opposed to a purely scientific *problem*—only when the elements involved are to be found not in the objectivity of the data but for the person *proposing* the enigma. It is thus on the side of the adult protagonists of the primal scene that we should place ourselves in order to determine whether the enigma in question relates to origins, that is, to the procreation of the human being. We would thus be obliged to admit that human coitus is a final stage of sexuality and as that sexuality is inhabited by a desire for procreation. From the beginning, Freud was unabatingly hostile to this idea; in the *Three Essays* of 1905,

---

8 "Fantasme originaire, fantasmes des origines, origine du fantasme," *Les Temps modernes* 215 (1964): 1133–68. English translation by Jonathan House in Dominique Scarfone's *Laplanche: an Introduction* (New York : The Unconscious in Translation, 2015) p. 100

for both men and women, he proposed a genesis of sexual desire that initially is disconnected from the child's desire, and only later are links established, links that are complex, contingent, and individually quite variable.

Before intoning, on the subject of primary fantasies (and in a way that we ourselves in fact did), a series of grand philosophical questions: where do we come from? where are we going? etc., it should thus be recalled that the desire for a child, whether conscious or not, is far from being general or preponderant and far from being an irreducible dimension of sexual desire. But that does not suffice. We should also recall that Freud does not fail to take into account the questioning of the child concerning origins and procreation. But he situates it precisely *elsewhere* than in the spectacle of the primal scene: in the arrival of a younger sibling. I will add that such an arrival is not a purely objective fact either: "We're going to give you a little brother" is also an enigmatic message coming from the other.

It is interesting to observe at this juncture that Freud treats the enigmas of birth and death in precisely the same terms. It is false, he says, that the investigation of birth results "from an innate need for causality."[9] Similarly, on the subject of death, "philosophers [he says] think . . . too philosophically," seeing in it a purely intellectual enigma: the man of origins—we can also read the child—does not believe in his own death. And he doesn't wrack his brains when confronted with the corpse of his enemy."[10] Here too the *enigma is conveyed to him via the message* addressed by the other at the time of his death: the death of a beloved.

To be sure, there is a limit to the category of the message: the one sent to us by the other who is leaving us forever. I mention it only in order to recall that mourning too cannot be reconceptualized without more than the two categories: material reality and fantasy; that is,

---

9 "On the Sexual Theories of Children," in *SE* 9:212.
10 "Thoughts for the Times on War and Death," in *SE* 14:293.

without taking into account the forever interrupted message, which is irremediably interrupted.[11]

Castration: The subject is complex, infused as it is, since Lacan, with a pathos that inflates its concept to the point of making it mean indiscriminately death, finitude, and quite simply the human condition. But already in Freud it was far from simple, even if we restore it, as he never tired of insisting, to its precise anatomical, genital context. This is because it is composed of different "ingredients," which are themselves situated at different "levels."[12] At the level of "theory" (the "theory of Hans and Sigmund"), it presents itself as a response or ordering and, as such, as a rampart against anxiety.[13] But at a deeper level it partakes of the character of an enigma: always posited or proposed by the other. Among the ingredients of the enigma, I shall pause a moment at the threat of castration. And I do so in order to note that we find in Freud a kind of index of the problem I am raising, the presence and interplay of two terms: *Drohung* and *Androhung*. And in the translation of the complete works, we have carefully differentiated one from the other. *Drohung*, which we translate as threat, and *Androhung* as a threat that has been uttered: a threat that has been addressed.

A pure threat is objective: a storm may threaten (except in the case where it is assumed that Jupiter brandishes his lightning); but it is precisely in that case that it becomes an *Androhung*. But a threat that is *addressed* cannot be reduced to its mere content, as in: we're going to cut it off. It cannot be assumed to be without an unconscious substratum. A father (or a mother) uttering "we're going to cut it off" cannot be purely and simply assimilated to the Law, as has been claimed since Lacan. Reducing matters to the legalistic and univocal aspect

11 See Jean Laplanche, "Le Temps et l'autre," in *La Révolution copernicienne inachevée*, pp. 374–79.
12 Ingredients and levels which I undertook to sort out in *Problématiques II: Castration. Symbolisations* (Paris: PUF, 1980).
13 Ibid., p. 170.

seems to me to have as its principal effect a masking of the underlying unconscious wishes. Might not the threat of castration be—on the part of the person uttering it—the vector of (or cover for) still other wishes? And, to mention only the most frequent of them, the unconscious desire to penetrate.

To conclude all too briefly, with regard to the primal scene and castration, I shall say that what is lacking, in Freud as well as in Lacan, is a taking into account of the enigmatic dimension, of alterity, on the side of the child's adult protagonists: the others of the primal scene, the others of the castration threat are as though they themselves were without any relation to their own unconscious, according to Lacan's formula, which is valid as well for Freud (and which I reject): "there is no Other of the Other."

Persecution

Is the human being definitively closed in on himself? Is he irremediably Ptolemaic, centered on himself? One might think as much were it not for psychoanalysis, and even on occasion from within psychoanalysis, when one observes it straining to reconstruct an exterior, objectivity, on the basis of pure interiority. Certain psychoanalytic constructions of objectality have nothing to envy in the most complex systems, specifically in the most delusional systems of the great idealists: Berkeley, Fichte, or even Hegel. In the last case, we are confronted with what is perhaps the most radical attempt to pull the other out of the hat of the same. The fundamental idea is that of alienation, an *Entfremdung*, or an externalization, an *Entaüsserung*. But however peremptory that "exterior" (or that "stranger") might be, it is not ultimately as serious as all that. It is, in the final analysis, in order to recognize myself that I create the stranger—in order, ultimately, to reappropriate him.

Contrary to such delusions centered on the self, psychoanalysis bears the seeds of a break with the Ptolemaic perspective. The seed is present in Freud's seduction theory as well as in the transference. But psychoanalysis is also prepared to reverse that movement, as though seduction and transference were ultimately but externalizations, alienations, the essential factor being to rediscover—or recognize—oneself through them.

There are other traces as well, other evidence of this priority of the other. Among them is the superego, which I mention only in passing, and psychosis—or, more precisely, persecution.

Before turning to Schreber, I shall recount, not without certain scruples, an allegedly humorous story, which many already know; for the laughter it elicits is inseparable from its unfathomable nature. It is the story of the madman who takes himself for a grain of seed and fears being eaten by chickens. He is admitted to a psychiatric hospital and treated not only by psychiatrists but by psychoanalysts. In what is called the "critique" of the delusion, the psychoanalyst proves himself worthy of his title by going far deeper than the classical psychiatrist: he is not satisfied merely to confront the patient with reality, but explains quite clearly how, starting with the proposition "I, a man, want to devour it, a chicken," one arrives—through a denial of the wish and in keeping with a derivation whose scheme was indicated by Freud[14]—at the proposition: "He, a chicken, wants to devour me, a grain of seed." And so all is elucidated, "critiqued," and the day comes for leaving the psychiatric hospital. It's an old-style asylum, located in the provinces and in a setting rather close to nature, with a chicken coop in the courtyard. Now barely does the patient leave the psychiatrist's office and pass in front of the chicken coop than he breaks into a run. The psychiatrist catches him: "But what's going on, you were completely cured; you *know* that all this is only an error and a projection of your own wishes?" And the patient replies: "I know perfectly well that I am not a grain of seed, and I know that it can't eat

---

14 "Psychoanalytic Notes on an Autobiographical Account of a Case of Paranoia (Dementia Paranoides)," in *SE* 12:63.

me; I even know that it doesn't want to eat me, that it *can't* want to eat me. But does the chicken know it?"

The nature of the question is irreducible. It is not an affirmation; nor is it a delusional belief: the belief was reduced, explained, and internalized. A *question* about the other is not something to be explained. It is the residue of any explanation. It partakes of the realm of confidence or distrust, of what might be called "fidence."

Persecution, of course, brings us to the Schreber case, which I assume is well known and concerning which Freud notes in passing that it may well be an important contribution to the study of religious psychology. But, if you consult the chapter in Ernest Jones's *Freud* on religion, and also Freud's texts explicitly devoted to the subject, you won't find a word about the Schreber case, which indicates an astonishing impasse with regard to what remains the most complete psychoanalytic elaboration concerning an individual's relation to God. "Schreber," then, is a case of erotic persecution by Flechsig (explicitly referred to as transference from the father), then by God. We are confronted with an extraordinary religious construction, which encompasses God in his multiplicity (the God above, the God below, as well as in front and behind, etc., the examination of souls, nerves, etc.), his relation to man, which consists of revelation and a fundamental incomprehension. It is something that, from my point of view—which is that of seduction—is quite extraordinary: God understands nothing of men and, we can undoubtedly add, he understands nothing of himself, ultimately encompassing the destruction of the world, its redemption, and its reconstitution anew.

But that destruction and reconstruction, if one reads the text attentively, is not that of the world in general, but rather of the human—i.e., interhuman—world, and, quite precisely, the sexual world. The reality at stake in this destruction-reconstruction is only incidentally material reality, what I call (in a slightly restrictive term) that of "self-preservation." We should note that the Schreber case is situated, in Freud's work, explicitly in that period in which sexuality and self-preservation are still—fortunately—clearly distinguished. And the debate with Jung, which we encounter in this text as well as in that devoted to "narcissism," bears the clear imprint of that distinction, which is plainly predicated against Jung's instinctual monism. This is crucial: the notion of "loss of reality" at this juncture is not yet unified, as it will be later on in the texts of 1924–1925 in which it is precisely self-preservation that will have disappeared as an independent dimension, finding itself totally incorporated in the second instinctual dualism. The texts of 1924–1925 on "neurosis and psychosis" thus suffer absolutely from an absence of distinction between sexual reality and reality . . . itself.[15]

Schematically put, Freud's Schreber case is composed of two parts: one concerning the content and the other explicitly devoted to the mechanism of paranoia.

Having decided to devote the lion's share of my presentation and critique to the second part, I should state emphatically that the first part of the Schreber text is a dazzling presentation of the interest this delusion has in terms of its conformity with psychoanalytic theory.[16] The brilliant and demonstrative use of psychoanalytic method pushes the limits that might be hoped for in "psychoanalysis outside of treatment."[17] But there is something more astonishing still: the psychoanalytic content of this first part will be entirely forgotten, totally neglected, once Freud moves on to the study of the "mechanism"—

---

15 "Neurosis and Psychosis," in *SE* 19.

16 A conformity on which Freud constantly insists, both at the end of his "Schreber" text (*SE* 12:78) and in his correspondence with Jung.

17 [Editor's note] In *New Foundations for Psychoanalysis* Laplanche refers to psychoanalysis *"exported* or *outside-the-walls,"* commenting: "I use this expression to separate myself from 'applied psychoanalysis,' which is . . . subject to critique insofar as it entails with it the notion of application. 'Application' would suppose that a methodology and a theory . . . abstracted from . . . the treatment . . . could then be carried without further ado—like an industrial application—into another domain, just as the applied science of the engineer in constructing a bridge is finally only an ingenious derivation from the fundamentals of physics or mechanics." New translation by Robert Stein (New York: The Unconscious in Translation, forthcoming)

by which I mean that its sexual content and the openings it offers onto the theory of seduction will be overlooked.[18]

That content will certainly be retrieved, but in the edulcorated and sublimated form of the father "complex," as we shall observe presently. For in short order Freud will recall that the fundamental theoretical problem, what remains to be explained, is the mechanism of paranoia, the form of its delusion and more precisely its persecutory form. Now the Freudian doctrine of the neuroses and psychoses is precise: the content, however interesting it may be (genital and pregenital sexuality, homosexuality, castration, etc.), is supposed to be the same in all disorders; it is universal: "But in all of this there is nothing characteristic of the form of disease known as paranoia, nothing that might not be found (and that has not in fact been found) in other kinds of neuroses. The distinctive character of paranoia. . . must be sought for. . . in the particular form assumed by the symptoms; and we shall expect to find that this is determined not by the nature of the complexes themselves but through the mechanism by which the symptoms are formed or by which repression is brought about."[19]

But we must attend carefully to what follows: there is going to be a major shift, a contradiction imposed by clinical practice on this doctrinal point. And yet the shift will not go far enough.

A major shift: while we should no longer speak in terms other than those of mechanism (defense and the return of the repressed), we are obliged to admit that "content" has its own impact, which is considerable: experience impels us "to attribute to the homosexual wish-fantasy an intimate (perhaps an invariable) relation to this particular *form* of disease" (161).[20]

In addition—and here we return to something more clas-

---

18 This contrast between the two parts of the Schreber case has been well observed by Bertrand Vichyn in his quite innovative thesis on paranoia, which was defended in 1988.
19 *SE* 12:59.
20 Ibid. (our emphasis).

sical—in the mechanism itself, we should distinguish between repression, on the one hand, and the return of the repressed, on the other. But Freud insists, and for him it is an important point of doctrine, that the two are not symmetrical: the return does not necessarily follow the paths of repression. And what determines the choice of neurosis is in fact the later phase of return which in principle is independent.[21]

Ultimately, what Freud argues in the second part focuses successively on these three points: the (homosexual) complex, the return (projection), and repression. But the paradox is that he will demolish precisely what he should—*doctrinally*--have imposed: the independence of the *return* mechanism, which theoretically is the one aspect specific to the "choice of neurosis," i.e., the independence of the mechanism of projection, since that is what is under discussion.

Projection, Freud tells us, lies at the core of paranoia: and there he kills it off in a single page.[22] He contents himself with a general psychological definition of it and then remarks that it is a universal process; with the result that paranoid projection is reduced to the model of so-called normal projection: I search in the external world and not in myself for "the causes of certain sensations" that are at first supposed to be interior. The model is overtly psychological, with a kind of recollection of the classical "neurological" meaning, according to which projection is conceived of as a point-by-point alignment between a specific zone of the brain and a specific peripheral sensory receptor. Such a model of "normal projection" is thus constructivist, somewhat in keeping with the sensualist model that is palpable in all psychoanalytic attempts at a so-called genesis of reality. The first not-me possession (to use Winnicott's term) undeniably goes back to Condillac and the famous "fragrance of a rose." Ultimately, as sketched in this page of the Schreber case, the model is indifferent to

---

21 Cf. Jean Laplanche and J.-B. Pontalis, "Return of the Repressed," in *Vocabulaire de la psychanalyse* (Paris: PUF, 1967).
22 *SE* 12:66.

the distinction between two realms of reality—self-preservation and sexuality—concerning which I have just praised Freud for maintaining their independence at this stage of his thought.

Finally, Freud's attitude concerning projection in this text is quite puzzling: on the one hand, we are referred without further ado to a future exhaustive study of projection, which will never be written. On the other hand, the *essence* of paranoia, which was allegedly to be situated in a projective "return" to the external world, turns out to be displaced onto what was said not to be specific to it, namely, the two other elements: the content and the process of repression. But, as if to further complicate matters, that projection, postponed indefinitely and, as it were, cast out of the passage that was to examine it, would, in various guises, come to haunt two other studies: one on repression and one on "complexes."

I will not enter into detail about the description of *repression* except to emphasize that there too we are in a totally ambiguous situation. Freud gives a canonical description, abstract in its generality, of *neurotic* repression with its three phases, and attempts simultaneously, but in vain, to integrate the paranoid process into it. It is not my intention to broach a confrontation between the psychotic process and neurotic repression, which would raise considerable problems. The principal underlying problem is, in my view, whether or not we are obliged, before all else, to reevaluate the theory of repression in light of a theory that I have called translational, linked to the idea of seduction and the message.[23]

---

23 The way in which Freud, in his discussion of the Schreber case, introduces a description of repression in general raises a number of questions. It should be noted, first of all, that Freud does not use the term in this context as a simple synonym for "defense." What Freud gives us is quite plainly a canonical description of the mechanism rather close to the one that will reappear in the article of 1915. Let us examine, then, a certain number of essential questions in order to clarify matters:
- What is the meaning of applying a model of repression in the unconscious to every form of psychopathology?

Despite all their ambiguity, Freud's description and discussion are extremely rich. But I am obliged to proceed obliquely to reach the major passage on projection, which merits mention and discussion, in the wake of comments of others:

> What forces itself so noisily upon our attention is the process of recovery, which undoes the work of repression and brings back the libido again on to the people it had abandoned? In paranoia this process is carried out by way of projection. It was incorrect to say that the perception which was suppressed internally is projected outwards; the truth is rather, as we now see, that what was abolished internally returns from without. The thorough examination of the process of projection which we have postponed to another occasion will clear up our remaining doubts on this subject.[24]

In summarizing the armature of Freud's reasoning, we find the following series of statements: it's a projection, but it is imprecise to say that it is a projection ("it was incorrect to say that the perception which was suppressed internally is projected outwards")—the examination of projection will clarify all this. It's a projection, but it's

---

- Can the schema of repression be used, so to speak, in psychosis in a reverse manner? This is a bit the schema of the 1924 articles (quoted below). Thus the disinvestment of the object would correspond, in psychosis, to the disinvestment of the representation in neurosis. But the analogy through symmetry does not hold for long: for instance, the "return" of the repressed takes place, in both cases, in the same direction.
- Another way of conceiving of psychotic defense in the context of repression would be to make of it a fundamental failure of the latter; a channel that is not alien to us but demands, in our view, an intensive reexamination, with the introduction of the "translational" dimension.
- Finally, in order to complicate things, we should keep in mind that there is also classical neurotic repression and a classical "return" in every concrete psychosis. *SE* 12:66.

24 *SE* 12:71.

not one, and "just wait and see" when I at last get around to speaking of projection!

Lacan, for those familiar with his texts (and specifically with his article on psychosis), cites this passage as an anticipation of foreclosure. "What was abolished internally returns from without" would be understandable as "what was foreclosed from the symbolic reappears in the real." Concerning which—once again—I would ask that we ask first of all which "real" is being invoked, among the (three) categories of the real.[25]

That text on psychoses is a great text—an inspired text. Its attitude toward Freud is Machiavellian in that Lacan criticizes Freud's classical successors (who are Lacan's adversaries), attributing to them certain ideas that are explicitly those of Freud, even as he ascribes to Freud ideas that are those of Jacques Lacan. In the critique of projection he initiates, Lacan attributes to his adversaries the following simplistic formulation: "The storage-room for props is inside, and they are trotted out as the need arises."[26] Now that formula is derived directly from Freud himself: "The world of fantasy . . . is the storehouse from which the materials or the pattern for building the new reality are derived."[27]

Lacan always refused to take a knife to Freud. Not the knife (according to the conventional image) of murder, but that of splitting and dialectics: summoning contradiction into play in Freud, who, within two lines, takes support in the good old theory of projection... only to reject it.

Were I in turn to introduce an element of discord into Lacan's text, I would say: the beginning of the text is breathtaking, revealing that the conception of delusion or hallucination cannot be dealt with adequately by a return to the primacy of the perceiver over the perceived—the old indestructible *percipiens*, whose functions of

---

25 See above, pp. 20ff
26 Jacques Lacan, *Écrits* (Paris: Seuil, 1966), p. 542.
27 "The Loss of Reality in Neurosis and Psychosis," in *SE* 19:187.

synthesis, and unity, and even whose uniqueness are challenged by Lacan. That beginning brings into relief in gripping manner what I call the dimension of the message and what delusion brings to the fore as irreducible alterity.

I will not deliver a lecture on Lacanianism. I don't know whether it is still fashionable these days to read Lacan. It would, in any event, be advisable to recommend it to those who are not inclined to orthodoxy in their reading. The text is not particularly easy. The central part, which presents Lacan's theory, gets increasingly difficult to grasp, given its seemingly mathematical or geometric schemata. I personally am of the opinion that the alterity of the other gets a bit blunted in the process. The persecutor becomes more and more abstract, "structured like a language," as one might put it. And, above all, less and less sexual. Such is the case for the introduction of the concept of foreclosure: the "foreclosure of the name of the father" is a curious euphemism compared to that which (in the case of Schreber) "returns in the real"—which is specifically an act of persecutory anal-sadistic sodomy.

This brings us back to Freud and the aspect he initially develops: the content of the delusion, the drive, homosexual desire, condensed in the formula: "I (a man) love him as a man." Can it be said that Freud, in the grammatical deduction of delusion he pro-poses, is already Lacanian? This is probably the case, in the way in which he develops as logical propositions all the forms of negation of that formula as so many types of delusion: persecution, jealousy, ero-tomania, etc. A structuro-logico-linguistic matrix of that sort, which is genuinely structuralist *avant la lettre*, finds nothing to envy in the per-mutational formulae that will allow Lacan, for example, to define his celebrated "four types of discourse." And yet we have good reason to examine Freud's deduction more closely without getting too carried away by the beauty of the demonstration.

(1) First of all, we may observe as symptomatic Freud's aston-ishment at the following: whereas the form of the illness should,

according to doctrine, be entirely dependent on its mechanism (i.e., on the metapsychology of return), experience forces us to acknowledge that persecution is in every case linked to a specific libidinal content. This, for Freud, remains an experiential fact, contradicting the theory, but does not in any way lead him to delve more deeply into the relation between what he calls projection and what he names homosexuality. On the contrary, he keeps them separate in his celebrated negations of the sentence "I love him." Projection remains a mechanism extrinsic to libidinal movement, like a supplementary and unexplained compulsion (*Zwang*). What shows clearly that projection remains extrinsic, without actually being determined by content, is its arbitrary use by Freud—at different times and *ad libitum*. Thus it is that we are given two quite different schemata. In the first,[28] the development is described as follows:

> I love him;
> I hate him;
> He hates me.

There are two quite distinct inversions, the first moving from love to hatred and the second corresponding to a subsequent projection (the ego being unable to tolerate hatred within).

But at another moment in the text[29] it is projection that is described as primary:

> I love him.
> He loves me.
> He hates me.

Here the transformation to hatred would be a merely secondary or accessory deformation allowing the projection not to be recognized.

(2) On the other hand, the homosexuality that *is* posited is a rather curious variant. At the same time as the Schreber case, Freud

---

28 *SE* 12:63.
29 Ibid., pp. 65–66.

was developing a complex psychogenesis of homosexuality in his *Leonardo*, a genesis by way of narcissistic identification with the mother. Subsequently, he would evoke another possible psychogenesis, also by way of a psychical conflict. Here things are quite different; we are in the presence of a kind of direct, preconflictual homosexuality, not transiting through the unconscious, a direct love for the father, one that is primary and, one might almost say, prehistoric.

(3) This homosexuality is not only strange in its genesis (or rather its absence of genesis) but also in its formulation, which tends to desexualize it, that is, to formulate it in terms of love and also hate. That desexualization is in glaring contrast with what is described by Schreber, which Freud followed in his first part, even though he barely takes it into account in what follows: on the one hand, an indivisible combination of sexual advances and persecution coming from God; on the other, the largely anal-sadistic character of God's behavior. Is reducing this veritable sexual harassment to a matter of love and hate really an advance in analysis?

(4) A final point, which is essential from my point of view: what Freud brings his transformations to bear on are neither fantasies nor scenarios. Compare what he describes here with, for example, the description of "drives and their vicissitudes"; there, the inversions, reversals, returns toward the subject's own person bear on libidinal actions: seeing, gazing, beating, etc. Here, in the case of Schreber, the reversals bear on abstract formulations of more or less desexualized sentiments: so-called instinctual impulses but *without* the wish-fantasies that, from the theoretical point of view, should serve as their representational-supports, the "ideational representatives."

Guy Rosolato, in his now classic article "Paranoia et scène primitive," placed an emphasis on theories putting masochism at the center of paranoid delusion.[30] Among the authors of such theo-

---

30 Guy Rosolato, "Paranoia et scène primitive," in *Essais sur le symbolique* (Paris: Gallimard, 1969), p. 236.

ries is R. Bak, who considered paranoia a "delusional masochism" and describes as an initial phase a "regression of sublimated homosexuality to masochism." It is a position that, in my view, reverses, and rightly so, the sequence of the Schreber text: homosexuality is sublimated and not primal; what lies at the root is masochism, as I have never stopped insisting since *Life and Death in Psychoanalysis* and my article *"La position originaire du masochisme dans le champ de la pulsion sexuelle."*[31] Pathological masochism, the masochism of Schreber, would be a particular (and assuredly aberrant) case of this primal position of masochism.

What is also remarkable is that Freud himself (as Rosolato, moreover, reminds us) will come very close to adopting that theory in 1919, long after Schreber, in "A Child Is Being Beaten." Commenting, with regard to his celebrated sequence, on its second phase, which is masochistic and unconscious ("being beaten by the father"), he expresses himself as follows: "I should not be surprised if it were one day possible to prove that the same fantasy is the basis of the delusional litigiousness of paranoia."[32]

That remark is crucial in my estimation and completely overturns the sequence previously described by Freud.

(1) With the formula "I am being beaten by my father" (which is, moreover, given as strictly equivalent to "My father is beating me," an equivalence in keeping with the structure of the unconscious fantasy), we find ourselves at the level of a concrete sexual scenario and no longer in the disembodied affective logic of the proposition "I love him."

(2) Freud, in "A Child Is Being Beaten," has phase 2, which is unconscious, follow a conscious lived experience (1) in which *the father beats* a little brother or sister.

(3) I have concentrated at some length, in a text on

---

31 In *La Révolution copernicienne inachevée.*
32 *SE* 17:195

interpretation,[33] on emphasizing the status as enigmatic message of phase (1): my father is beating a younger sibling, *in front of me; he shows it to me*. I attempted to show how repression, which is activated between (1) and (2), can be conceived, on the translational model, as a partial translation of the message with "whatever lay at hand"—the partial failure of translation leaving an untranslated, but distorted, "anamorphic," residue: the unconscious fantasy.

With what we may intuit of psychosis, this model could only be invoked in order to reveal its radical failure—the failure that Freud at times calls repudiation, at times disavowal, and that Lacan calls foreclosure. In advancing only step by step, we may perhaps be obliged to assume that ultimately, in psychosis, there is only a minimal difference, or no difference at all, between phase (1) and phase (2). What precedes "my father is beating me" would then be… "my father is beating me"—with, to be sure, the whole sexual (and eventually metaphorical) dimension of that act. This harmonizes well with what we know of Schreber's father, as well as with the absence of a younger sibling who might have been beaten in the presence of his or her elder brother.

Are we then to assume that in psychosis the message remains unchanged, waiting, suspended? In what state? And where?

Models crowd in on us, and all of them expose us to the danger of including them "within": despite everything "within a subject." Our dissatisfaction with the notions of repression and unconscious is notorious; but need we, for all that, reinvent other modes of inclusion? The crypt presupposes the ego; the splitting of the ego presupposes the ego, on both sides of the split. Foreclosure? It is still me—or I— who forecloses.

For my part, I one day proposed, with the translational model of repression in two phases, the image of a first phase in which the sex-

33 "L'Interprétation entre déterminisme et herméneutique" (1991), in *La Révolution copernicienne inachevée*, pp. 385–416, and in *Essays on Otherness*, op. cit. pp.138–165.

29

ual-presexual enigmatic message from the other is, as it were, actually implanted in the body. In short, in which it is not taken into account by an ego or a subject. We should, in fact, insist on this: primary repression is correlative with the constitution of the ego, whoever it is who says "I." The imperative, then, is managing to think a process that is not in the first person, nor even, perhaps, in any person at all. But every model, whether it is one of foreclosure or seclusion, risks being captured by identitarian thought: a mode that is ultimately Ptolemaic. Which is reassuring, to be sure . . .

Revelation

During these days of discussion, we are allegedly speaking about religion. I am absolutely no expert on the field—not even on Catholicism, which is the religion of my family and my youth—and even less on other religions, their history and their specificity. Here too a work like Rosolato's on sacrifice offers admirable in-depth knowledge—a veritable mine of information—and also a crucial set of reflections and comparisons.[34]

Today I would like to consider religion from the perspective of *revelation*. "Revealed religions": not only the three religions "of the Book," but many more: even, it would appear, that of the Etruscans.

I do not want to conceal that the choice of the theme of revelation corresponds to my vision of psychoanalysis and to the priority that I accord to the message emanating from the other. I might have sought documentation on the theology or philosophy of revelation, but I have done so only sporadically. I have, however, consulted a quite interesting text by Fichte, dating from 1792–1793 and titled *Versuch einer Kritik aller Offenbarung* (An Attempt at a Critique of All Revelation).[35]

---

34 Guy Rosolato, *Le Sacrifice* (Paris: PUF, 1991).
35 *Attempt at a Critique of All Revelation*, ed. Allen Wood, trans. Garrett Green (Cambridge: Cambridge University Press, 2010).

It is a text with an amusing history: we find ourselves in the glory years of an aging Kant, and Fichte, an illustrious nobody, publishes his text in the form and with the title of a critique. His publisher, in his shrewdness, assumes it advantageous to publish the work anonymously, and everyone immediately concludes that the text in question is Kant's fourth critique. In short order, the philosophical public issues assessments of great acclaim. Whereupon Fichte, out of honesty, but also out of a concern to reclaim what was rightfully his, reveals that he is, in fact, the author: an immediate reversal of the critical reception ensues, insisting on the worthlessness of the text . . .

The work, in my view, opens up a theory of communication, and thus a potential decentering, whereas Kant remains within what I have called the Ptolemaic dispensation. The central paragraph of the text, titled "Formal Exposition of the Concept of Religion," is basically an exposition of the concept of *Bekanntmachung*. *Bekanntmachung*, during the German occupation, was the general heading of the posters plastered on the walls, which, out of mockery (and perhaps influenced by surrealism), we recast as *bécane machin* (the "whatchamacallit machine"). A *Bekanntmachung* might announce that bread-rationing cards would be distributed at a particular time, but also that a specific individual was about to be executed . . . It was a *notification* or *announcement*, the latter term allowing one to distinguish, as Fichte, moreover, does, between the announcer, the receiver of the announcement, and what is announced. Fichte, then, proceeding in a Kantian manner, develops two points: the *necessity* of the *Bekanntmachung* and its *possibility*. As for the "necessity," he shows that with the exception of truths demonstrated a priori, the entire realm of what we know is "historical," and is thus transmitted—communicated, announced, made known (*bekannt gemacht*)—to us through the mediation of an other. This is even the case for most of the truths that happen to be demonstrable to the extent that we don't resort to that demonstration on each occasion, contenting ourselves instead with the reasoning of another. We live almost exclusively in the realm of historical truth—

that is, of what is announced by another.

As for the "possibility" of *Bekanntmachung*, it raises a typically Kantian problem: whereas the sensory world is entirely determined, subordinate to a perfect determinism by causes said to be "efficient," the "communication" of a truth must be of a different order, obeying a finality. Fichte's response in this case is strictly Kantian: the existence of a free subject (presupposed by an act of communication from subject to subject) is a postulate of the moral law.[36]

What is important in this discussion is the promotion of the category of communication emanating from the other and the subordination of revelation—as a special case ultimately lacking in much specificity—to that category. I posit this provisionally, noting at the same time that in Fichte's *Bekanntmachung* it is plainly not a matter of a message that might be enigmatic, compromised by the unconscious.

Let us inquire for a moment into the title of this colloquium, "Beginnings," or rather into its subtitle, "Neurotic Formations, Reli-

---

36 Fichte is referring here to the third antinomy of pure reason according to Kant, and directly pits the determinism of the sensory world against the necessity of positing a free subject, who is plainly the moral subject.

The question would be one of knowing whether this antinomy would not be more precisely formulated by pitting against determinism (the world of physical laws) the ineluctability of a communication of truth, which postulates that such a communication is not governed by a physical causality: if my interlocutor is an "automaton," an "animal-machine," I should probably be interested only in the laws that dictate its movements and not in the alleged contents of what it utters. The Kantian antinomy remains extrinsic: it opposes to each other a thesis and an antithesis situated on two different (phenomenal and noumenal) terrains, those of science and morality, and can cohabit without genuine conflict. The true antinomy is far more acute and conflictual; it gnaws at every affirmation, or rather at every *communication* of the thesis of complete determinism: at the very instant that I write "neuronal man," I contradict myself by addressing a reader and attempting to convince him according to an order of reasons and not an order of neurons.

The antinomy could thus be reformulated as follows: 1) man is a natural being, and all his acts should be able to be explained according to the laws of nature (*Critique of Pure Reason* (London: Dent, 1934 [1781]), pp. 270–74); 2) communication from one man to another, and particularly that of the preceding assertion, postulates that I do not understand such communication to be determined by the laws of nature.

gious Formations." Whether dubbed formations or models, there are a plurality of religious models in Freud, a diversity and perhaps a unity that is difficult to maintain. First of all, as Rosolato clearly reminds us,[37] a distinction should be made between the model for rituals, which is the model of obsessional neurosis, and the model or models for belief. But, within the category of belief, the Freudian model is more complex and more fragmentary than appears to be the case. There is, first of all, what is given straightaway in *The Future of an Illusion*, which is precisely the schema of illusion: according to Freud's definition, a belief that conforms to a wish and cannot be proved. Delusion falls quite explicitly under this rubric, as a component of illusion, that component concerning which it can be demonstrated that it is in contradiction with reality. The insufficiency of that theory of delusion is obvious: an illusion could become a delusion depending on the state of our knowledge at any particular moment. Whoever believed in spontaneous generation before Pasteur's discovery was in a state of illusion, but once Pasteur demonstrated the error it constituted, that error became a delusion. Regarding individuals of differing levels of

---

There have been numerous attempts to escape this antinomy, whose two terms are ineluctable, by attempting to find a utopian point of dehiscence in which freedom might be introduced: what I call a solution of the "pineal gland" type. It is well known that Descartes alleged that the "soul," at a specific point in the brain, could act on the body by influencing the *direction* of the movement of "animal spirits." Such a change in direction would not necessitate the intervention of an additional force. This is a conception based on an erroneous statement of the principle of the conservation of energy in the form of a so-called conservation of the quantity of movement. The modern "solution"—of the "pineal gland" type—is to attempt to introduce "freedom" or "meaning" through the door opening onto relations with Heisenberg and quantum theory.

The third antinomy, in the form I give to it above, is bearable (from the speculative point of view) only thanks to the recognition of the fact that science is not and never will be a complete totality, and that determinism—as much as its opposite: the communication of truth—is a regulating principle of theoretical practice. I say "from the speculative point of view," since, in any event, in daily life, it is completely tolerated, like an inconsequential consequence, including by the adepts of an absolutist determinism, from the moment that they enter into communication.

37 Rosolato, *Le Sacrifice*, p. 72.

knowledge, but also once one civilization is compared to another, the problem becomes virtually insoluble: at what precise moment do we begin to delude ourselves by believing in spontaneous generation? In defining delusion, can we be satisfied with putting it in the balance against "rational criticism"?

I return to the model of illusion applied to religion. The wish underlying it, in a first analysis, is linked to the helplessness of the human being (who is an adult as Freud begins his analysis), his inability to help himself when confronting the forces of nature, the cruelty of fate and death, and ultimately the suffering and privations imposed by life in common. It is a conception of which it has been noted that it has nothing specifically psychoanalytic about it and is, in fact, a legacy of Enlightenment philosophy, ultimately by way of Feuerbach. Freud himself addresses that very objection to himself in *The Future of an Illusion*, and he answers it with due clarity. That consolatory function for the adult is but the manifest aspect of religious belief. What is latent is the Oedipus complex, and more precisely the paternal complex (here I am summarizing, quite briefly, Freud's presentation). But theoretically there would be two paths for deriving the religions of modern adults from the paternal complex. On the one hand, the individual path, consisting in tracing things back to the helplessness and ambivalence of the child-individual confronting a father. But Freud was never satisfied with that path. In the "Wolf Man," for example, he finds it insufficient to trace a path from the Wolf Man's beliefs to his personal relation with his father. The adult religious construct cannot be reduced to the fantasies and desires of a given child confronting a father. It is never, in any event, an individual creation, but rather one that is cultural. What is required in each case is an articulation between an individual Oedipus complex and the Oedipus complex of humanity. In point of fact, insofar as religion is concerned, it is humanity's childhood, its prehistory, that is dominant, with *Totem and Taboo*, on the one hand, and *Moses and Monotheism*, on the other— with, however, a clear difference in accent between the way in which

34

religion is characterized as "infantile" in texts dating from the 1920s and the evaluation of "progress in spirituality" in *Moses*.

The childhood of the individual or that of humanity? Can we establish a correspondence between the Oedipus complex of the one and the Oedipus complex of the other? In the *Moses* book the key word is at last pronounced and supplies the title of a subchapter. It is a major point of reflection: the word *analogy*. How are we to conceive of the analogy between an individual and a people? The problem is fortunately not posed in all its generality, but with reference to a precise question, memory, or, still more precisely, transmission.

How many times did Freud attempt this analogy, trying at times to shed light on transmission in the case of the individual, at others, with regard to collective transmission!

In *Civilization and Its Discontents*, it is the grandiose fresco deploying in space-time, before our eyes, the archeology of ancient Rome (taken as a model of preservation by the unconscious in individual "memory").[38]

In the *Leonardo*, a poorly understood passage[39] compares two ways of writing history—*Geschichtschreibung*—and two types of individual memorization: one (the chronicle) that notes things down day by day, the other an orderly and retroactive reconstitution. It may be noted that in this case it is no longer a question of either repression or the unconscious.

In the *Moses*, contrary to the two preceding texts, it is the individual process that comes to the rescue by shedding light on collective memory. In the history of peoples, several kinds of transmission are evoked, which are to be distinguished clearly, precisely when what is at stake is religion.

First of all, *transmission by communication*, that is, tradition. Freud devotes several lengthy developments to it, specifically in com-

---

38 Cf. Laplanche, *La Révolution copernicienne inachevée*, p. 398.
39 *SE* 11:83.

paring religious tradition to the epic. What is essential is that linear tradition, the pure and simple transmission by what is manifest and by language, is insufficient for religion.

The second model is *repression and return of the repressed*; this is the case that is central to the *Moses* volume. Mosaic doctrine had to be effaced by the murder of Moses in order to return with the force of a symptom. "A tradition that was based only on communication could not lead to the compulsive character that attaches to religious phenomena . . . it would never attain the privilege of being liberated from the constraint of logical thought. It must have gone through the fate of being repressed, the condition of lingering in the unconscious, before it is able . . . to bring the masses under its spell."[40]

I will come back in a moment to this model of collective and historical repression, with latency period and return, but I first will mention the third model, which comes to be juxtaposed with the two others. It is that of atavism, the *hereditary transmission* of memory-traces. Freud lingers over it for a while, offering as proof, as we know, elements discovered by psychoanalysis—that at least is the claim—such as the symbolics of speech leading to an original or primal language as well as the idea of primal fantasies. This is the celebrated phylogenetic model of *Totem and Taboo* and of the "Overview of the Transference Neuroses." I prefer not to discuss it as such; I have already done so frequently.

How does the model intervene here? Presumably in support of Freud's position, but actually in order to confuse the issue. In support, since it is a matter of proving the existence of a transmission that might be called internal and does not proceed by way of tradition, "culture," and "speech." But this model of phylogenetic transmission confuses matters since it is a model of inscription through repetition, by summation, and not a model of repression.[41] In addition, it is a

---

40 *SE* 23:101.

41 Freud is explicit in this regard: "under what conditions does a memory of this kind enter the archaic heritage? . . . if the event was important enough, or repeated often enough, or both." *SE* 23:101.

model of inscription mediated necessarily by way of the biology of each individual. Whereas, in the evolution of the Mosaic religion, it is precisely a matter of something quite different: the repression of a single event, eventually in two phases (and not the additive multiplicity of repetition), and, in addition, its inscription in the individual-Jewish people, considered not as a genetic succession of individuals, but as analogous, in its totality, to what Freud, in other texts,[42] calls great-individuals (*Grossindividuen*).[43]

What then would be the analogy between the Moses episode, as Freud views it, and repression? We are dealing with a genesis, but of what?" Religion? Surely not: the Moses volume does not revise any of the explanations already proposed. Is it the genesis of monotheism? Yes and no, but ultimately no, since monotheism, that of Akhenaton, has a prior origin. Freud himself seems disconcerted to realize that he may not have gained anything by replacing a Jewish monotheism by an Egyptian monotheism.[44] And this is all the more the case in that a sociological explanation seems quite natural insofar as Egypt is concerned: the constitution of a great centralized empire might naturally lead to a unitary religion. The problem is thus: what happened between the Egyptian belief and the one ushered in by Moses? Belief, as if by a miracle, becomes revelation and election. But revelation and election are not enough. That Moses chose his people and revealed monotheism is not enough to give it the force of a compulsion: what is required is repression.

---

42 For example: "Thoughts for the Times on War and Death," in *SE* 14:278.

43 In point of fact, there is an even more important underlying confusion: Freud's assimilation of repression with a consigning to memory, a certain kind of memory. Here I am obliged to allude to my personal conception: in my view, the differences are fundamental: memory bears—virtually—on every perception or every experience; repression bears exclusively on a message—or what signifies . . . (see, in this volume, "A Brief Treatise on the Unconscious," Chapter 3).

44 This is emphasized by Marie Moscovici in her preface to the French translation in the OCF.

Individual-society. It is here that the "analogy" comes up against a major and, in my opinion, quite simple difficulty: in order for a message to be repressed, an ego performing the repression has to be constituted. Repression takes place in the first person. The constitution of the ego is correlative with repression. But in that case the notion of a collective neurosis—when it is taken *literally* and not as a sum of individual neuroses[45]—immediately encounters the following impossibility: how, in collective terms, is one to conceive of a locus and a status for the repressed? On the other hand, the notion of a collective *psychosis* remains attractive, and it is not without justification that the status of collective paranoia has been claimed for religion, notably by Rosolato, for the three monotheisms, and also by Eugène Enriquez and Jean-François Lyotard more specifically for Judaism.

If the paranoid process has no subject or ego that represses, or (to cast things in a more nuanced way) if paranoia corresponds to a sector in which there is no ego that represses, it is tempting to take things literally concerning the collective "great-individual" as well. It is suggestive to say, for instance—as does, I believe, Lyotard—that a sacred text may be the locus of an untranslatable (and initially unutterable or "foreclosed") message.

Religion and paranoia. Freud was far from heading down that path. The importance of the linkage is not spelled out, even in the case of Schreber. On the subject of religion, Freud does indeed speak of *Wahn* or delusion[46] in *Moses and Monotheism*, but this entails a curiously revealing problem in translation. The French translator of the Gallimard edition, Cornelius Heim, takes the trouble to explain that, in the space of three lines of Freud's text, *Wahn* is to be translated once as *illusion* and once as *delusion* (*délire*). From my perspective, of course,

---

45 "Collective hysteria" can be considered as a sum of individual hysterias. There is a convergence of unconsciousnesses and, above all, a site of convergence for agencies of repression: the leader with whom the *egos* identify.
46 *SE* 23:130.

he is wrong with regard to the theory of translation since he makes an ambiguity in the text inaccessible by changing the French word used to translate *Wahn*. But what is remarkable is that what he does can appear correct, given our interpretation of a certain movement in Freud's thought; for it is *Freud himself* who constantly reduces delusion to a simple variety of illusion.

I will not head down the path of a delusional model of religion. On the other hand, I will say a few words concerning the seduction-based model in religion, encompassing the delusional model as a particular case. The notion of seduction seems to me readable, in an almost omnipresent way, in the Bible. Concerning the word itself, an examination would be called for, going back to the Greek of the Septuagint or the Greek of the New Testament (πλαναω = to lead astray or seduce); it is certain that the verb "to seduce" is found, specifically for seduction by Christ and also for seduction by God, notably in Jeremiah. But from the word *seduction* to the *fact* of seduction a certain broadening is called for. The fact of seduction is found as early as in Genesis: a knowledge that is forbidden is proposed and is, moreover, proposed by someone who is duplicitous, if one is willing to include the Tempter *within* God himself. *Temptation* is perhaps inseparable from *revelation* and *seduction*.

What then is the case for those ingredients, these prerequisites of seduction, namely the message and the enigmatic? In my view, this is precisely what is lacking in Freud's theory, in his theory of religion as well, of course, as in his general theory. What Moses transmits, according to him, is the monotheistic belief of Akhenaton; it is a dogma (*Lehrsatz*), an object of belief (*Glauben*), that is repressed with the murder of the founder. The repression only adds compulsive force to Akhenaton's monotheistic belief, but not to any *message* from him—which is never mentioned.

The question of the enigmatic is even more characteristic. Considering it from the perspective of the unconscious of the speaker, none of the protagonists of the story has an unconscious: neither Moses nor

Akhenaton nor, above all, the primal father. The father of the hoard communicates nothing; he has no unconscious. No more—to bring things closer to us—than do the fathers of the Wolf Man, the Rat Man, Little Hans, or Dora. At the origin of the Oedipus complex, there is no Oedipus complex. In the case of Moses, it is the succession of repressions that creates a substitute for the priority of the other. Repression creates, as if *ex machina*, the compulsive force, the *Zwang*, of religious belief. The enigma is, as it were, displaced forward in that succession without ever being located in the simultaneity of an enigmatic message, in the compulsion of a "to-be-translated." As is known, I see the origin of the temporalization of the human being in the "drive to translate" and I situate the motor of this process not in the translator, but in the internal, atemporal, simultaneous imbalance of the enigmatic message, which provides the force of a "to-be-translated."[47]

All this is far from Freud. But is it that far from a certain conception of "revelation"? That God is a god who speaks and compels listening is evident throughout the entire Book, which is but a variant of the paradigm "Hear O Israel!" That God is enigmatic and compels translating appears evident in the entire Judeo-Christian tradition of exegesis. That this enigma presupposes that the message is opaque to itself plainly raises a different question. Does God have an unconscious? I leave that debate (or even that anathema) to the theologians, here quoting Rosolato: "The enigmatic aspect of (primal analogical) signifiers is transposed and received in religious mysteries."[48] In this sense, one can consider the mystery of the Trinity, with the bloody conflicts to which it led, as a failed attempt at appropriation, at translation, of a primal enigma?

As far as enigmatic messages and seduction stories are concerned, Job provides us with a fine example. The parallel with Schreber imposes itself on more than one score: with the primal destruction of the world and its final reconstitution, the parallel with the duplicity of

---

47 Cf. for example "Le mur et l'arcade" (1988), in *La révolution copernicienne inachevée*, pp. 287–306.
48 *Nouvelle Revue de psychanalyse* 46 (1992): 243.

the seducer (which is of the same order as the "perfidy" about which Schreber spoke), if one were willing to include in it, in a sulfurous unity, Satan himself; even the parallel with the anal aspect of the persecution, detectable in the dung heap, and in the stinking excrement that Job himself has become. Finally and above all the parallel with the repeated effort at translation, justification, delimitation, and mastery, which is at the heart of the debate between Job and his interlocutors.

This translation is the work of an ego, its completed aspect is dogma, even under the domesticated form of the enigma that is religious mystery or the modalities of belief.

Belief: Glaube, Glauben. The term is difficult to translate; in Freud, for example, it is sometimes rendered as 'belief' and sometimes as 'faith' (article of faith, faith as a theological virtue, etc.) One word in German, two words in French as well as in English and in many other languages. Is a language having only word for two in a state of richness or infirmity? The word *Lust* is similar meaning both pleasure and desire, Freud hesitates between a polysemy in the German, in which the confusion is fertile, and a kind of incapacity to establish indispensable conceptual differences.[49] In the case of *Glauben*, I have no hesitation in saying that we are dealing with a fundamental infirmity of the German language. The difference between faith and belief is barely perceived by German speakers, and it takes a long time to explain it to them. When it is perceived, it is poorly understood. Thus there is a philosophical dictionary which, having observed that German has no term corresponding to "faith" (*foi* in French), assimilates it to the religious aspect of belief or even to its affective aspect. In general, the distinction is not even perceived: this is the case for Freud himself. A passage that shows this clearly is found in the article titled "A Religious Experience." Freud's interlocutor is an Englishman who

---

49 Cf. *Traduire Freud* (in collaboration with A. Bourguignon, P. Cotet, F. Robert), "Terminologie raisonnée" article on "Lust" (Paris: PUF, 1989).

describes in a letter how he lost and regained his faith when faced with a person on a dissecting table—a person who plainly makes him think of his mother. Freud, after magisterially analyzing the situation, proceeds to a fragment from another letter in which the correspondent expresses the wish that God give Freud "the faith to believe." French would render the phrase without any difficulty as *la foi de croire*, but Freud reveals his incomprehension by translating it spontaneously (but quite flatly) as *das rechte Glauben*, meaning literally "the right belief."

Benveniste posits that "it is what can be said that delimits and organizes what can be thought."[50] Is it the case even when it is a matter of languages belonging to one and the same civilization, such as German, on the one hand, and English and French on the other? How, for example, should one translate the following celebrated passage from the second preface to Kant's *Critique of Pure Reason*: "I must, therefore, abolish knowledge in order to make room for belief (*das Glauben*)?" Kant, I have stated, is an apostle of the Ptolemaic (and not the Copernican) dispensation, and this despite his reference to Copernicus.[51] One of the chapters of the same Critique of Pure Reason is titled *"Meinen, glauben, wissen"* (Of opinion, belief, knowledge), defining in that manner various possible positions of the knowing subject in relation to the object. There is obviously no question, in that triad, of translating *Glauben* as "faith" —it being solely a matter of belief . . .

Faith (foi). The *Robert* dictionary initially distinguishes what it calls an "objective" meaning, that is, a meaning emanating from the speaker or the enouncer, to take up Fichte's distinction referred to above: as in the case of one who is "faithful to his word" in expressions such as *jurer sa foi* and *violer sa foi*. Opposed to this, there would be a "subjective" meaning: trust in the other's word, which thus falls on the side of the recipient or "announcee." In religion, one speaks

50 Émile Benveniste, "Catégories de langue, catégories de pensée," in *Problèmes de linguistique générale* (Paris: Gallimard, 1966), p. 70.
51 *La Révolution copernicienne inachevée*, pp. viii–ix.

of the faithful, but one also says that God is faithful. It is the intrinsic constraint of the message that demands translation.

And then, all of a sudden, as a counteroffensive to that priority of the message emanating from the other, one observes a veritable invasion by belief, a kind of reconquest of faith by belief—by way of the Kantians, by way of Freud, and, quite obviously, by way of psychoanalysis. Entire studies have been published on belief without at all inquiring into faith. I am thinking of a special issue of *La Nouvelle Revue de psychanalyse* on belief,[52] in which no one sought to follow a clue supplied by J.-B. Pontalis in his introduction, which bears the title "Se fier à sans croire en" (Having faith in without believing in." "Don't believe psychoanalysis!" he says. "Have faith in it," he adds. That sentence may well be untranslatable in German and in Freudian. I find it completely in agreement with the idea that the transference, like faith, comes from the other.[53]

---

52 *La Nouvelle Revue de psychanalyse*, no. 18 (1978).

53 "Opinion, knowledge, and belief" (according to Kant's expression) are modalities of the subjective attitude when confronting truth. They are mutually convertible: what is believed can be known, through the intermediary of verification. That is, in fact, how Freud extricates himself from the objection that almost the entirety of our life is founded only on belief in "dogmas" (*Lehrsätze*) transmitted by others: one can always go and see for oneself, perform the demonstration oneself (cf. *The Future of an Illusion*, beginning of chapter 5).

Opposed to the man of belief (and knowledge), the only type known to Freud, is the man of faith, in this anecdote recalled by Claude Imbert, concerning Saint Thomas: "A disciple asks Thomas: 'Master, if I were to tell you that there was a winged ox in the courtyard, would you believe me?' 'I would tell you to go back and look again.' 'But if I came back saying to you, one more time, there is a winged ox in the courtyard, how would you answer?' 'Then,' said Thomas, 'I would prefer to believe that God decided to perform a miracle rather than think that a son of Dominic decided to deceive me.'" Claude Imbert, "For a Structure of Belief: Anselm's Argument," *Nouvelle Revue de psychanalyse*, no. 18 (1978): 43.

We should emphasize that the faith in consideration here is not faith in God, but in a modest disciple, who cannot "want to deceive." Saint Thomas does not at all ascend the series of causes as Claude Imbert suggests ("your words are the sign of what you saw, and what you saw is the sign of the thing."): his faith rests on the "fidelity" of the son of Dominic. The Cartesian hypothesis of the "evil genius" would surface here as a major piece in the debate. On the other side, the other Saint Thomas, who "believes only in what he sees" and to whom it is replied: happy is he who has not seen and who "adheres" (to use Chouraqui's word).

Conclusion

At the outset, I adopted a critical position regarding notions that are nonetheless central to psychoanalysis: fantasy, persecution as a projective delusion, and myth.

I did not, of course, intend to deny their existence or their importance, but rather to attempt to show that they are correlative with a process of closure in relation to the address of the other, an address both enigmatic and seductive. I also ought to say: a sexual address. The distinction between the vital order and the human order—which is cultural and sexual—is crucial. When I speak of a primal decentering, of a fundamental Copernicanism, I am not speaking in general, but specifically with regard to the sexual domain.

The confusion between the sexual and self-preservation, accepted by Freud after 1920, is probably not without influence on the impasse at which the discussion of the "oceanic feeling" proposed by Romain Rolland was to end. The *ocean*, should one opt to retain that word, is quite simply the sexual. It is only in that realm, the realm of the message of psychical reality, that movement is centripetal and not centrifugal. "Psychical reality" is not created by me; it is invasive. At the outset there is too much reality in the domain of the sexual. And it is to that "too much reality" that the model in Freud's "project for a scientific psychology"[54] can be applied: the ego treats a part of that influx of reality with the purpose of attenuating the level of investment and integrating it into its system. But there always remains an irreducible residue of alterity—which may be what Romain Rolland calls oceanic feeling and would be precisely the perception of the enigmatic as such.

---

54 Jean Laplanche, *Life and Death in Psychoanalysis*, pp. 96ff. Baltimore: Johns Hopkins University Press, 1976

Reductionism. With regard to religion, there is an obvious reductionist intent in psychoanalysis. That attitude is not, however, specific, either on the side of the "reducer" or on that of the "reduced" since the reduction is not aimed solely at religion, and, in addition, the psychoanalytic undertaking is part of a much larger historical movement. The reductionism regarding religion is often but an avatar of a more general reductionism correlative with the illusion of the centrifugal. I create the object, the reality, based on my fantasy. I am obliged to traverse a "first not me" in order to reach objectality-objectivity. I create persecution based on my inner demons. Revelation is merely the correlate of myth, a creation of the collective imagination. In all this one invariably discovers the "indestructible *percipiens*," projection as a universal mechanism, normal and pathological—which is to say, even neurological.

What is opposed to this reductionism, in all domains, is the inalterability of what at one point I called "transcendence." I once spoke of a "transcendence of the transference": the term is more or less well chosen, since it is not a matter of verticality, nor of surpassing, and even less of self-surpassing. If it required accepting things in the sense of the expression: "I transcend *myself* toward," I would not retain the term *transcendence*.

What is at stake, however, is the existence of a vector and the direction of that vector. What is called in engineering a "guide" (and occasionally a "pull line") is this: one has what is called a duct, a large tube through which one attempts eventually to pass cables or smaller tubes. In that duct, at the time it is laid, one leaves a rope to which the cable can subsequently be attached in order to pull it. Instead of pushing the cable, in a centrifugal motion (by "projection"), one pulls it precisely toward the exterior, where the guide finds its starting point. The movement of the cable remains quite centrifugal, but a prior relation had been established; there was a preexisting opposite vector, allowing the cable to be pulled.[55]

I have attempted to trace that vector emanating from the other in three parallel domains: infantile seduction, persecution, and revelation:

other ----- → ego 1) infantile seduction
other ----- → ego 2) persecution
other ----- → ego 3) revelation

This priority of the other does not preclude centrifugal and then reciprocal movements, interactions, from occurring. But they are guided (in the precise sense of the engineer's "guide") by the primal, centripetal vector.

This priority of the other does not preclude attempts to establish a hierarchy, a genesis, a correlation, or even a reduction among the three parallel vectors. The persecutory vector (2) is assuredly an avatar (but also evidence) of vector 1. As for vector 3 (revelation), I wanted only to recall its relation to the two others without any a priori will either to denigrate it by subordinating it or, inversely, by granting it any priority.

After all, does "religion" lose or gain by being confronted with the major coordinates of the human condition? It was in the sense of just such a confrontation that I chose to recall, following Fichte, that revelation is but a variety of *Bekanntmachung;* I opted to recall as well

---

55 As I was proposing this image of the guide, I came upon this passage in Freud: "We begin to see that we describe the behavior of both jealous and persecutory paranoiacs very inadequately by saying that they project outward on to others what they do not wish to recognize in themselves. Certainly they do this; but they do not project it into the blue, so to speak, where there is nothing of the sort already. They *let themselves be guided* by their knowledge of the unconscious . . . " "Some Neurotic Mechanisms in Jealousy, Paranoia, and Homosexuality," in SE 18:226 (my emphasis).

The need for a centripetal "guide" to subtend the centrifugal projection seemed clearly to be intuited by Freud. It is precisely there that he introduces the "communication from unconscious to unconscious." A concept to be debated anew, based on the general theory of seduction.

that faith, which cannot be reduced to belief, and which, as an autonomous movement having its origin in the other, is not only a religious sentiment in the narrow sense of the term.

SUMMARY

Seduction, persecution, revelation

To seduce, to persecute, and *to reveal* are active verbs. To speak of a "fantasy of seduction," a "delusion of persecution," or a "myth of revelation" appears as a reversal of passivity into activity, in which the subject, centered (or rather recentered) on itself, pretends to be at the origin of what it has primally submitted to. It would be appropriate to ask whether, in alleging their original passivity, the neurotic, the paranoiac, and the religious individual are not "in a certain sense correct" (Freud): not only insofar as the "content" of their fantasies, delusions, and beliefs is concerned but also regarding the centripetal (and not centrifugal) vectorization of the intervention of the other.

Concerning *seduction*, it is posited that it is not primarily a fantasy but a "real" situation to be found at the core of the two other great allegedly primal scenarios: castration and the primal scene. But in order for that assertion not to be confused with an event-based realism, it is important to bring to the fore the third category of a reality that is constantly reduced to those of material reality and psychological reality: the reality of the message, and, more specifically for analysis, of the enigmatic message.

The priority of the other in *paranoia* is reexamined with regard to the Schreber case. The sexual other and his intrusion constitute the essential component of the analysis conducted by Freud in the first part of his study. But in the second part what triumphs is desexualization (in the name of love) and a recentering on the subject, both of them visible in the so-called first sentence, from which Freud would derive everything: "I (a man) love him (a man)."

Finally, the religious realm is an occasion to refer to Fichte's notion of *Bekanntmachung*, the "announcement" by the other that he places at the inception of a "critique of all revelation," and additionally to the notion of *faith* (finding its source in the other), to be differentiated clearly from that of belief, which is alone available to Freud and lends itself too easily to devalorization as "illusion."

We have been intent on underscoring the existence of a single vector emanating from the other, irreducible to any projection by the subject, in the three parallel realms of primal seduction, paranoia, and religion—and that despite whatever the articulations, priorities, or even "reductions" one may be tempted to propose between them.

II
Notes on *après-coup*

First of all, I want to emphasize that the whole of the problematic of *Nachträglichkeit* (*après-coup*, deferred action) is itself shaped by a process of après-coup. It is the French reading and translation of Freud that gave the concept of après-coup its importance. If, for example, you take the index of the volumes of the *Gesammelte Werke* of Freud, you will not find either *nachträglich* or *Nachträglichkeit* mentioned. The *Gesamtregister*, which dates from considerably later—more precisely 1968, which is after the publication of *Vocabulaire de la psychanalyse*— does indeed have one or two entries for the adjective *nachträglich*, but they are not very significant. If you consult the indexes of the works of Freud's principal successors, you will obtain an equally negative result. It is consequently in France, and in close relation with problems of translation, that the importance of *Nachträglichkeit* has made itself felt. That importance was first revealed by Lacan, who, in 1953, drew attention to the term in a precise (although limited) sense, but he did not envisage the broader implications of the concept for Freud's work. He was concerned solely with its occurrence in the case of the Wolf Man and paid no attention to its use in the 1895–1900 period.

These "notes" are based on a conversation of Jean Laplanche with Martin Stanton. They were published in Jean Laplanche, *Seduction, Translation, and the Drives* (London: ICA, 1992), ed. John Fletcher and Martin Stanton, and subsequently expanded and revised by the author.

It was Pontalis and I who drew attention to the general importance of the concept—initially in *"Fantasme originaire, fantasmes des origines, origine du fantasme"* (1964), then in *Vocabulaire de la psychanalyse* (1967). I have pursued the elaboration of the concept in *Vie et mort en psychanalyse* (1970), in *Problématiques* (1981–1988), as well as in *Nouveaux fondements pour la psychanalyse* (1987).

I am currently working on a more substantial article on the "après-coup of *Nachträglichkeit*." In it I present a detailed study of the use Freud makes of the term and the way in which it differs from my conception; I will consequently offer no more than a schematic version of my argument here. I will develop it along three general axes: first, the use of the concept in Freud's work; second, the problem of its translation; and finally, my own conception of après-coup. Here too, I should emphasize that one can examine attentively what Freud said without being in agreement with his thinking, and that is in fact my situation!

Let us begin, then, with Freud's conception of the après-coup. He uses the terms *nachträglich* and *Nachträglichkeit* during a significant portion of his active years, from the time of his correspondence with Fliess, through *The Interpretation of Dreams* and the "little Hans" case (1908), to the "Wolf Man" (1914–1918), and even beyond. Thus it is possible to follow the development of those terms in the general context of his work. They do not, however, ever acquire sufficient substance as concepts for Freud to have devoted an entire article to the concept of après-coup. We can observe the initial evolution of the term in Freud's correspondence with Fliess. Several elements can be isolated as evidence. The adjective *nachträglich*, which is drawn from current German usage, is employed by Freud in several ways. Roughly speaking, three uses can be distinguished: first, there is the sense of an ulterior or secondary meaning—which relates a second consciousness to a primary one. Strachey and Masson customarily translated it as "subsequently"; it thus simply takes on the temporal sense of "later." The second usage follows the temporal direction from the past toward the future, and the third the reverse, from the future toward the past. The second usage, from the past toward the future, is closely tied to the theory of seduction: it implies the deposit of something in the individual that will be reactivated only later on and will thus become active only in a "second phase"—which constitutes the theory of seduction. It should be noted that this theory of seduction was extremely mechanical because Freud had never thought that one might reverse the direction of time. One might use the example of the delayed-action bomb to illustrate this point: the first memory is like a delayed-action bomb that would be detonated by something extrinsic. There is nothing retroactive to be found in this case. But there is a third case that does include a valence of retroactivity. There are a certain number of passages that speak of things perceived in a first phase, then understood retroactively. Such passages are rather rare in Freud.

I will restrict myself here to making some contextual remarks concerning these three uses. If he has a choice between a deterministic conception, which proceeds from the past toward the future and a retrospective or hermeneutic conception that proceeds from the present toward the past, Freud will always choose the former. In point of fact, he never even tries to reconcile the two conceptions. I refer here to the letter to Fliess of October 3, 1897, in which he recounts an episode from his self-analysis and comments: "A harsh critic might say of all this that it was retrogressively fantasied instead of progressively determined. The *experimenta crucis* must decide against him."[56] My other contextual remark concerns the appearance of the noun *Nachträglichkeit*. As you know, the word is rather rare in German. It is surprising that the noun does not make its first appearance until a relatively late letter to Fliess of November 14, 1897.[57] That letter intervenes after what is called the abandonment of the theory of seduction, at a time when

56 *The Complete Letters of Sigmund Freud to Wilhelm Fliess: 1887–1904*, trans. Jeffrey Moussaieff Masson (Cambridge: Harvard University Press, 1985), p. 270.
57 Ibid., pp. 203–8.

Freud becomes even more "deterministic" (in the sense that future and present are both determined by the past). The letter is entirely focused on the organic determination of repression and consequently on the phylogenetic origin of ontogenetic development. It is on the terrain of the determination of the development of the sexual stages of the individual by phylogenetic stages that Freud posits the après-coup, and it is thus in no way a matter of the reversal of a temporal progression. As a result things are not that simple. Whereas we would like to see a double—and even contradictory—usage of *Nachträglich-keit*, in reality what we find is a highly deterministic usage.

Since this vision might be reproached with being based solely on texts from before 1898, I will briefly illustrate Freud's consistency in rejecting temporal reversibility in his subsequent texts. Three texts are important in this regard: *The Interpretation of Dreams,* "Little Hans," and "the Wolf Man." In that sequence, Freud finds himself increasingly in the grips of a theoretical confrontation with Jung, defending his views on the reality of the "actual" primal scene, in the sense of a scene actually experienced. Freud made a few concessions, but never wavered in his conviction that what comes before determines what comes after. This is why it seems totally false to me to assimilate the Freudian concept of *Nachträglichkeit* to the Jungian notion of *Zurück-phantasieren* (retroactive fantasy). [58]

Let us move on to my second point, which concerns *transla-tion.* Numerous terms have been proposed for this term as for many others. One has to decide whether or not translation should proceed according to context—that is, if the term has to be "interpreted." If so, neither in French nor in English can one render *nachträglich/ Nachträglichkeit* by a single term. This approach is well illustrated by

---

58 I am criticizing here recent attempts to assimilate Freudian usage of the term *Nachträglichkeit* to the hermeneutic tradition, specifically through parallels with Jung's concept of *Zurückphantasieren.* "Freud's *Nachträglichkeit* and Strachey's 'Deferred Action': Trauma Constructions and the Direction of Causality," Helmut Thomä and Neil Cheshire, *International Review of Psychoanalysis* 18 (1991): 407–27.

Strachey, who translates them by a whole series of terms, depending on the context: "deferred action," "subsequently," "in a deferred fashion," "subsequent," "after-effect," "deferred effect," "deferred nature of the effect," "later," etc. To the extent that one decides to "interpret" in this manner, and impose a meaning on a text that is essentially open, a single translation remains impossible. Let us now take the example of two translations of *Nachträglichkeit* that seem to compete with each other: "retrospective attribution," proposed by Helmut Thomä, and the classical "deferred action," proposed by Strachey. Two examples to illustrate: in *Studies on Hysteria*, Freud speaks of the "*nachträgliche Erledigung der Traumen*,"[59] and in his letters to Fliess he writes, "*Phantasien sind Dinge früh gehört erst nachträglich verstanden*."[60] In the first example, it is absolutely impossible to translate *nachträglich* as "retrospective attribution," which would give an absurd translation: "the liquidation of the trauma by retrospective attribution." It is equally absurd to translate the second sentence by "fantasies are things that were heard before and understood solely by deferred action." It will be seen in these two examples that the interpretative translations are narrowly dependent on the context in which Freud uses the term *nachträglich*. We should thus decide either to separate and split the term in translation or to select a term allowing readers to stick with Freud's term and reinterpret it for themselves. That is why I am proposing a non-interpretative translation: I suggest the term *après-coup* in French and *afterwards* in English. In all cases in Freud, it is possible to use *après-coup* as well as *afterwards* and *afterwardsness*.

I would like now to speak of my own conception of *Nachträglichkeit* and emphasize that it differs both from Freud's conception and from that of Jung (or hermeneutics). As an introduction, I would like to take a passage from *The Interpretation of Dreams*, which has not been commented on by other authors. The focus is an associa-

---

59 *Studies in Hysteria*, in SE 2:204–5.
60 Letter to Fliess of April 6, 1897, *Gesammelte Werke* 1:229.

tion to the "Knödel" (dumpling) dream:

> In connection with the three women I thought of the
> three Fates who spin the destiny of man, and I knew
> that one of the three women—the inn-hostess in the
> dream—was the mother who gives life, and further-
> more (as in my own case) gives the living creature its
> first nourishment. Love and hunger, I reflected, meet
> at a woman's breast. A young man who was a great
> admirer of feminine beauty was talking once—so
> the story went—of the good-looking wet-nurse who
> had suckled him when he was a baby: "I'm sorry," he
> remarked, "that I didn't make a better use of my oppor-
> tunity." I was in the habit of quoting this anecdote to
> explain the factor of après-coup in the mechanism of
> the psychoneuroses.[61]

The text is significant in that it shows that in 1900 Freud still
regarded *Nachträglichkeit* as an important concept that had to be
explained to his students. In this anecdote one can detect the two possible temporal directions at work in *après-coup*. The first direction is
evoked when the adult male, upon seeing the child being suckled at
the breast of his nurse, retrospectively imagines all the erotic pleasure
he might have derived from such a situation if he had only known.
Here we have a genuine example of *Zurückphantasieren* (retroactive
fantasy) and hermeneutics: he reinterprets the function of giving the
breast in terms of his present situation. It is an utterly Jungian conception. The other temporal direction is equally present, since we cannot
forget that according to Freud oral sexuality is not a sheer invention
of the adult. He believes that the child at the breast derives an erotic
pleasure in suckling that he describes, moreover, in the *Three Essays on
the Theory of Sexuality* as the first oral erotic experience. In this context,

---

61 *SE* 4:204–5. Translation modified to replace "deferred action" with après-coup.

if the sexuality of the adult is awakened by the spectacle of the infant at the breast, it is because it has retained and conserved traces of his own infantile sexuality. There are thus two interpretations of the anecdote that are possible, one progressive and one retroactive, but they remain independent and isolated from each other.

I would like to intervene at this point in Freud's account in order to give my own point of view, which is not a choice between those two possibilities. In no way does it imply opting either for the hermeneutic position or for Freud's deterministic position. What Freud excludes or does not want to see in this example is quite simply . . . the wet-nurse. The only reality he takes into account is that of the two interlocutors equally "centered on the subject"—i.e., the infantile subject and the adult subject; one sucks on the breast, the other experiences erotic pleasure. Freud does not acknowledge here the wet-nurse and *her* sexuality. He has completely forgotten his theory of seduction and does not take into account the pleasure of the seductress, wet-nurse or mother, who will take on such importance in the study on Leonardo. He treats the breast as an object for the infant and not as an erogenous zone for the nurse. Once one introduces a third term into the scene—namely the wet-nurse and *her* sexuality, which is no doubt vaguely intuited by the baby—it is no longer possible to consider après-coup as a simple combination of two opposing vectors. The third term is what has passed to the child from the adult: the *message* of the wet-nurse to the infant.

A second element that I would add in order to transform the concept of après-coup is the idea of translation. In my view, après-coup is inconceivable without a model of translation: it presupposes that something has been proffered by the other, which is retranslated and reinterpreted après-coup. On the one hand, I introduce the notion of the *other*, and on the other hand there is the model of *translation*. Even if we focus all our attention on the retroactive temporal direction, in the sense in which someone reinterprets his past, that past cannot be purely factual, a raw and untransformed *datum*. Rather, it contains in an immanent manner something *prior—a message* emanating from the other. It is thus impossible to advance a strictly hermeneutical position—since the *past already encompasses something, as a deposit, that demands to be deciphered,* which is the message of the other person. But doesn't modern hermeneutics forget its own beginnings, when it was—in the religious interpretation of the sacred texts—a hermeneutics of the message?

In concluding, I would like to say that Freud's concept of après-coup contains both a great richness and a certain ambiguity that combines a retrogressive motion and a progressive motion. I want to justify this problem of different directions, to and fro, by arguing that from the beginning there is something that goes in the direction of the past toward the future, from the other to the individual in question, from the adult toward the baby, which I call the implanting of the enigmatic message. This message is then retranslated, following a temporal direction that is alternately retrogressive and progressive (in agreement with my model of translation—detranslation—retranslation).

III
A Brief Treatise on the Unconscious

Preamble

1. The unconscious in question in this essay is the one discovered by Freud, within and outside of clinical practice, one that continues to be—such is what we postulate—the object of psychoanalysis.

What I attempted to bring to the fore in 1959, and to elaborate subsequently,[62] is a rather specific conception of the unconscious concerning its *mode of being* and its *genesis*. Like every theory, it exists at a distance from the facts, but is intent on accounting for their reciprocal relations—above all with regard to what is called clinical psychoanalysis, understood as what is uncovered and what happens in the psychoanalytic setting. To put things differently, my endeavor consists in placing what is foundational in psychoanalytic *practice* in relation to the foundational process of each human being insofar as it is characterized by the creation of an unconscious.

2. Historians are capable of debating endlessly the originality of Freud's discovery and the novelty of the psychoanalytic unconscious. Freud himself wavered between a feeling of having discovered

---

Nouvelle revue de psychanalyse 48 (1993).

62 See in particular *Problématiques IV: L'Inconscient et le ça* (Paris: PUF, 1981), where the report of Laplanche and Leclaire to the Bonneval Congress (1959) is reproduced: "L'Inconscient, une étude psychanalytique." See also *Nouveaux fondements pour la psychanalyse* (Paris: PUF, 1987), pp. 44–48 and 128–48.

a *terra incognita* and, on occasion, a willingness to attach his efforts to an older line of thought—as when, surprisingly, he invokes his allegiance to Schopenhauer's "unconscious will."[63]

My intention is not to enter into a debate over the history of ideas, about which there are others a thousand times more competent. I want only to emphasize that it is primarily in relation to the psychoanalytic *method*—which is to say, the altogether original and minutely described paths of access to the unconscious—that the originality of this new domain is repeatedly asserted.[64] On the other hand, it is in the way Freud conceptualizes the unconscious, thus situating it *topographically* and *genetically*, that Freud's ambiguity surfaces. Alongside texts (such as that of 1915) giving preponderance to the process of repression, and thus to a creation of the unconscious in the course of each individual existence, there is a constant temptation to situate the unconscious in one or another genetic lineage, in which it occupies a position of first (or primordial) element. Which yields a psychological lineage: "Everything that is conscious was first unconscious." And a line of ascent within the biological individual in which the id is the "great reservoir of drives" and constitutes the unrepressed part of the unconscious, one that would open directly onto the body. Finally, the lineage of the species and "phylogenesis": either by way of so-called primal fantasies that would constitute the core of the unconscious or under the rubric of a metabiological and metacosmological speculation that would take the unconscious of drives back to an immemorial atavism.

Thus, in Freud's thought, the mechanism of repression is pit-

---

63 I have commented on this penitential ritual of "Canossa" in *La Révolution copernicienne inachevée*, p. xviii.

64 Let us recall once again that the first issue in the definition of psychoanalysis, to which clinical practice and theory are both subordinated, is to be "a procedure for the investigation of mental processes which are barely accessible in any other way" (*SE* 18:235).

ted against a dynamic of emergence from a "primal"[65] realm, quite "naturally" assimilated to the unconscious and lending itself to a whole range of "romantic" reminiscences (in the broadest sense of this term).[66] But there is worse: the point of view of repression tended more and more to subordinate itself to that of emergence—thus the notion of a *primal repression*, the creator of an unconscious site, becomes sporadic after 1915; repression thereafter would be essentially secondary, that is, bearing on drive-impulses that were already present and surging from the primordial (but not primally repressed) unconscious.

3. The positing of a primally biological "id" of this sort, one necessarily preformed, went directly counter to the novelty implicit in the notion of the drive, as a sexual process that, in man, is not adapted to a pre-established aim. It made short shrift of Freud's deepening of the mechanism of repression and of its successive phases (specifically in the "Schreber Case," 1911, and "The Unconscious," 1915).

4. Last but not least, the relegation to secondary status of the repressed unconscious compromised the specificity of the psychoanalytic realm as a sexual realm. As soon as the unconscious is assimilated to a primordial id,[67] which itself is not only plugged into the body but also into a biologistic orientation (and even a vitalism), the forces in play become vital forces, independent at the outset from the sexual and from fantasy, which is inseparable from the sexual. The terms *life instinct—death instinct* designate perfectly those forces, which are predetermined in their finality, that can be defined in terms desirous of their independence both from the orgasmic and from fantasy: the

---

65 Cf., on this theme, *Le fourvoiement biologisant de la sexualité chez Freud* (Paris: Synthélabo, "Les empêcheurs de penser en rond," 1993), English translation by Donald Nicholson-Smith, *The Temptation of Biology: Freud's Theories of Sexuality* (New York, The Unconscious in Translation, 2015)
66 See below, p. 71.
67 I have shown in *L'inconscient et le ça* certain positive aspects of the notion (and even more of the term) "id," once one is prepared to disconnect it from the legacy of Groddeck, which is persistent in Freud himself. I oppose to the idea that there is, from the outset, at the bottom of man, "it," that of a process of repression, which creates in me a veritable "it"—more "it" than nature itself, one might say.

constitution of more and more inclusive units, on the one hand, or a return to the inorganic, on the other.[68]

To summarize our position, the stakes linked to an accurate conception of the unconscious go far beyond the domain of pure theory. They touch notably on 1) the foundation and comprehension of analytic practice; 2) the originality of Freud's discovery and the rupture it instituted in the history of ideas and even in the history of man; 3) the notion of drive; 4) the specificity of the sexual-fantasmatic domain, reaffirmed in practice as well as in theory.

With regard to these stakes, I will limit myself in this context to five essential points, of which several are on the order of an emphasis on ideas already articulated whereas others (3 and 4) entail developments that are more unfamiliar.

I.   The realism of the unconscious.
II. The process of repression.
III. The consequences of repression on the (celebrated) characteristics of the unconscious.
IV. The unconscious in life and in treatment.
V.   The unconscious and metaphysics.

I. THE REALISM OF THE UNCONSCIOUS

It was under the provocative banner of "the realism of the unconscious" that the communication by Laplanche and Leclaire to the Bonneval Colloquium of 1959 was presented. I find nothing essential to change regarding this point[69] and will be content to retrace rapidly the most salient elements.

---

68 I say "desirous of their independence," since fantasies linked to the notion of a life instinct and a death instinct are obvious, from the myth of Aristophanes to the images of Nirvana or a mineral, glacial, cosmic state, in which energy levels are close to zero.

69 In 1977–1978 (*Problématiques IV*), I elaborated retrospectively an extended reflection on this text, which still strikes me today as acceptable for the most part, with the single exception of a futile discussion pitting the unconscious as the condition of language against language as the condition of the unconscious, which, even with the best of intentions, remained enthralled to a certain Lacanian problematic.

1.   The reduction of the unconscious to a hidden *meaning* appears to me to be the constant temptation drawing Freud's discovery backwards into a millennial hermeneutics. Now it is conjointly in the elucidation of symptoms (in the broad sense, including slips of the tongue, parapraxes, dreams, etc.) and in the method for accessing them that the originality of "unconscious formations" can be asserted—as opposed to simple cases of polysemy, which are inherent in all systems of communication. The Freudian notion of a compromise formation implies a sort of bastardized production between (at least two) causal series, one of which, the unconscious chain, acts by way of displacement and condensation. A botched action, to take that convenient example, is not a simple act in everyday life beneath which interpretation would discover hidden meanings; no doubt the simple act of "boiling soup" may be (more or less legitimately) incorporated into different contexts relating it to a biological meaning (self-preservation), a sexual meaning (preparing the totemic feast), one that is sociological (higher classes and urban populations no longer eat soup), etc. But the symptom, the irruption of the unconscious, occurs only if I turn over the pot, or if I add too much salt when one of my guests suffers from hypertension.

What is called, in a term consecrated by usage (and allegedly derived from psychoanalysis), content analysis may bear equally on any text at all, with the purpose of giving one or several "readings": "the unconscious of a text "is by definition unlimited; every discourse is, according to Umberto Eco's expression, an "open work." Freud's approach, however, is entirely different, when what is at stake is the "subtlety of a bungled action"[70]: on a birthday card, a word "totally alien to the context" is introduced then crossed out: evidence of the irruption of an *other* causal chain.[71] What comes from the unconscious intervenes like an (inherently conflictual) reality at the heart of the

---

70 *The Subtleties of a Faulty Action* 1935, SE 22:233–38.
71 But not, for all that, of a chain of *meanings* or of a "signifying chain." [Editor's note: see Laplanche's 2003 "Displacement and Condensation" in *Freud and the Sexual* (New York, The Unconscious in Translation, 2011 pp. 133-138.)]

conscious "text," which, as a result, takes on an air of diminished coherence—at times riddled with gaps and at others, inversely, with moments of unjustifiable emphasis or insistence. In brief, the notions of defense, conflict, compromise, condensation, etc., lose all their impact when psychoanalysis is reduced to a new version of hermeneutics: a hermeneutics in which the "sexual meaning" would come to be superimposed on the infinite number of other possible meanings.

2.   The "realism of the unconscious" aimed at removing certain impasses affecting Freudian theory. I will recall two of them.

First of all there is the unresolved opposition between the functional hypothesis (in which a *common* representational content, a memory, belonging, according to the way in which it is "invested," either in the system Ucs or in the Pcs/Cs, and the topographical hypothesis (unconscious and conscious inscriptions are distinct and can coexist; one does not abolish the other). I discussed this point, which is not at all academic, at length in 1959[72] and above all in 1977.[73] What emerges first of all is that the "reification" hypothesis of two separate and independent traces of a common "event" is imposed, however strange it may seem, by "impressions drawn from analytic work," namely the fact that a "becoming conscious," however advanced it may be, does not abolish the unconscious inscription. The functional hypothesis, on the other hand, seems most at ease when it is not a matter of accounting for the return of the repressed, but of the reverse path, that is, of accounting for repression. If it is the "mnemic trace," the *representation of an event*, that is repressed, that is, which passes from a conscious state to an unconscious state, there is no need to attribute to it a double inscription.

Not without boldness, Freud thus allows two hypotheses to

---

72 "The Unconscious: A Psychoanalytic Study" in *Problématiques IV*, pp. 276–81, English translation by Luke Thurston with Lindsay Watson in *The Unconscious and the Id*, pp 234-238.
73 *Problématiques IV*, pp. 73–104 *The Unconscious and the Id*, pp. 58-86

coexist that are difficult to reconcile: repression is conceived on the model of a recollection consigned to memory; on the other hand, once that repression is accomplished, the unconscious inscription, in its peculiarity, reveals itself as something other than a mere recollection. But such a contradiction may also lead to questioning a proposition—all too widely accepted—according to which repression would be simply a particular case of committing to memory, the unconscious recollection being simply a deeper, more recessed reminiscence than an ordinary "preconscious" memory. What is the relation of repression to memory as memory is generally studied in psychology? The path on which I have deliberately set out consists in considering the element or unconscious "trace" *not as a memorized representation but as a sort of waste product of certain processes of memorization.*

A second impasse in Freud's theorization, which is also inherent in the attempt to include repression in a theory of memory and consciousness, is linked to the celebrated opposition of the terms *Wortvorstellung/Sachvorstellung*, quite accurately translated in the Standard Edition as "word-presentation" / "thing-presentation." Those two compound terms signify that the content of the "presentation" is, in one case, the word and in the other more or less the "mnemic image" of the thing. In addition (and despite all the nuances that it would be appropriate to introduce at this point), the thing-presentation, which is characteristic of the unconscious, is essentially constituted, according to Freud, by visual elements, whereas the word-presentation is acoustic by nature, composed of words capable of being *pronounced*.[74]

Now it is precisely at this point that the theory of the unconscious is placed—*incorrectly in my opinion*—within a psychological theory that makes the emergence into consciousness of a chain of thoughts dependent on the possibility of associating it, element by element, with acoustical verbal traces, capable of being brought back to life, reuttered,

---

74 And this even in *The Ego and the Id*, in which the "mnemic residues of things" are assimilated to "optical mnemic residues," while the "verbal residues are essentially derived from acoustical perceptions." *SE* 19:20–21.

at least incipiently, and thus perceived internally. That theory, which is already present in the *Project for a Scientific Psychology*,[75] is deserving of the greatest interest, in the context of "an account of normal processes"; it is indeed the one that is taken up anew in the celebrated formula: "The conscious presentation comprises the presentation of the thing plus the presentation of the word belonging to it, while the unconscious presentation is the presentation of the thing alone."[76] But it is precisely that link—the "plus" that should join word-presentation and thing-presentation—that is problematic in analytic work.

Thus it was necessary to ask what kind of reality is to be attributed to unconscious elements and to refuse to see in them mere "mnemic images" of things, more or less distorted replicas of events or objects. It was in order to convey this that I proposed the term *représentation-chose* for the translation of *Sachvorstellung*, not as a more accurate translation but as a provocative mistranslation.[77] What I want to convey with it is that the unconscious element is not a representation *referring* to an external thing whose "trace" it would be, but that the transition to unconscious status is correlated with a loss of reference. The representation (or, in more contemporary and truer terms: the signifier), in becoming unconscious, loses its status as representation (or signifier) and becomes a thing that no longer represents (signifies) anything other than itself.

---

75 Part 3: "The Origins of Psychoanalysis."

76 "The Unconscious," in *SE* 14:201.

77 See, for instance, *Problématiques IV*, p. 96ff. *Problématiques V*, pp. 112–13.

My friend Daniel Widlöcher will forgive me for being amused at seeing him ascribe to Freud the notion of "thing-representation, which is, properly speaking, foreign to him. See "Temps pour entendre, temps pour interpréter, temps pour comprendre," *Bulletin de la Fédération européenne de psychanalyse*, no. 40 (1993): 24–25. And, when he asserts that such unconscious representations "refer to nothing other than themselves," without realizing it he is moving in the direction of Laplanche's meaning (1959) and not of Freud's.

As for his suggestion that we call thing-representations "action-representation," it in fact corresponds to the idea that the alien internal entities still remain active, that they are "causes" in the "metaphysical" sense of the term; see part 5 below, and also *La révolution copernicienne inachevée*, p. 392.

3.   The "realism of the unconscious" assigns itself the objective of giving a precise meaning to the notion of "psychical reality," which Freud constantly used but which he never really defined autonomously other than on rare occasions, whereas most of the time he reduces it to psychological reality, that is, in the last analysis, to our subjectivity as we experience it.[78]

In distinguishing not two orders of reality, as Freud most frequently does (external material reality and internal psychological reality), but three, i. e., by adding the reality of the message, or that of the signifier, I must acknowledge that this evokes rudimentary tripartite divisions attempted by Freud himself, as well, of course, as the tripartite Lacanian scheme: Real, Imaginary, Symbolic.[79]

Clarifying matters in summary fashion, I will say that I do not at all adhere to the two first categories in the sense given to them by Lacan, satisfying myself, on the contrary, with Freud's solid opposition:

            Freud: external reality – psychological reality

and not   Lacan: the Real – the Imaginary

As for the third category, I consider the Freudian term *psychical reality* to be the index of a reality that has been neglected up until now but cannot be assimilated to the Lacanian "Symbolic," whose narrowly linguistic and supra-individual or structural (and, in a word, metaphysical) character I reject (see below, p. 92 ff).[80]

---

78 Concerning all this, see in particular *Problématiques V*, pp. 89–101. See also "Séduction, persécution, révélation," *Psychanalyse à l'université*, no. 18 (1993): 72.

79 See, for example, *Problématiques IV*, pp. 89–91.

80 In tribute to Lacan, and even after all my disagreements with "Lacanianism" have been taken into account, at least two aspects should be emphatically noted:
- *the man and master* was an extraordinary source of stimulation for thought and research in a somewhat monotonously repetitive post-Freudian world;
- the *thinker* imposed the certitude, unprecedented in the Freudian realm, that the unconscious and drives do not emerge from the obscure depths of "life," but that their genesis and nature are inseparable from the human sphere and interhuman communication.

From both these perspectives, a rereading of the striking *Function and Field of Speech and Language in Psychoanalysis*, trans. Alan Sheridan (London: Tavistock, 1977) is in order.

The category of the message or of the signifier as something "signifying for" or "addressed to"[81] is absolutely different from that of the Symbolic: the message may be verbal or nonverbal, more or less structured, or only marginally implicated in a structure. The Lacanian model of language, borrowed directly from Saussure and the structuralists, is ultimately valid only for a perfect, "well-made," univocal language in which the fixed differences between signifiers (the "values") determine (and indeed render superfluous) the relation of a signifier to a specific signified.[82] In sum, I understand the category of the message or the "signifier for" in terms of the full extension given by Freud to language, including the language of gestures and every other mode of expression of psychical activity.

And yet that category is insufficient to account for what we call "unconscious psychical reality." One needs to supplement it with the strange transformation effected by repression and resulting in the formation of a thing-presentation or, put differently, a designified signifier.[83]

4.   Ultimately, the realism of the unconscious is closely connected with what I have called its "clinico-theoretical deduction,"[84] that is, a kind of demonstration of its necessity on the basis of the primordially asymmetrical situation of the adult-child relation. I will return to this

---

81 Cf., for example, *Nouveaux fondements pour la psychanalyse*, pp. 47–48.

82 As in mathematics; cf., for example, *Problématiques IV*, pp. 129–34.

83 To the extent that one introduces the notion of thing-presentation, the opposition of presentation of the thing/presentation of the word becomes irrelevant for the psychoanalytic unconscious:

1) A word-presentation (or verbal presentation) becomes in the unconscious, exactly like a (visual) thing-presentation.

2) The presentation of the thing has an interest for psychoanalysis and is "treated" by repression only to the extent to which it conveys a message and is "signified" or "addressed to."

On the other hand, this opposition retains its value for a psychology of memory in which what is at stake is the remembering of a preconscious memory (see above, p. 63–64 and below p. 69 ff).

84 *New Foundations for Psychoanalysis*, p. 151.

in a few lines, but what I want to emphasize first is that this model of repression is not intent on accounting solely for the genesis of the repressed (the existence of the repressed) but also for the production of a certain kind of reality, called "unconscious" (the nature of the repressed).

II. THE "TRANSLATIONAL MODEL" OF REPRESSION

Having repeatedly elaborated and attempted to perfect[85] this model,[86] here I will indicate only some essential points, stressing recent developments.

1.   The translational model of repression is conceivable only in the context of the theory of seduction. The thing-presentations that form the core of the unconscious can be conceived as what eludes the first attempts of the child to forge an interhuman world by translating the messages coming from adults into a more or less coherent vision. The partial (but necessary) failure of such attempts stems from the fact that these messages are enigmatic for the very person emitting them which is to say they are *compromised* by the adult's unconscious. The only emphasis that I will supply at this juncture will be a reminder that the adult-child relation is eminently suited to the reawakening of conflicts and desires issuing from the unconscious:[87] all messages are not equally enigmatic, but especially enigmatic are those emitted under certain conditions of reactivation.

---

85 The most recent references are *New Foundations*, chapter 3, and "Interpretation Between Determinism and Hermeneutics," translated by Philip Slotkin in Jean Laplanche, *Essays on Otherness*, (London, Routledge, 1999) ed. John Fletcher pp. 138–65.

86 Which stems, as is known, from Freud's Letter 52 to Fliess.

87 See, among others, my allusion to the article of Milton Malev, "The Jewish Orthodox Circumcision Ceremony," in *Problématiques II*, p. 239 ff. Circumcision itself can be viewed as a symptomatic act, a "message compromised" by the unconscious of adults. See as well, concerning the "explicit threat of castration" and its seductive value: "Seduction, Persecution, Revelation," this volume, Chapter 1.

2.   The model of the substitution of signifiers or *metabola*, as proposed already at Bonneval (1959), still seems valid to me. Derived from a schema of Lacan, it was sharply criticized, no doubt because it was simultaneously too much and too little indebted to Lacan. It has the genuine though limited interest of furnishing a suggestive model for thought. I have taken it up a number of times, both in *Problématiques* and in my *Nouveaux fondements*.[88]

I will recall that it is a question proposed to the subject in the presence of a message (a signifier S_1) of undertaking a "translation" by substituting a new signifier (S_2) for the initial signifier S_1. S_1 and S_2 are frequently in a complex relation composed of resemblances, contiguities, and even oppositions.

The initial formula was written as follows:

$$\frac{S_1}{s} \times \frac{S_2}{S_1} = \frac{\dfrac{S_2}{s}}{\dfrac{S_1}{S_1}}$$

in which the translation process is being compared to the action of a multiplier $\dfrac{S_2}{S_1}$ on a multiplicand $\dfrac{S_1}{s}$.

The formula, as reproduced here, corresponds to the first translations of adult messages that the child creates for himself. According to the formula of Freud himself, these translations are accompanied by failures of translation that are—precisely—the first acts of repression which is to say they are instances of primal repression.

The principal merit of this schematic representation of the process is to confront the mind with the paradox of a residue of translation, which no longer signifies anything but itself: $\dfrac{S_1}{S_1}$

_____

88 *New Foundations*, pp. 130–33.

But, in simple equations such as this, mathematics emphasizes the conservation of quantity and is incapable of giving an account of the disruption entailed by psychical *metabolism*. So we must understand that the two halves of the diagram do not really correspond to an equality (suggested by the equal sign) but rather to a transformation (which could be indicated by an arrow).

On the left, it is a question of a message to be translated (M_1) and not of a signifier (one does not translate an isolated signifier). On the right we discover both the partial translation of the message (M_2) as well as the repressed signifier(s) S_1/S_1.

A schematic representation giving a better picture of primal repression would thus be something like:

$$\frac{M_1}{s} \times \frac{M_2}{M_1} \to \frac{\dfrac{M_2}{s}}{\dfrac{S_1}{S_1}}$$

This allows us to understand that the repressed signifier S_1 is the untranslated residue of message M_1 and not the message in its totality. The message is partially translated and partially repressed.

3.   The crucial point for understanding the translation model of repression is to grasp firmly the idea that repression cannot be considered a particular version of consigning something to memory.

Among the innumerable texts Freud devoted to memory, mnemic traces, and remembrance, only a few are concerned with the problem of fixation in memory. The most remarkable is a passage in the Leonardo book plainly suggested by the problem of the childhood "vulture" memory.[89] To make himself understood, Freud compares the way in which a human individual stores his memories to the way in which history is written at the collective level. There would thus

---

89 *SE* 11:82.

be two rather distinct ways of writing history (or historiography, *Geschichtsschreibung*): one, in the manner of chroniclers, consists in a "continuous, day by day record of present experience" and the other casts a "glance back to the past, gathers traditions and legends, interprets the traces of antiquity that survive in customs and usages, and in this way creates a history of the past." This second historiography plainly distorts matters as a function of contemporary interests and the aversion provoked by many a past event. It should be noted that in the second case two phases of inscription are explicitly required, since the *a posteriori* reconstruction does not take place on the basis of nothing: an initial inscription of "traces of the past" was indeed required, but these are not traced by the historian. Inversely, I will add, the historian-chronicler is not a mere recorder of facts. At a time when audiovisual recording had not yet supplanted the chronicle, he had at least to transcribe things that had been experienced, and to do so in a text as faithful and neutral as possible. The path from experience to text is assuredly not innocent, but in relation to a history "rewritten" considerably after the fact the difference remains immense. Freud's favorite example concerning such rewriting is that of Titus-Livius composing, at the beginning of the modern era, a history of the origins of Rome: the huts of the founders of Rome are transformed into sumptuous palaces, the tribal chiefs into kings of illustrious origin, etc.

According to Freud, for the individual, in a manner parallel to the two historiographies, there would be two types of memorization. The first, "entirely comparable" to the history of the chronicler, would be a "man's conscious memory of lived experiences of his maturity." The second would be that of childhood memories which "correspond, as far as their origin and reliability are concerned, to the history of a nation's earliest days, which was compiled later and for tendentious reasons."[90]

---

90 Ibid., 83–84.

I note the following points:

Memorization for the (normal) adult is alleged not to entail any essential distortion. We are dealing here, to be sure, with an ideal model, which the psychology of daily life cannot accept in unmodified form.

The committing to memory of childhood experience is alleged to occur a posteriori, but, to be sure, it posits an initial phase in childhood, that of the deposition of traces. Here then we find quite precisely the model of après-coup or of trauma in two phases. What undergoes distortion and rearrangement in memory are not childhood events (which are by nature inaccessible), but rather the early deposition of their traces.

Finally, we should emphasize that here we are dealing with a model of *conscious memory*, the result of the secondary elaboration in which Freud is interested here is the conscious memory—quite precisely, the "screen-memory." But to utter that term (*Deckerinnerung*) is to indicate that it covers over and prevents the emergence of something: precisely the repressed.

There has been so much interest in the "childhood memory of Leonardo da Vinci" focused on the question of to which real event it corresponds that, as a result, seeing it for what it is has simply been neglected. It is not a repressed unconscious element but rather is a screen-memory to which the model of a distorting and repressive memorization can be applied. Moreover, the Leonardo text[91] being one of the principal occasions in which the function of seduction reemerges, I do not think it at all arbitrary to apply the model of the repressive *metabola*, while simplifying, to be sure, its elements.

M_1—the message inscribed in an initial phase, which we will designate, in a considerable simplification, as the "vehement caresses" (of the mother).[92]

---

91 Ibid., pp. 120–23.
92 Ibid., pp. 115–16.

M_2—the screen memory—call it the "fable of the bird," thus avoiding the secondary controversy of the kite vs. the vulture.[93]

The repressive *metabola*, characterizing the après-coup phase, might be schematized as follows:

$$\frac{\text{vehement caresses}}{s} \times \frac{\text{bird-related fable}}{\text{vehement caresses}} \rightarrow \frac{\dfrac{\text{bird-related fable}}{s} \quad S_1}{S_1}$$

A long commentary would be necessary:

(1) The "vehement caresses"[94] of the mother are messages addressed to the subject, Leonardo. Their initial inscription does *not* necessitate a translation; it is purely and simply an implantation. In still other words, they are perceptual elements, but perceptual elements which "signal" something;[95] they do not need to be transcribed into signifiers, since they are, from the outset, "signifiers to."

(2) These "vehement caresses" are *enigmatic* messages. Their signified is partly sexual, perverse, unknown to the mother herself.[96]

---

93 See J.-P. Maïdani-Gérard, Léonard de Vinci: mythologie ou théologie? (Paris: PUF, 1993). What Freud discussed with his "Egyptian" hypothesis relating to the goddess Mout, what J.-P. Maïdani-Gérard discussed anew, with the Christian hypothesis of the theme of the Immaculate Conception, is the ideological context, the "language of translation" in which the substitute message M2 is situated.

94 *SE* 11:115–16.

95 They are *Wahrnehmungszeichen* (perceptual indices). See, for instance, *New Foundations*, pp 130ff., and *La Révolution copernicienne inachevée*, pp. xxv–xxvi.

96 "A mother's love for the infant she suckles and cares for is something much more profound than her later affection for the growing child. It is in the nature of a completely satisfying love relation, which not only fulfills every mental wish but also every physical need; and if it represents one of the forms of attainable human happiness, that is in no little measure due to the possibility it offers of satisfying, without reproach, wishful impulses which have long been repressed and which must be called perverse." *SE* 11:117.

(3) My schema would be deficient if it allowed one to believe that what is rediscovered at the unconscious level is nothing other than the "enigmatic signifier" with which we began. In point of fact, we should insist on the notion that the enigmatic adult messages undergo a reconfiguration or dislocation. Certain of their aspects are translated while a number of "anamorphic" elements are excluded from the translation and become unconscious. This is why, despite the success it has enjoyed, the term "enigmatic signifier" is inaccurate as a designation for the complex and compromised message of the adult. In contrast, at the unconscious level, the term "designified signifier" strikes me as being more correct. In my model, I leave it in its algebraic formulation $S_1/S_{1'}$, being no more able than Freud was to pursue the "analysis" of Leonardo.

In no way should we assimilate the analysis of Leonardo to an analytic treatment. It is lacking essential elements—transference and working through under pressure of the primordial enigmatic situation—that cannot be added in absentia. And yet the paths explored by Freud in his investigation are not without interest: first of all, he makes use of a method close to that of free associations, utilizing material freely juxtaposed from Leonardo's notebooks. In addition, despite appearances, he does not attempt to discover the meaning(s) of the bird-related fable. On the contrary, he dismantles it, relating it to the ideological, cultural, and linguistic elements that intersect in it and give it an appearance of consistency. Ultimately he finds correlations, associative links between these elements of the fable and those of the primordial situation (itself partially conjectured thanks to historical information about Leonardo's family), which allows him to approach a designified-signifier, something orbiting around the smile, the penetrating kiss . . . a veritable object-source of the drive and a part of the artistic creativity of Leonardo.

III. THE FEATURES OF THE UNCONSCIOUS AND THEIR EXPLANATION BY WAY OF REPRESSION

On more than one occasion, Freud enumerated the features of the system unconscious or those of the id, which he quite properly views as identical. What means does he use to achieve this conclusion?

The idea that only what is directly accessible to consciousness is knowable in the psychical apparatus (or outside of it) is extremely debatable. Through sheer reverence for the term *unconscious*, and by virtue of the "essential closure" affecting it in the person in question (*ego*), might we have lost Freud's daring when, in "A Child Is Being Beaten," he claims to know and articulate a fantasy that, in most cases, can absolutely not become conscious ("I am being beaten by my father"). Even if it were the case that Freud was wrong regarding the object of his inference, at least the implications of the procedure were perfectly assumed: *one can speak of* the unconscious and detect—and even reconstruct—some of its contents.

Beyond what can be observed directly (which does not at all imply accurate knowledge!), facts and extant realities can be inferred from other more indirectly observable phenomena. This is the case for numerous physically existing realities. Thus the atom had long been deduced before being observed.[97] And thus, in astrophysics, the "black holes," which *by definition* are not visible (as they absorb all rays), are detectable only indirectly through their gravitational effects. It is by way of just such an *indirect* procedure that Freud bases his claim regarding the id: "What little we know of it we have learnt from our study of the dream-work and the construction of neurotic symptoms."[98] Ultimately, properties of what exists and even what exists itself can be deduced from a model, which itself is forged by

---

97 The fact that the atom is not observed but deduced allowed a certain idealism of the "constructed" scientific object to reign for a considerable amount of time. The atom, it was claimed, is no more than a bundle of equations.
98 *New Introductory Lectures*, in SE 22:73.

contact with observed facts. Let us recall, following Popper, that a contradiction between one of the consequences deduced from the model and a fact of experience will have as a result a "falsification"[99] of the model, entailing either its abandonment or its deep modification or its integration as a particular case within a more general model.[100] This model may also be of different sorts: static, that is describing a relatively stationary state,[101] or genetic, that is "predicting" the properties of an object on the basis of its production. In this sense, the translational model of repression is "genetic" since it describes the production of the unconscious and it should thus be possible to deduce not only the existence of the unconscious[102] but certain of its properties—its consistency, one might say.[103]

1. *Unconsciousness and Atemporality*

For several reasons I am linking these two problems, which, in my view, cast light on each other. Freud, in considering them

---

99 I retain the word *falsification*, which does not encompass all refutations. Falsification refers to the failure of a theory with regard to one of its major *consequences*.

100 A famous example: Einstein and Newtonian physics. Another example of falsification: Freud's abandonment of the theory of seduction because certain of its consequences contradicted experience.

101 Einsteinian physics described the bending of light rays by gravitation before that could be observed.

102 See "The Wall and the Arcade," in *Jean Laplanche: Seduction, Translation, and the Drives*, pp. 197–216.

103 One further remark on the fact that the id possesses primarily negative characteristics. Freud connects this to the fact that the id "can only be described in opposition to the ego" (*New Introductory Lectures*, in *SE* 22:73). But such a characterization "in the negative" can also be understood in terms of genesis to the extent that the latter *does away with* certain aspects of the conscious psychical network (as indicated in the Bonneval Report, with its chapter on the fiction of a language in a reduced state," *Problématiques IV*, pp. 297–300). Note, moreover, that for one of the major characteristics, we are dealing with a kind of negation of negation: "the absence of negation in the unconscious."

Ultimately, from the perspective of proof, negative characteristics (no man is a quadruped) lend themselves to falsification as much as positive ones (all men have thumbs opposable to the other fingers of the same hand).

separately, gave priority in an ineluctable manner to the problem of becoming conscious[104] and mortgaged himself to a conscientialist theory, whereas, in my view, his conception of the system unconscious is driven by something other than the light of consciousness with which we illuminate (or fail to illuminate) one or another preconscious memory or affect. In this regard, I have little to remove from—and only would add a bit to—my short account in "The Unconscious and the Problem of Consciousness" of 1959.[105]

In two recent articles on time,[106] I propose to distinguish four temporal levels, of which two are aligned with our object: the psyche of the human being.

"Level II is perceptual time, that of immediate consciousness; it is also . . . the time of living beings. Level III is the time of memory and of the individual project, the temporalization of the human being."[107] I situated Freud's contributions at those two levels that were, unfortunately, poorly differentiated by Freud himself. Level II, that of immediate temporality, is described by him in elaborations of a psychophysiological cast, in which "time" is viewed in relation to perception and its rhythmicity. As for level III, Freud, without having actually thematized it, contributed a decisive notion: that of après-coup. I also indicated that the confusion of those two levels, and above all the interference of problematic II (which is extrapsychoanalytic) in problematic III was one of the forms taken by the forced reintegration of psychoanalysis into general psychology.[108] And yet one can see that on occasion the distinction is clearly present in Freud: in the passage on Leonardo noted above, the consignment to memory in the manner of the "chronicler" corresponds to level II of temporality, the consign-

---

104 *Bewusstwerden* or "becoming-conscious."
105 Section I. (C) of "The Unconscious: a Psychoanalytic Study" in *Problématiques IV*.
106 "Psychoanalysis, temporality and translation" in *Jean Laplanche: Seduction, Translation, and the Drives*, pp. 161–77; Jean Laplanche, "Time and the Other," translated by Luke Thurston in *Essays on Otherness*, pp. 237–41.
107 Ibid., p. 239.
108 Ibid., pp. 240–41.

ment to memory in the manner of a rewriting that corresponds to level III.

From the perspective of the "unconscious," the level of perceptual temporality and immediate consciousness mainly concerns the preconscious-conscious relation, that is, access to my personal archives. On the other hand, it is at the level of *temporalization* conceived as a narrativization, a translation of enigmas emanating from the other, and then of an ongoing "self-theorization," that repression is to be situated—precisely as a failure of that temporalization and as a deposition of untranslated residues.

That being the case, the word *consciousness*, which should be heard in our psychoanalytic term *unconscious*, is not the immediate, vital *consciousness* rooted in perception. The use of the word consciousness by a Hegel in expressions such as "unhappy consciousness," "pious consciousness," and even by Freud himself in "consciousness of guilt" (*Schuldbewusstsein*) brings us closer to what is at stake. In the word *con-sciousness*, we should allow etymology (*cum-scire*) its full importance—as, in each human being, a relatively organized and coherent (*co-haerens*) "knowledge"[109] of oneself, one's entourage, and one's fate. This "self-knowledge," constituted après-coup, and thus taking up the past from the point of view of the present with an eye to the future, this movement of translation, has its origin in the "unmoved mover" of the enigmatic address emanating from the (external) other.[110] It necessarily leaves out something of that address, something untranslatable that becomes the unconscious, the internal other. That internal other, in turn, functions as an agent, a source-object, constantly seeking to penetrate into con-scious existence (which is something *entirely different* from emerging into the light of consciousness-perception).

From this perspective, the adjective "atemporal" (*zeitlos*) does

---

109 Which is, to be sure, nonscientific and for the most part based on fantasy or ideology; as is the case for infantile sexual "theories."
110 "Temporalité et traduction," in *La révolution copernicienne inachevée*, p. 325 ff.

not designate an extrinsic quality of the "other thing" in us, but its very being, determined by its genesis: exclusion from the work of temporalization specific to the Pcs/Cs system.[111]

While the term *atemporal*, or *timeless*, can thus be considered more pertinent than that of *unconscious*, the exclusion of what is "atemporal" in relation to consciousness is much less direct and essential than may have been thought.[112] *A priori*, nothing prevents contents of the "atemporal," thing-presentations, from acceding to consciousness without passing through temporalization (the system Pcs) and without losing their full participation in their "system": ecmnesic resurgences with or without hypnosis, hallucinations.[113] Conversely, the simple addition of a word-presentation to a thing-presentation—which Freud ultimately sees as the essence of access to consciousness—is quite insufficient when it is a matter of reintegrating the thing-presentation into the space of temporalization.[114] At the very least, what is required is the work of analytic treatment.

2. *Absence of Coordination and Negation*

I find nothing to add on this score to the fundamental

---

111 "The processes of the system Ucs are *timeless*, i.e., they are not ordered temporally, are not altered by the passage of time; they have no reference to time at all. Reference to time is bound up, once again, with the work of the system Cs" (or "system Pcs" in the 1915 edition ["The Unconscious," in *SE* 14:187]).

   It could not be formulated any better. And yet Freud's hesitation between "system Cs" and "system Pcs" indicates his uncertainty with regard to what I am calling "consciousness II" (immediate consciousness) and "temporalizing con-sciousness III," which corresponds, for him, to the system Pcs.

112 For purposes of convenience, I am designating by this term, *Bewusstheit* in German, consciousness II, linked to immediate temporality. This is Freud's system perception-consciousness.

113 See *Problématiques IV*, etc.

114 We should recall that the nature of the thing-presentation depends on neither the (visual-auditory) sensorium nor the (verbal or nonverbal) content through which it emerges. A word-presentation, upon being repressed, becomes a thing-representation. Nothing prevents such a word-based thing-presentation from acceding directly to consciousness through an attempt at reutterance: dream sentences, verbal hallucinations.

description of the system Ucs or the id, taken up by Freud on several occasions, for instance in the *New Introductory Lectures*:

> It is filled with energy reaching it from the drives, but it has no organization, produces no collective will, but only a striving to bring about the satisfaction of the needs of the drives subject to the observance of the pleasure principle. The logical laws of thought do not apply in the id, and this is true above all of the law of contradiction. Contrary impulses exist side by side, without cancelling each other out or diminishing each other; at the most they may converge to form compromises under the dominating economic pressure towards the discharge of energy. There is nothing in the id that could be compared with negation.[115]

Lack of coordination and absence of contradiction[116] obviously go together, the principle of the excluded middle being essential to the coordination of thoughts. The same holds for the notion of "value," which is crucial in semiology and allows specific signifiers to be marked by their difference with neighboring signifiers. It is precisely those linkages, differences, and coordinations that are abolished by repression. Freud already noted, and properly so, that repression worked in a "highly individual" manner.[117] But despite his assertion of "the very great extent to which repression and the unconscious are correlated,"[118] he was reticent when confronted with the hypothesis of explaining the characteristics of the unconscious in terms of the process of repression. When the notion of the id appeared later on, the description of a system without either coordination or

---

115 *New Introductory Lectures*, in *SE* 22:73–74.
116 For an isolated formulation going in the opposite direction, and which I consider to be a slip, see *Problématiques IV*, p. 103, note 1.
117 "Repression," in *SE* 14:150.
118 Ibid., pp. 147–48.

"collective impulse," imposed in large part by analytic experience, would be maintained, even though it appears minimally attuned to an endogenous origin of the id, if the latter is conceived as "taking up into itself the needs of the drives."[119] In fact, nothing in the observation of living *organisms* allows us to assert such a *disorganization* of needs, which would, moreover, be incompatible with life. And if one were to admit, in agreement with an increasingly prevalent perspective in Freud, that "in the id, which is capable of being inherited, are harbored residues of the existence of countless egos,"[120] and notably those organizers that are the complexes (*organized groups* of representations) and primal fantasies (typical fantasmatic structures[121]), the contradiction with the former description of the unconscious system would be even more striking.

That the id (the system Ucs) is the result of repression, and that repression is to be understood in terms of a translation-based theory are *my* hypotheses. At the least, they have the advantage of accounting for the features of the system as Freud drew them from analytic experience. To put things succinctly, translation treats the message as a coherent whole, whereas untranslated signifiers are not coherent with each other and do not form a chain; repression, the negative face of the translation of the enigmatic message, has the effect of dislocation.

Here I propose to illustrate this precise point (translation dislocates what it rejects) without in any way claiming to give an example of repression, in the psychoanalytic sense—if only by virtue of the fact that we are dealing with a case of interlingual translation, but for many other reasons as well.

---

119 *New Introductory Lectures*, in *SE* 22:73.
120 *The Ego and the Id*, in *SE* 19:38.
121 This becomes most palpable in the *Moses* study: with the massive return of the notions of instinct, phylogenesis, and even with the notion that "the course of events in the id, and their mutual interaction, are governed by quite different laws than those prevailing in the ego" (*SE* 23:96). For this is something entirely different from saying, as previously, that they "exist side by side without being influenced by one another" (*SE* 14:186).

Consider the translation of the French sentence: *"L'étalon court dans la ferme."* The two words *etalon* and *ferme* have homonyms.

> *étalon* 1 = horse intended for reproduction (English: stallion)
> *étalon* 2 = legal unit of measurement (English: standard)
> *ferme* 1 = agricultural land that is exploited (English: farm)
> *ferme* 2 = a collection of things bound together (English: truss)

The English translation, according to meaning and context, obviously chooses *étalon* 1 and *ferme* 1, which yields: "The stallion is running in the farm." What is thus left aside are the signifiers:

> *étalon* 2 = legal unit of measurement
> and *ferme* 2 = truss

But those abandoned signifiers have no syntagmatic or paradigmatic relation between them. They do not form a second "signifying chain"; to paraphrase Freud, they persist side by side without either influencing or contradicting each other.[122]

It is explicitly from the *absence of negation* in the unconscious that Freud derives the absence of an unconscious representation of *death*.[123] Without wishing to delve any deeper here into that rather

---

122 The choice, in this example, of homonyms rather than polysemic terms, takes on an additional meaning. It should be remembered that a word's *polysemy* consists in the fact that there are several meanings, which are in a relation of (metaphoric or metonymic) derivation between them. *Homonymy* designates two words pronounced (or even written) identically and having no relation of derivation between them, referring to different histories and contexts, and often having different etymologies. The interest of homonyms is to illustrate the notion of *compromise*, in symptoms, dreams, parapraxes, etc., as a *mechanical signifying confluence* of two causal series, and not as a "second meaning" hidden beneath the first.

   Thus, in Freud's brief article (referred to above, p. 61 n. 70), the word *bis* is a perfect homonym in this sense, since it belongs simultaneously to Latin (*bis* = twice) and to German (*bis* = up until), and plainly one cannot say that there is a superimposition of two *meanings* of the same word such as might be entertained by hermeneutics

123 "What we call our 'unconscious' knows nothing that is negative, and no negation; —in it, contradictories coincide. *For that reason* it does not know its own death, for to that we can only give a negative content," "Thought for the Times on War and Death," in *SE* 14:296 (my emphasis).

complex question,[124] I would insist on noting that Freud should have extended that inference to the notion of castration, to which (in proper Freudian doctrine) we can also only give a "negative content."

But in a more general manner, the notion of an "unconscious complex," whether "oedipal" or "castratory," is particularly in need of being reexamined to the extent that a complex corresponds to a structure with its complementarities, coordinations, reciprocities, and exclusions. If the Oedipus complex is a major variant of kinship structures, a basis for the exchange of persons, goods, and ideas, it is hard to perceive how such "binding" of the contemporary soul would find its place in the realm of the "unbound." The presence in the unconscious of elementary (but uncoordinated) impulses regarding parents is not to be rejected for that reason. This is not the case for castration, an idea wholly sustained by negation at the heart of the phallic-castrated opposition,[125] and which can *only* be conceived as an organizer imposing, at higher levels, its binary logic, with, as its most tangible benefit, the binding of the anxiety caused by the attack of the drive within the fear of a danger that can be discerned and mastered.

3. *The Unconscious and the Primary Process*

A renewed consideration, however, ought to lead us to nuance those last assertions: we frequently admit, following Freud, that in the unconscious the primary process reigns, characterized by the mobility of investments and by the mechanisms of displacement and condensation. Now such mobility, implying incessant exchanges between unconscious signifiers, appears to be quite difficult to recon-

---

124 Are there, in general, ideas in the unconscious?

What is the relation between that thesis of Freud's and those concerning the representation of death in children and primitives, once the idea that the unconscious is what is most "primitive" in us has been rejected?

If death is revealed to me by the death of the other, what kind of metabolism and repression then process that message?

125 See articles on the "castration complex" and "foreclosure," in *The Language of Psychoanalysis; Problématiques II, passim; New Foundations for Psychoanalysis*, pp. 36–37.

cile with the conception of thing-presentations as fixed and separated from each other by the process of repression.

We may note, first of all, that it is in relation to dreams and, more generally, to the formation of symptoms that the primary process is discovered. More precisely, it is postulated as characterizing the unconscious work culminating in dreams, jokes, symptoms, etc. That work, moreover, most often bears on "residues" that are not unconscious, but preconscious.

On the other hand, in favor of the fixity of the unconscious, in clinical experience we find striking manifestations to which certain formulations of Freud bear witness: most prominent among them is "repetition compulsion," which, in *Beyond the Pleasure Principle*, is described as the model of the return of the same, practically of the identical. In *The Problem of Anxiety* that compulsion is designated as the "resistance of the unconscious" and defined as "the attraction exerted by the unconscious prototypes upon the repressed drives."[126]

The solution is, in fact, close at hand if one keeps in mind the distinction between primal and secondary repression: the second being characterized precisely by the existence of an attraction exercised by what is primally repressed. There would thus be reason to distinguish *schematically* two levels in the system unconscious: that of the primally repressed, constituted by unconscious prototypes, characterized by their fixity and the effect of attraction they exercise, not on each other, but on the representations that pass within their reach; and that of the secondarily repressed, to which the primary process is applied. Not to mention, of course, the momentary attraction of preconscious residues subject in turn to displacement, condensation, and overdetermination in the course of symptom formation.

If one considers that, despite its strangeness from the perspective of logical thought, the primary process nonetheless constitutes a kind of binding and if one recalls that the sexual death drive is a prin-

---

126 *SE* 20:159–60.

ciple of unbinding, whereas the sexual life drive (or Eros) functions in agreement with the principle of binding, it will be admitted that the deepest level, that of what is primally repressed, is the privileged locus of the sexual death drive ("a pure culture of alterity"), while in the secondarily repressed, the locus of the primary process, both types of drive begin to struggle with each other and to compromise.[127]

It is clear that this stratification of unconscious contents and processes entails a nuancing of the conclusion of the preceding section: it is from the "primal" unconscious that the presence of complexes ought to be excluded. Yet even if one discovers them at the level of the secondary unconscious, they nonetheless assume very special forms in which *contradiction* does not yet exist: the castratory wound is present in it as a perforation, "button hole," or even a cut, but not as a cutting off.[128] One can slice a body into a thousand pieces; one can slice it incompletely. But to slice off the piece called phallus is an act of negation, culminating in the category "castrated." As such the castratory *removal* does not belong to the unconscious.[129]

4. *The Unconscious and Affect*

I would not be coming back to this question (however summarily) were it not that it lends itself to accusations concerning my intention. Denying the presence of affects in the unconscious would be tantamount to promoting an intellectualist mode of psychoanalysis, failing to leave room for affective relations, the expression of sentiments, etc. Among the accused in this procedure are to be counted Freud's text of 1915, Lacanian theory, and also, of course, the conception of the author

---

127 A conflict that is pursued at higher levels, between the ego, the superego, and the id: "The struggle which once raged in the deepest strata of the mind . . . is now continued in a higher region, like the Battle of the Huns in Kaulbach's painting," *The Ego and the Id*, in *SE* 19:39.

128 See my commentary on the prehistoric paintings described by Leroi-Gourhan, *Problématiques II*, pp. 268–69.

129 "In analysis, we never discover a 'no' in the unconscious," "Negation," in *SE* 19:239.

of these lines, from 1959 until the present. In a few words then:

1. My theory of repression, derived from that of Freud in 1915, reinterpreted by way of the notion of translation, implies that "in the unconscious" there are "thing-presentations." And thus no affect . . . but not any "representations of" either!

Conceiving of the contents of the unconscious as psychical "things," "internal alien entities," entails an intellectual effort. The only question is whether or not it is profitable!

2. The messages that are the object of the first translations are neither essentially verbal nor "intellectual" either! They include, for the most part, affective signifiers, which can be translated or repressed: a smile (in the case of Leonardo), an angry gesture, an expression of disgust, etc. Those signifiers, if they are repressed, will be stripped of meaning, exactly as more "intellectual" signifiers are. The "exclusion" of affect is in this case but a general consequence of the exclusion of the signified.

3. The locus of affect is primarily the body and secondarily the ego. Affect is the experience of the way in which the body and the ego are *affected*. This amounts to saying that the unconscious (or the id) affects the ego, and does so according to different modalities, ranging from anxiety to the most elaborate affects, by way of shame, guilt, etc. To exclude affect from the unconscious, to situate it *differently* in the topographical model, thus in no way means excluding it from analysis!

4. The claim of rediscovering repressed affects in the unconscious strikes me as deriving from the old theory of dual personality (or even multiple personalities) on which Freud drew briefly while emerging from the first cases of parahypnotic treatment (Anna O.). According to that theory, which depended a bit too much on appearances, there would have been one (or several) unconscious personalities alternating with the conscious personality, but equally complete with affects, representations, a quite specific moral conscience, occasionally a different language, etc.

But if Freud drew for a while, dialectically, on the argument in favor of a "second consciousness,"[130] he very quickly demonstrated its limitations. The unconscious is thus in no way another "self" in me, ultimately more authentic than me, a Mr. Hyde alternating with Dr. Jekyll, one with his hatred, the other with his love.. It is the other-thing (*das Andere*) in me, the repressed residue of the other-person (*der Andere*). It *affects me*, just as the other-person once affected me in the past.

IV.   THE UNCONSCIOUS IN LIFE AND IN TREATMENT

1.   *The Ptolemaic Unconscious*

In *The Unfinished Copernican Revolution*,[131] I attempted to show the movement through which, on the basis of an initial Copernicanism (a gravitation of the human child in the orbit of the sexual adult), man enclosed himself—in a Ptolemaic system. That closure is correlated with a permanent movement of translation, but it is one that bears two faces: translation properly speaking, issuing in the dominant ideology of the ego, and repression, the other face, which pushes thing-presentations into the unconscious. These are quite simply included in the ego, contained by it through a continuous counterinvestment; as such, they participate fully in the Ptolemaic dispensation. But, at the same time, they constitute an irreducible kernel and, as it were, a quintessence of alterity: and as a result, a promise of reopening.

The everyday manifestations of the unconscious, the "formations of the unconscious," do not elude such closure: they make their appearance in the narcissistic space of the ego and, in addition, by way of the machinelike mechanics of the primary process, they are not to be considered as messages. Dreams are most often dreamt without being recounted and without communicative intention: the model of the "tub," as I have called it, schematizes quite well its initial

---

130 "The Unconscious," in *SE* 14:164.
131 In *Essays on Otherness*, pp. 52-83 translated by Luke Thurston.

"unrelatedness,"[132] its narcissism. This could be shown equally well for symptoms, which are not relational or allocutory from the outset, unless it be in the use of their secondary benefits. There are bungled acts, cases of *lapsus calami* without witness and without "address"— without even a virtual "address."

2. *Openings in Life*

There does, however, exist a *compulsion to recount* certain dreams. Can we consider it to be purely internal, as the maintenance of an allocutory opening at the core of the most "closed," 'private" phenomenon?[133] Without taking a categorical stand, my tendency would be to give the determining role to "provocation" by the other.[134] I do not believe that a dream becomes an address *solely* by being recounted: it is the fact that the dream coming "to be told" can cause it to turn into an address. That "version," or turning toward the other, seems to me to be of an entirely different nature than the "transferences" that are common currency in all dreams and are but modalities of displacement and condensation, the image of one person surfacing in the place of that of another or being superimposed on it. Such transferences are modalities of the "filled-in" transference:

> An unconscious idea is as such quite incapable of entering the preconscious and . . . it can only exercise any effect there by establishing a connection with an idea which already belongs to the preconscious, by transferring its intensity on to it and by getting itself "covered" by it. Here we have the fact of "transfer-

---

132 Here I take up a development in *Problématiques V*, pp. 57–59, which moves from closure to opening.
133 Ibid., p. 79.
134 "Transference: Its Provocation by the Analyst," translated by Luke Thurston in *Essays on Otherness*, pp. 214–33.

ence," which provides an explanation of so many striking phenomena in the mental life of neurotics.[135]

The interpreter of dreams, the soothsayer, and the prophetess are indispensable characters in every culture; one seeks them out because they are supposed to know more about such strange phenomena, thus renewing in a way that is undeniable the relation to the adult "who knows more." More generally still, I have postulated as one of the major dimensions of the cultural realm this provocation by the enigma of the other. Cultural messages, "creations," are situated beyond any purely pragmatic intent (bringing about a specific effect on a specific addressee, using specific means). They are, at bottom, provoked by the "unnamed audience," "scattered in the future" that will or will not receive such bottles cast into the sea.

"Culture" itself seems to me one of the precursors of the analytic situation, specifically by way of the "hollowed-out" transference that it establishes.

3. *The Opening of Analytic Treatment*

The "tub of analytic treatment," as I have attempted to show, is quite different from the tub of the dream; and it is so for the quite simple reason that it includes the other, the other-person, within its enclosure. It is thus not paradoxically that we can assert that it constitutes a locus of unheard of, literally unprecedented *opening* in human existence. We should recall in addition that if the id does indeed stem from earliest utterances, what characterizes its specificity is that it *does*

---

135 *The Interpretation of Dreams*, in *SE* 4–5:562–63; The *Journées de Bonneval*, according to the "argument" of the current issue of the *Nouvelle Revue psychanalytique*, have "curiously neglected" the transference. And, just as curiously, so did Freud's article of 1915 and most of his elaborations on the unconscious and the id: "Bonneval," it would appear, was in excellent company! Perhaps one should have begun by articulating the alterity of the unconscious with the alterity of the other of childhood, thus attempting to approach a relation of the unconscious to the other in the transference that would not be the mere duplication of the "cliché" figured by the "filled-in" transference. See "The Dynamics of Transference," in *SE* 12:99.

not speak. What can restore the id to language (and more generally to expression) can be only the result of a complex process, which is that of analytic treatment. It is sustained in a variety of ways—maintaining the enclosure of the tub; the inner attitude of the analyst, consisting of listening, rejection, and respect with regard to the enigma of his own unconscious; the method of free associations and the freedom to speak[136]; and finally, through interpretation and construction, with interpretation (in the strict sense) being *tendentially* on the side of the analyst and construction on that of the analysand.[137]

I can only reformulate at this point a certain number of things: it is in the hollow of the enigma proposed by the analyst that the analysand comes to lodge and re-elaborate the resonant void of his own earliest enigmas. This takes place by way of a dismantling of his own (notably oedipal) constructions, a tracking of signifiers toward the repressed, and ultimately new construction-translations, necessarily originating in the analysand, into which the latter attempts to infiltrate something of the repressed. "Necessarily originating in the analysand," since it should be forcefully asserted that if the human being is constantly translating—translating messages emanating from the other, then self-translating—he is his own hermeneut. But hermeneutics (i.e., translation) has as its obverse repression and cannot elude it. The analyst, on each occasion that he pretends to translate or assist in translating, *assists in repressing.* For it is not for the analyst to be the hermeneut, not even via the psychoanalytic ideologies which are never far from hand. What is called, for instance, "psychoanalytic reading," and whose banality so fatigues us, is quite directly a means of repression.[138] The *hermeneut,* well before psychoanalysis and no

---

136 *Problématiques V*, passim.; Where has it been possible to say, where has one succeeded in saying, at any stage of human history, what is said in analysis?

137 Jean Laplanche, "Interpretation Between Determinism and Hermeneutics," translated by Philip Slotkin in *Essays on Otherness,* pp. 161ff.

138 Reading in terms of the death instinct or the depressive position, oedipal readings or reading in terms of the castration complex, reading according to the Law . . . Readings, readings . . . The theory of seduction is not a "language" to be read but an effort to understand analytic practice.

doubt after it, *is the human being*. What is acute in psychoanalysis is not part of that universal tendency but opposed to it: in that sense, and even as it acknowledges the role of the hermeneut, psychoanalysis is quite precisely an antihermeneutics.

What part of the id is integrated into speech? And what part—the "unconscious prototypes"—remains anchored and perhaps unchanging? Finally, and above all, what part of the hollowed-out transference can be transferred, at the end or upon interruption by the analyst, eluding a Ptolemaic closure that seems all too natural? These questions do not have a general answer, allowing us at most to envisage a typology of processes and ends of analysis . . .

V. UNCONSCIOUS AND METAPHYSICS

The most active tendencies in contemporary psychoanalysis seem caught between two temptations, which I will characterize for convenience as phenomenological and metaphysical.

1. *The phenomenological tendency*: I discussed this tendency as early as 1959, while studying the endeavors of Georges Politzer. One of the most notable representatives of this tendency (even if his success has not been commensurate with the quality of his efforts) is Roy Schafer in the United States. To summarize things briefly, what is at stake in every case is restoring to the human being his status as "first-person" subject, the author of his acts and his signifying intentions. All descriptions in terms of metapsychology, apparatus, system, etc., would be alienating descriptions in which psychoanalysis would be complicit with an all-too-natural inclination toward "abstraction" and "realism." Those last terms are Politzer's, but Schafer's critique, which is more elaborate, and executed by a thinker who is a connoisseur of ego psychology and a seasoned practitioner, proceeds along exactly the same lines: "it is not the agency [the ego] but the person who perceives, judges, and thinks"; the unconscious is the subject's "self-trickery," which finds an accomplice in the psychoanalytic theory of a "mind-place," etc.

I call these attempts "phenomenological" in the broad sense; even if they are also inspired by other philosophies, they posit that it ought to be possible to rediscover the intentionality of a subject at the heart of all his psychical acts and to account for them completely.[139] To be sure, such a phenomenology assigns itself a less insurmountable task than one intent on accounting, through a more or less transcendental constitution, for the world of apperception of all *cogitata*.

Consider first of all that in Politzer, and even more in Schafer, this attempt at disalienating the subject or the person passes before all else by way of theory or "language." Proposing a "new language for psychoanalysis" (first in books, but also in analytic treatment) would be the essential step to be taken for the subject to reassume mastery of—and responsibility for—his psychical acts.[140] Now, even supposing that one could count on such a system of programmed "self-theorization,"[141] it would be effective only if it accounted for the fact that language "in the third person" is, in spite of everything, so successful. In other words, resistance and defense, before being part of theory, are parts of the human being himself, and thinking focused on disalienation ought to encompass thinking of alienation.[142]

Second, the entire Freudian experiment was constituted as the discovery of an other-thing in us, acting not according to meaning, but to modalities that are causal. The critique of the "realism of the unconscious" continues to collide with that same experience, which notably bears the name of "repetition compulsion," and to attempt to compete with "mechanistic" descriptions of dream-work, which

---

139 There is an excellent critical account of Roy Schafer's thought by Agnès Oppenheimer, "Le meilleur des mondes possibles: A propos du projet de R. Schafer," in *Psychanalyse à l'Université* 9, no. 35 (1984): 467–90. See as well *Problématiques V*, pp. 226–29.

140 Roy Schafer, *A New Language for Psychoanalysis* (New Haven: Yale University Press, 1976).

141 To invoke a term I have used.

142 See *Problématiques V*, pp. 226–28, in which I resort to these polemical formulations: "Metapsychology is dead . . . but it does not know it" (Politzer); "the subject is not alienated . . . but it does not know it" (Schafer).

remain unequaled up to the present day.

Finally—and this is my personal contribution—in refusing to recognize in ourselves a foreign body as hard as iron, "disalienating" thought deprives itself of the path leading from the other-thing in us to the other-person that is its origin. It fails in this to discover that the internal alienation is the residue of a fundamental excentration whose center is the adult other for the child, whose gravitational pull is to be situated in the enigmatic message. Thus, in promoting a new "language,"[143] one fails to give value to the category of the message, to the "signifier to," and, ultimately, to the other.[144]

2. Speaking of the *metaphysical tendency*, I shall refer to Freud and Auguste Comte, first of all in order to do away with the allegation that one need be a metaphysician, or else one is not a philosopher. As though there did not exist a critical philosophy, a positive philosophy, a Freudian philosophy, and several others.

Forgotten and little read these days, Auguste Comte enunciated a "law of three estates" through which the evolution of the (collective, but also individual) human mind would necessarily transit: the *theological estate*, in which phenomena are conceived as "produced by the direct and continuous action of supernatural agents"; the *metaphysical estate*, in which "supernatural agents are replaced by abstract forces, veritable entities (personified abstractions) conceived as capable of generating on their own all observed phenomena, whose explanation would consist thereafter of assigning to each its corresponding entity"; the *positive estate*, finally, with the notion of law as a constant relation between phenomena.

Freud, for his part, rallied to a sequence, which, despite its slightly different terms, is not that far away: visions of a successively

---

143 Quite in the sense of Poincaré and Condillac of a "well-made language."
144 A phenomenological psychology misses the other-thing. A phenomenology of perception misses the other-person. See Jean Laplanche, "The Unfinished Copernican Revolution" translated by Luke Thurston in *Essays on Otherness*, p. 72, note 38.

animistic, religious, and scientific world.[145] "Animism," according to
Freud, is quite close to Comte's theology, their common point being
the intervention of *anthropomorphic* agents. As for metaphysical concepts, when Freud speaks of them, it is in a fashion rather less precise
than Auguste Comte, including religious notions such as original sin,
God, etc.[146] Let us retain, then, the Comtean definition of metaphysics as a creation of abstract entities to which is ascribed a real power,
a definition that is not without finding further resonance in Freud
when he assimilates a *certain* philosophical thought to schizophrenic
thinking, which is satisfied with words in place of things.[147]

Creating abstract entities and attributing an intrinsic efficacy
to them: the procedure is beginning to have currency, specifically in
a kind of French neometapsychology or metaphysics. The transition
from adjective to noun lends itself to this tendency particularly well. I
have already indicated the Lacanian sequence:

Symbolism → symbolic → the Symbolic
But examples abound:
Mother → maternal → the Maternal
Origin → the originary → the Originary[148]

Quite recently, we have been taught that it was time to "bring
ourselves up to date concerning the central notion of the Negative."[149]
The capital letter arrived as the seal of a derivation drawn from the
greatest metaphysician of all time, Hegel:

---

145 *Totem and Taboo*, in *SE* 13:77.
146 This is the famous passage on "the transformation of metaphysics into metapsychology," *The Psychopathology of Everyday Life*, *SE* 6:259. I have offered several
observations concerning the "repatriation" of the metaphysical notions of thing-in-
itself, cause, and archeology in "The Wall and the Arcade" in *Seduction, Translation,
and the Drives*, p. 210, and "Interpretation Between Determinism and Hermeneutics," in *Essays on Otherness*, p. 144.
147 "The Unconscious," *SE* 14:200.
148 I have used this word, specifying nonetheless that I did not ascribe to it a transcendent or causal value, as a category to be observed in experience.
149 Program of the XII Journées occitanes de psychanalyse, November 1993.

Negation → negative → the Negative.

And yet, in the texts of Freud invoked, one can indeed find the term *negation* (or *Verneinung*), and the adjective *negative*, but not, to my knowledge, the metaphysical entity *das Negative*.[150] Yet all the difficulty lies there: whereas a qualification (such as that of: negative) may be found in various occurrences, one will solemnly say that "the Negative" manifests itself in "different figures," and the trick will have been performed. Thus, as August Comte recalls, would "phlogiston" generate the "different figures" of fire . . .

They will be lying in wait for me, and I'm aware of it. And, for once, our metaphysicians can join their voices with those of Politzer and Schafer and say: "But what then of 'the unconscious'? Is it not the very exemplar of an entity forged from an adjective? Didn't Freud give us *the* example of the metaphysical concept par excellence? And it is of no avail, exploiting the hypocrisy of translators, to have shorn it of a capital letter!"

I will ask, incidentally, our metaphysicians of the Negative whether they have, in fact, already exhausted the joys of the metaphysics of the Unconscious, so much do they experience the need to plunge, in Baudelaire's words, "to the depths of the Unknown to find the New."

But, above all, I will plead guilty; not for myself, nor for Freud, nor even for "the unconscious," but for the "unconscious things," the veritable "words" (or signifiers) "taken for things"; taken for things in the mechanism of "rejected" translation. It should be fully admitted that "the unconscious" is not a metaphysical entity, but a collective notion encompassing "entities," which, *for their part*, have taken on "metaphysical" or "metapsychological" value. Those entities function according to the "metaphysical" principle of causality, removed as they are from the laws of meaning.

---

150 Whereas, moreover, German, the metaphysical language par excellence, lends itself all too easily to a nominalization of the adjective or verb.

To conclude, then, on a note from Comte: whereas he refuses to accord a separate place, between physiology and sociology, in the classification of positive sciences, to psychology, it is amusing to observe that "theology" and "metaphysics" stage a return in force precisely *in that place*, with psychoanalysis, which entails an *anthropomorphism* of agencies and a *metaphysics* of intrapsychic entities. But it is a return that is effected *in the human being* and not in the classification of sciences, and from that place anthropomorphism and metaphysics are not about to be evicted.

IV
The Training Analysis:
A Psychoanalysis "on Command"

Let us turn the calendar back to a precise period: one ending in what is called the "schism" of 1963, between a Lacanian group and a group (the Association psychanalytique de France: APF) that would be "recognized" by the IPA (International Psychoanalytic Association).

It will not be a matter of recounting a history which is rather well known in its details and very diversely appreciated in its motives. I would like simply to bring to the fore, from the point of view of the analyst's "formation," a perspective that has never been described as such.

An Indicator

The request for recognition by the IPA, formulated with the support of the entire membership of the Société française de psychanalyse (SFP), the debates, meetings, and investigations that accompanied that procedure, can properly be regarded as a kind of "detonator"— or, better, as a "catalyst." It remains that its significance was deep and its repercussions unsuspected.

This text is a revised and expanded version of an article already published under the title "Une révolution sans cesse occultée," in the *Revue internationale d'histoire de la psychanalyse* 2 (1989): 393–402.

But first of all we should not forget that Lacan was not being dragged into this request, even if he allowed his "students" to assume everyday political tasks. It is certain that, at the time, he saw in it the privileged path of a conquest, the door to be opened for an international dissemination of his "cause" (which was identified as *la Cause*). Failing to advance on that path, Lacan and the zealots of expansionist Lacanianism subsequently discovered other paths. The explicit constitution of an ILA (International Lacanian Association) would long since have been completed were it not for a number of internal dissensions. Ideological imperialism, both institutional and political, is one of the undeniable components of Freudianism. Lacanianism is but one of its most accomplished manifestations.

Let us return to the SFP's application for recognition. Without delving into individual motivations, it is possible to assert that among "Lacan's pupils" several themes converged: repairing the blunder of the elders (including Lacan) who were foolish enough to resign in 1953; rejoining a community of thought and opening new possibilities for exchange; leading that community to acknowledge an association quite different from the SPP (Société psychanalytique de Paris), in which, to be sure, Lacan's thought played an eminent role, but did so along with that of others (Lagache, Dolto . . .).

This is where the "cunning-of-history" effect comes into play. The weeks and months of internal discussions and external negotiations, the commissions and depositions, were to catalyze, for all of Lacan's students directly implicated, the unveiling of, the becoming conscious of (or the "taking" consciousness, as one says of the moment when a mayonnaise "takes") of elements previously diffuse, half-silenced, or considered to be marginal, all of which concerned the conception of the analyst's formation:

(1) The practice of short (and even ultrashort) sessions. Individuals were able to flaunt longer sessions they were having or had had with Lacan; but tongues began to wag on the subject of waiting rooms filling up, exercises in tricks using two doors, etc.

(2) The systematically cultivated fusing of training analyses—on which Lacan insisted—teaching (the seminar), and the
manipulation of individuals in accordance with their idiosyncrasies,
for the greater glory of the Cause and its Prophet.

(3) But, above all, the fact that Lacan was not disposed to
renounce those "practices" in any way was suddenly indicative
of their importance. All at once what had only been intuited was
abruptly perceived: beyond the theoretical contributions (which, we
agreed, had been unjustly banned), there was Lacanianism as an exercise in power and feudal submission, the propagation of the doctrine
being inseparable from personal allegiance, and the latter finding its
preferred vehicle in Lacanian practice (in the broadest sense).

Thus what might have seemed incidental to us (to me) in our
naïveté—incidental in the sense of haven been taken to be the idiosyncrasies of a man and a practice—had become a major issue. The
very conception of the analytic process was at stake: the analysis of
the patient and, even more, the analysis of the "candidate."

Shall we say that contact with the IPA simply served to free us
from a certain Lacanian enthrallment, allowing us to rejoin the orthodox group and its accepted practice concerning training? That would
be inadequate and imprecise.

Growing Awareness

It is here that history enlists a second—and even more diabolical—
exercise in cunning. The IPA served to enlighten us with regard to
Lacan's training practices, but Lacan, and the critique of his practice,
served to reveal what was latent, not only in the entire contemporary
analytic movement but in the inspiration of Freud himself.

What exists, since Freud and in keeping with what is
undoubtedly the decisive impulse of Sándor Ferenczi, is the *training
analysis* as the decisive centerpiece of the analyst's formation. Better not to quibble over words, which too often have served only to

confuse matters: "training analysis" (*Lehranalyse*), "teaching analysis" (*Bildungsanalyse*), "personal analysis" (*Selbstanalyse*) are all terms that have in common integrating the analysis of the candidate into an aim that is ultimately delivery of a "finished product": an analyst who has received "the most suitable formation" (*die geeignetste Ausbildung*). Every practice in the world, all groups combined, whatever the school in which they claim membership, carefully maintains most or all of the following points: a "training analysis" can be conducted only by a superanalyst, since it entails a "plus" in relation to ordinary analysis. A training analysis is *undertaken* with the prior approval of the institution ("admission to training"), which thus confirms that such an "analysis" is to take place while admitting at the outset that the analysand is legitimized in his "ideal" of becoming an analyst. The training analysis is *pursued* entirely under the sign of that common *purpose*, which can be seen in the following questions: When will I be admitted to the teaching program? When will I be allowed to begin taking on analysands under supervision? What opinions will you (you, my analyst) give me or are you going to give about me?, etc. The problems turning round and round in the "pre-congresses" of the IPA on the subject of training ("specifics of . . . difficulties specific to . . . characteristics of the transference in . . . the training analysis") or even the extreme question, shamefully maintained: can the analyst, at one moment or another, give an opinion on his analysand? All these are only symptoms of a situation accepted without discussion since Freud: a training analysis *entails*—while considering the analytic method only as a means—an *end* extrinsic to the process of analysis and which is from the beginning consolidated by the connivance of three authorities: the institutions (and their ideals), the analysts (and their ideals), and the candidates (and their ideals or ambitions).

To raise the question of the "goal-representation" in relation to the training analysis is thus absolutely not to say: in that case every analysis ought to be therapeutic. In the same way as for the "training" analysis, it may be wondered to what extent an analysis that accepts uncritically its therapeutic purpose remains an analysis. For the same question can be asked about a so-called therapeutic analysis: ought the conception of health as imagined by the patient who arrives in search of an analyst and the ends he aims at in asking for an analysis be accepted as presuppositions such that one would ultimately be obligated to lead the patient where he wants to go? In both cases, for the one whose focus is "training" as well as the "therapeutic," the problem is determining whether an analysis can be engaged without there being what Freud calls a "suspension" of "goal-representation"—aims as apparently valid and reasonable as: I want to become an analyst; I want to stop suffering from a specific symptom; I want to resolve a specific unbearable marital situation, etc.; or, if children are at stake, I would like this child to perform better at school . . . The question is whether those objectives ought to be accepted at the outset of an analytic process, or whether they are not themselves an integral part of what is to be analyzed. The question is, above all, to determine whether the professional objective, once approved by the institution *and* by an analyst assigned to that end, can be put into play in the analysis in other than a fictitious way. It is indeed claimed that the desire to become an analyst "is to be analyzed" like any other desire. But it becomes only a sham analysis as soon as, so to speak, the institution awaits the analysand at the office door; like a mother, in the waiting room, awaiting her child whom she is *having analyzed* so that he will become "well-behaved."

To return to our historical concern, what Lacan showed openly—the only analysis is a training analysis; instruction, training, and the analysis of the candidate are all one; to enter into analysis is to adhere to the ideals of the group and its leader, etc.—all that exists everywhere and without, generally, anyone who dares to admit it.[151]

---

151 At the time of the split, I recall the confidential remark of one of the senior members of the group breaking with Lacan; it was more or less as follows: "Neither illusions nor idealism, friends; there is no doubt that every training analysis influences those who are analyzed." In brief, everyone has dirty hands, and Lacan committed the error of showing them.

But this situation harks back to the founders: Freud, who quickly accepted "self-analysis" as the best means to forge the best analytic instrument possible. Freud, who even with regard to *analysis in general* occasionally makes revealing formulations: "it turns out that the assumption of there being an unconscious enables us to construct a successful procedure by which we can exert an effective influence upon the course of conscious processes."[152] Ferenczi, who posits that the "training" analysis should delve to greater depths than the "therapeutic," but precisely as a function of the *professional ends* it assigns itself.

On that basis: professional ends, ideals of the analytic movement, the group, and the leader, propagation of orthodox doctrine and practice, etc., everything follows . . . including the "short session." Did Freud not assert that he conducted short analyses (several months) in order to be able "to extend his influence" to more disciples?[153] The calculation is simple: five minutes instead of forty-five, or five months instead of forty-five; the gain is the same. One has "trained" nine times as many propagators of the faith.

Thus a growing awareness with regard to Lacan could only be completed by a symmetrical increase in awareness with regard to prevailing practices, all stemming from Freud: a Freud who wanted himself to be the founder of a church as well as a pioneer of the unconscious.

A Revolution

At the heart of the APF, freshly emergent from Lacanianism, the problem was quickly cast in these terms: restore autonomy to the personal analysis to the maximal extent or continue to consider it as part of a setup aimed at "the most suitable form of training."

1969–1971. Is it possible, in a few lines, to convey the essential aspect of what was played out? In 1969, under my presidency and at my behest, a proposal to modify procedures for accreditation was

---

152 "The Unconscious" in *SE* 14:167.
153 Abram Kardiner, *My Analysis with Freud* (New York: Norton, 1977).

presented, debated, and ultimately rejected. In 1971, under the presidency and at the behest of Pontalis, a new proposal, ultimately quite close to the previous one, was discussed and adopted. It instituted the regulation according to which we currently function.

What was acquired in 1971:

1. *The elimination of the training analysis,* undertaken "on command" as a function of the institution's desire to "produce" analysts.

- the elimination of prior interviews;
- the elimination of the list and title of training analyst;
- candidates are known to the APF only at the time of admission to supervision; their request is receivable whosoever their original analyst: titular member, associate, or student of the APF or member of another group. The point is not a formality. Annual statistics show that our training committee examines each candidate without objection to the person or the affiliation of his analyst.

These points are not a concession to a soft liberalism and have nothing to do with problems of "democracy." They bear witness to a radicalism regarding the conception of analysis. Wherein we do not situate ourselves as midway between the SFP and the Lacanian École, since both of them order up personal analyses with the aim of obtaining a finished product conforming to the ideals of the institution.

2. *An entirely new procedure for validating the candidate's analytic work in his supervised cases:* one no longer confides in the unmotivated decision of the supervisor, since it is the content of the supervision and the capacities of the candidate that are the object of a deeper—and collective—evaluation.

3. The only list of teaching analysts that remains is that of "analysts practicing at the training institute." This is not a masked list of training analysts, but the list of supervisors, which may, moreover, be revised annually.

The inspiration of all these rules can be encapsulated in a single word: ensuring a maximum of extraterritoriality in the practice of analysis and, most of all, in the analysis of whoever proposes to become an analyst himself. Without any illusion as to all that works against that autonomy in relation to utilitarian or ideal aims, the rules established at the APF avoid creating or even favoring an "unanalyzable" content: the kind of "specifications of technique" in accordance with which the analytic institution would order up (from its training analysts) analysts conforming to standards.

Cover-ups

It is remarkable that this heterogeneous character of practices at the APF (as much in relation to dominant practices as in relation to the Freudian ideals themselves) is constantly and repeatedly concealed— by others as well as by ourselves. It is, to be sure, the rule that any individual consents to perceive the other only in accordance with his own model. In France, we may mention, at a number of years' distance, I. and R. Barande,[154] for whom "differences are minimal between the SPP and the APF in their common application of the standard norms of the IPA," and the *Agenda de psychanalyse*, according to which "training analysts" at the APF are named in a special list called the "list of analysts practicing at the Training Institute"![155]

Within the international movement, our conception is quite simply unknown—by individuals as well as by groups or administrative entities. Our method of producing analysts is, no doubt, from time to time described in an incomplete and bastardized manner, in one international "report" or another: one "variant" among others in a multitude of "ways of proceeding." But it entails a fundamental misperception in which all parties are complicit. I would invoke as

---

154 I. and R. Barande, *Histoire de la psychanalyse en France* (Toulouse: Privat, 1975), pp. 53–54.
155 *L'Agenda de la psychanalyse*, no. 1, p. 22.

principal witness the celebrated "precongresses" intended to debate questions of training. Each member society is asked to delegate a certain number of "training analysts," a category taken for granted and amenable to common—international-psychoanalytic or quite simply Freudian—sense. But it is comical to observe the way in which we respond: not with "a training analyst? Don't know what you mean. We already told you as much and we're going to explain things further," but by straining to translate "training analyst" into APF French. We scratch our heads: no doubt they mean supervisors? Or analysts serving in the training institute? Or "titular members?" An ethnocentric translation, as they say:[156] thanks to which they would have no problem retorting to us: after all, you're not so different! You too have training analysts since you send them as delegates to congresses!

Just as remarkable is the manner in which the debate on fundamental issues is frequently oriented: not in terms of a suspension and calling into question, for each analysis, of prior aim-representations or ideals, whether "therapeutic" or professional, but through a balancing of one in relation to the other. One thinks one can escape that mortgage of ideals by a facile concession: to be sure, every analysis, even of a candidate, is also therapeutic, etc.

To sum up, on one point—which is fundamental, if any is— the conception of analysis: here we are, fully part of the IPA and the psychoanalytic movement in its entirety and completely opposed to the universally prevalent practice and ideology. But in the name of a misperception expertly maintained by all, everyone . . . appears not to know it. It should be admitted that if there were a *genuine* awareness of the situation it would be imperative—if not to exclude us (a practice that is quite rare)—to at least say why we are not excluded!

If a "revolution" is perpetually "hidden," even to those who have carried it out, it becomes necessary to yield to the evidence: the revolution is poorly consolidated and needs to be maintained in a

---

156 The English "He had bacon and eggs," translated as "Il prenait son café au lait."

"permanent" manner. At all times, and under the most diverse pretexts, the (legitimate) requirements of professional training have their effect on what can never be integrated into this kind of goal: the personal analysis of someone (let us not say: of a candidate).

In conclusion: if every analysis is a "formation," it cannot be so in the sense with which that fine term *Bildung* has never ceased resonating in German ears: a movement through which the individual, by way of the strangest adventures of a trip to "foreign" lands, makes contact with what is most deeply his "own."

Analysis is that voyage which attempts asymptotically to make once again "our own" (*eigen*) what is most foreign in us (the unconscious).

In relation to this conception of analysis and the fine formulation "Wo Es war, soll Ich werden" as cultural movement (*Bildung*), the idea of a formation suitable to a professional goal (*die geeignetste Ausbildung*)[157] is quite simply a contradiction.

Without denying that a "suitable formation" remains indispensable for the future analyst, we would deliberately maintain outside of it, outside of every professional and ideological end as well as every institutional control, what can only be an extraterritorial process: the personal analysis.

---

157 "The Question of Lay Analysis," *SE* 20:252.

V
Forces at Play in Psychical Conflict

For this clarification of neurotic conflict, Freud's two texts of 1924, "Neurosis and Psychosis" and "The Loss of Reality in Neurosis and Psychosis," if not as models to be applied, at least can serve as a point of departure. For Freud, there is explicitly a question of inserting conflict into the framework of his new theory of the psychical apparatus. But three oddities draw our attention from the outset:

(1) The description of conflict is essentially in terms of the structure of the mental apparatus, and yet, curiously, that version of the structural[158] model does not invoke solely the three agencies that have been in place since 1920: ego, id, and superego. Abruptly, a new "agency" appears as an autonomous force: "reality." As a result, the conflict resides in the way in which the ego finds itself caught between two principal forces and is obliged to ally itself with one or the other. In neurosis it is reality that would win out at the expense of the id. In psychosis it would be the reverse.

Presented at the 2nd Colloque international Jean Laplanche, Canterbury, July 15, 1994

158 [Editor's note: In English psychoanalytic texts, Freud's first model of mind—Ucs/Pcs/Cs—is usually called the "topographic" model and his second model—Ego/Superego/Id—is usually called the "structural" model. This may suggest that one is more descriptive and less structural than the other. In French, each of Freud's models of the mind is referred to as a *topique*: the first *topique* and the second *topique*. This permits, as in this sentence, a model of the mind that is close to, but not identical with, the structural model also to be called a topography.]

(2) Concerning the drives, which classically are opposed to each other in the psyche (defense, symptom, compromise, etc.), the new opposition between "life drives" and "death drives"[159] completely fails to find its place. Far from there being a struggle between them, the two great drives are encompassed in the id and share a common fate.

(3) As for the former opposition, that of sexual drives and drives of self-preservation, its absence is not surprising, since it disappeared as a major axis of Freudian thought after 1915, but nevertheless is cruelly felt precisely whenever there is a question of reality.

On Reality

On the basis of a robust "realism," Freud always distinguished between two types of reality: material external reality, to which we accede by perception, and psychological reality, corresponding to perceptions of what emanates from within, initially feelings of pleasure-displeasure, then affects, and finally representations, fantasies, logical arguments, etc.[160]

It is not a matter of challenging this first opposition, but of establishing distinctions within it, pondering which forces (or "drives") are in play, and also of wondering about the possibility of a third type of reality, transverse to the other two.

Concerning *exterior reality*, it is utterly simplistic to speak of the "real exterior world" without specifying it and without taking into account the forces that polarize it. Simply to say that "for the ego, perception plays the part which in the id falls to [drive]"[161] is to establish a symmetry without rigor by conjuring away the question of

---

159 Whatever the meaning one is inclined to attribute to them. See below, p. 166 ff.
160 Psychological reality is not specific to the human being. It develops in every living creature, growing in complication with the complexity of the central nervous system.
161 *The Ego and the Id, SE* 19. [Editor's note: here and elsewhere, when necessary, we have modified the Standard Edition to be consistent with Laplanche's thinking and to retain the clarity of Laplanche's translation of Freud. Modifications are indicated by square brackets.]

force. The exterior world sketches lines of force only through investment by a living being. One is even justified in supposing that the exterior world can *be perceived* solely as a function of such an investment. What is indifferent is not noticed by the living creature. The air we breathe irrupts violently only when it becomes suffocating or is lacking.[162]

For a given individual, we can describe in an elementary way the forces that animate reality according to three paired oppositions: sexuality/self-preservation, attraction/repulsion, living (and, more narrowly, human) environment/inanimate environment.

Let us provisionally put aside sexuality in order to concentrate on the domain of *self-preservation* or adaptation. This is the domain that is generally made to coincide with the notion of "reality" in general, "realism" having adopted as a guiding maxim "life before all else" (*primum vivere*)—before philosophy or even before making love. Following the attraction/repulsion polarity, the realm of self-preservative needs has the contours of an environment (*Umwelt*) composed of poles of attraction (objects of need) and negative poles (dangers). Those needs are inscribed in the individual by way of more or less fixed or adaptable mechanisms, inherited phylogenetically. But it is here that the difference between two types of environment (living/inanimate) intervenes, and it is incumbent on us to distinguish clearly between species, depending on whether they are directly plugged into an inanimate environment or whether that insertion occurs through the mediation of another living being. For a certain number of living species, these mechanisms are directly preadapted to the object of consumption or the situation to avoid (appetite for a specific source of nourishment; instinctive knowledge of a precise danger).

---

162 See D. Lagache: "In their behavior, living organisms deal with positive and negative values, or with value-objects and not with objects in the sense that common knowledge or scientific knowledge bestows upon this term, divesting reality of all subjective import." "Psychocriminogenesis" in The Work of Daniel Lagache: Selected Writings (London: Karnac 1993) p. 95.

For other species, access to material objects and to knowledge of factual danger are inseparable from the mediation of the "socius." In the case of the human being (which is the only one to concern us here), Freud emphasized forcefully a congenital ignorance of *dangers*; and, as for *desires* directly preadapted to an object, specifically the desire for nourishment, it appears that they too are inexistent. The baby initially has no "thought" of the milk; it is only by way of the attraction and the proposition of the breast, its warmth, the nesting that it proffered, etc., that the infant accedes to the notorious food-value."[163] The human world of self-preservation, as opposed to what transpires in the case of numerous animals, is thus from the outset, and in its entirety, an interactive world, oriented by reciprocal vectors without their being, for all that, uniformly complementary. Fully as much as "self-preservative," this force field, insofar as it is interhuman or interanimal, can be called the field of "tenderness" (Freud) or "attachment" (modern psychology—ethology).

It is paradoxical but true to say that this domain of self-preservation with regard to the human being is described only by way of abstraction. Present at birth in the form of innate instinctual dispositions, it is quickly *covered over, disqualified*, by another play of forces, those of human sexuality.

But before introducing sexuality, it is indispensable to delineate a third order of reality, not *alongside* material reality and psychological reality, but transverse in relation to them: the reality of the *message*, whose materiality may be characterized as "signifying." This realm of reality is one that Freud intuits occasionally, identifying a "psychical reality" distinct not only from material reality but also from merely psychological reality and, so to speak, more indestructible and resistant than it. It is notably the case for what he names "uncon-

---

163 A term employed by Lagache to emphasize the fact that the environment is not neutral, but oriented by values, which are so many vectors of force. But, precisely, the vector of nourishment as a relation to the inanimate is not a primal vector for the infant as it is for the paramecium or newly hatched salmon attached to its yolk sac.

scious wishes reduced to their ultimate and truest expression,"[164] or, in accord with our realism of the unconscious, the "de-signified signifiers" ("thing-representations") that populate the unconscious.

The materiality of the message outside of any "psychical" insertion into external reality might be figured as the presence of a tablet of hieroglyphics abandoned in the desert. But the message and the signifier are not, for all that, reducible to verbal language alone: an arrow indicative of direction, drawn on the wall of a cavern, is also a message; as are a smile, a threatening gesture, or even the destruction by an American airplane of an Iraqi missile base. The realm of reality specific to the message includes the following features: 1) the message is not necessarily verbal, or even integrated into a semiotic system, but it is always inscribed in a (signifying) materiality; 2) the message, before representing something (a signified), always represents an other for someone: it is communication, address; 3) the message, by virtue of its materiality, is dedicated to polysemy.

It is at this juncture that it is useful to discuss the distinguishing characteristics of the *adult* message addressed to the child. Like any other, this message is open to numerous interpretations. But we say it is "enigmatic" in a very precise sense which exceeds all polysemy. Indeed, the adult message, addressed to the child on the basis of a dialogue, a reciprocal dialogue of self-preservation, turns out to be inhabited, compromised, by the unconscious sexuality of the adult. If it appears as enigmatic to the child, it is undoubtedly because it exceeds the nursing infant's possibilities of understanding and mastery; but in addition and more fundamentally it is because in its duplicity it remains opaque to the understanding of the very person emitting it. The term "compromised" message refers to an essential notion in psychoanalysis intended to account for the psychopathology of everyday life including actions, speech acts, writings, etc., all addressed to an other and all affected by an "interference" from the unconscious of the emitter.

---

164 See *Traumdeutung*, in *Gesammelte Werke* 2–3:265.

The sexual message thus *inhabits* the self-preservative message. But, as opposed to the latter, it does not imply a reciprocity of the request-response sort and is fundamentally asymmetrical, finding its origin in the (adult) other.

It is here that the theory of leaning on and of generalized seduction becomes necessary. Not being able to take it up in detail, I will limit myself initially to the following diagram showing how the self-preservative, interactive message of the adult is paired with a unidirectional message of a sexual nature.

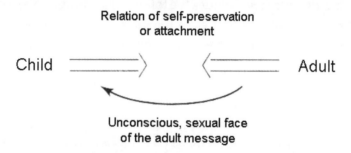

Relation of self-preservation
or attachment

Child   Adult

Unconscious, sexual face
of the adult message

We will be alluding to the rest of the process further on. But what is significant here for the *problem of reality* is that—at each of its *stages*, on each of its *levels*, in each of its bodily *locations*—the relation of self-preservation is infested, invaded, and soon completely over-written by sexual meanings.

What is called pansexualism in psychoanalysis is the theory positing that sexuality accounts for the totality of the human being. Yet we are positing that theoretical pansexualism is but the reflection of a *real* pansexualism, that is, of a movement by which sexuality reinvests the entirety of human activities. Sexuality is not everything, but it is everywhere.

At the conclusion of this overview of "reality" and its impact on psychical conflict, we may offer the following summary: exterior reality can intervene as a force only to the extent that it is invested. The investment of self-preservation (needs) in man is entirely mediated by interhuman relations. These, in turn, are totally infested, compromised, on the adult side, by the participation of the adult's sexual unconscious.

Like a neutral country invaded by two foreign armies battling each other, not only to share its territory but to exercise supremacy with regard to other spoils, such is the situation of the domain of self-preservation in the human being, invaded by sexual conflict. The self-preservative forces remain feeble and incapable of exercising any significant influence. Scarcely capable in themselves of conflict, their fate remains entirely dependent on sexual conflict. It is well known that the human being, once sexualized, remains inaccessible to purely adaptive concerns. He feeds himself or deprives himself of nourishment "for love of" or "out of hatred against" and not in order to survive. The bizarre impulses and follies of human beings, their destructive or altruistic ideals, are not amenable to intimidation. The *compulsion* of love or perversion mocks every interdiction. To that extent, the idea of a "real danger" being the key to repression and neurosis (as it emerges from a certain reading of *The Problem of Anxiety*) does not hold up for a second in the face of experience. Castration was never a "real danger": it intervenes as a psychical force only on the basis of a threat that has been uttered (*Androhung* and not *Drohung*), and the latter in turn cannot be separated from the unconscious sexual meanings present in the person uttering it.[165]

The realm of self-preservation is thus not directly party to psychical conflict. It is the field on which psychical conflict is deployed and eventually what is at stake in it. Hysterical blindness[166] is not the result of a conflict between a nonsexual, adaptive visual function and sexual impulses, but it is the consequence, for the visual function, of

---

165 The threat of castration is itself seduction in the broad sense in which we define it. As for the "theory of castration," its metapsychological status is quite different.
166 "The Psychoanalytic View of Psychogenetic Disturbance of Vision," in *SE* 11:209–18. See also the first chapter of *Inhibitions, Symptoms and Anxiety* with regard to inhibition, *SE* 20:87-90

a conflict between antagonistic sexual forces. It is that particular position of self-preservation that justifies its situation at the borders of psychoanalytic therapy and its "tub.[167]

The Apparatus of the Soul

On several occasions Freud asserted that the psychical apparatus could be understood only by way of its genesis in the individual. He did not always remain faithful to that perspective, notably by appealing, in his description of the psychical "agencies," to roots or innate cores. This is notably the case for the id, whose conception, alongside a positive intention, conveys the risk of returning to innate instinctual (and no longer drive) forces.[168]

Another risk, which is in no way less significant, consists in believing that what is described by the "metapsychology" is a more refined, precise, and "extensive" version of psychology: the expression *dynamic psychology*, which is occasionally employed, serves to promote just such an error. And it is against it that we make use, following Freud, of the slightly outmoded term the *apparatus of the soul*, by which we mean, quite precisely, the *sexual* psychical apparatus.

Psychoanalysis undoubtedly exceeds its rights in pretending to supplant cognitive psychology, whose legitimacy remains intact. But there occurs, in the world of "interior" psychological reality, something comparable to the process of "real pansexualism": the sexual apparatus of the soul tends to reclaim as its own, to invade and to appropriate the domain of psychological reality, which is in principle independent, but, in the human being, is independent only in an abstract way.

---

167 See *Problématiques IV*, pp. 207ff, and *Problématiques V*, e.g., pp. 81, 156, 181, 211. The discourse of self-preservation can be "heard" in analytic treatment only insofar as it evokes, triggers, and even generates sexuality.
168 See *The Temptation of Biology: Freud's Theories of Sexuality* (New York, The Unconscious in Translation, 2015) and *The Unconscious and the Id* (London, Rebus Press, 1999) for the problematic of the id. Freud's return to instinct (*Instinkt*) is emphasized in his final texts, for example: *Moses and Monotheism*.

The Freudian division of the apparatus of the soul into an id, an ego, ideal agencies, and a superego, remains an indispensable guiding thread. Distinctions between an *ego* and a *self*, or between the *ego* and the *I*, are eminently subject to criticism and arising primarily from ideological exigencies: the *self* is a way of restoring an alleged autonomy to a rational ego while neglecting its narcissistic component. Inversely, the introduction of an "I," whatever the pretexts for such a split, leads us back to a philosophy of the "subject" that is not innocent.

But the agencies of the apparatus of the soul can only be conceived in terms of their origin: the impact on a developing biological organism of enigmatic messages emanating from the other. Thus if one were obliged to introduce an agency or "instance" other than Freud's classic cases, it would not be an "instance of the letter,"[169] an abstract power issuing from structuralist theory but an instance of the other.

This priority of the (external) other in the constitution of the soul-apparatus will be duplicated by the instance of the internal other: the id. For the latter is not there primordially and for all eternity: it is that part of the message emanating from the external other that never succeeded in being completely translated (integrated, metabolized).[170] It is, so to speak, a "quintessence" of otherness.

The constitution of the soul-apparatus, in its topographical aspect as much as in the forces at work (the economic-dynamic aspect), is correlative with the process of repression. The latter, in turn, is to be understood in the framework of the generalized theory of seduction: implantation of the enigmatic signifier, its reactivation après-coup, attempts at mastery, the failure of translation resulting in the deposit of source-objects in the id. I will not return to this sequence, my objective being to discuss how the already constituted apparatus of the soul functions in normal/neurotic conflict.

---

169 Lacan, "L'Instance de la lettre . . . ," in *Écrits* (Paris: Seuil, 1966).
170 See *New Foundations for Psychoanalysis*, part 2, and, "Ponctuation," in *La révolution copernicienne inachevée*.

Some Supplementary Remarks on the Structural Model

The structural model is a point of view of the ego in the sense that every model of the mind is from the point of view of the ego—finding its origin in the ego and reflecting the ego's interests. This is in agreement with Freud's intuition: "the psyche is extended, but does not know it." Quite so: the ego is certainly a part of the psyche (the apparatus of the soul), but it is also hegemonic: it lays claim to being the whole and is potentially the whole.[171] That the ego can be described as extended must be understood in relation to its narcissistic origin. As we know, narcissism is not to be conceived as an initial monadic state, but as a libidinal investment "of the ego," or, more precisely, as a libidinal investment that *constitutes* the ego in the image of the other body as a totality (the body of the other—but also my body as other). Narcissism is nothing other than narcissistic identification.

The Forces of the Drive: Binding and Unbinding

We come now to the forces involved. In direct alignment with the theory of seduction and the pansexualist "invasion," we assert that they are solely of a sexual nature. It is within sexuality that the separation between the sexual forces of unbinding (Freud's death drive) and the sexual forces of binding (Freud's Eros) is produced. It is imperative to understand that repression itself creates the drive forces of unbinding. The threat to the organism bent on self-preservation constituted by the strangerness (*étrangèreté*) of the message emanating from the other (a strangerness grounded in sexuality) ultimately ends up confining that strangerness in the repressed unconscious. The reasons for that unbinding, and for the primary process governing the unconscious contents, are to be sought nowhere else than in repression itself. It acts in a "highly individual manner" (Freud), breaking

---

171 At the risk, when it is that whole, of no longer having any power: in the dream, the ego, fixated on the wish to sleep, is dilated to the point of again coinciding with the limits of the body-ego; but it allows far greater play to the primary process.

connections between the elements of the message, and above all dis-connecting the link between signifier and signified. The unconscious contents are the residue of that strange metabolism,[172] which "treats" the messages of the other, but fails to "treat" the strangerness itself. It is those "designified signifiers" that pursue their existence side by side in the unconscious, or contract between them the most absurd alliances (i.e., by displacement-condensation).

The binding forces are no less erotic than those that unbind, and it is quite legitimately that Freud designated them by the name of Eros, which "tends to establish ever larger unities." But the error of the founder was in having wanted to annex the totality of the erotic to Eros, whereas Eros is only the "bound" aspect of sexuality.

Eros's center of action is the ego; Eros replenishes itself end-lessly with libido invested in *totalities*: in this sense object-libido and ego-libido are strictly correlative: if man lives by love, it is indissocia-bly by love of the ego and love of the (total) object.

In light of all that, should we solidify the conflict as though it were produced between two antagonistic forces defined once and for all as drives that unbind and drives that bind, annexed to two immutable psychical "instances" or agencies, the id and the ego? It seems not. On the one hand, it is the same sexual force (libido) that is found on both sides, and it would be scarcely conceivable that there not be conversions from one form into the other. We are well aware that an extreme case of the will to bind can result in an extreme bout of unbinding.[173]

Binding and unbinding are thus best conceived as two princi-ples (types of process, modes of functioning) at work at all structural levels. This is tantamount to saying that the structural limits and the economic-dynamic play of forces coincide only in an extremely crude approach to the question: there are both elements that are more

---

172 On the subject of the metabolic, see *Problématiques IV*, pp. 135ff.
173 See the analysis by Jacques André of the Terror during the Revolution in *La révo-lution fratricide* (Paris: PUF, 1993).

unbound and those that are less unbound in the id, and likewise are more or less bound in the ego.[174]

We should also guard against the great injustice we would risk if we purely and simply assimilated binding to the ego, and the ego to narcissism. Maintaining that the starting point, the bud of the ego, is to be situated in a specular identification with the image of a fellow creature should not bring us to neglect the identificatory contributions and successive rearrangements that come to enrich and dialecticize that "instance" or agency. Correspondingly, the fact that the ego always remains the pole that *binding* actions are attached to does not imply such actions merely impose rigidity. Even if many neurotic defense mechanisms preferentially appeal to narcissistic rigidity, more supple modes of binding the drives are commonly in play.

Schematically, we can distinguish two types of binding: binding by means of a *form* imposed from the exterior, as a "container" for aggressive elements of the drive, and binding by way of *symbolization*, that is, by integration into the sequences, networks, and symbolic structures capable of putting in order the largest possible share of the strangerness of the drives.

Among those "binding" elements, one should rank in first place the great "complexes," Oedipus and Castration, and all the great

---

174 Freud, in his *New Introductory Lectures*, proposed a comparison with a country whose various populations are divided *grosso modo* solely according to geographical criteria: the Germans, who raise livestock, in the hills; the Magyars, who grow crops, on the plain; and the Slovaks, who fish, on the shores of the lakes. The terrible current situation of the Yugoslavian conflict may allow us to give some currency to the comparison. The level of physical geography (plains, mountains, lakes, etc.) is but a ground, which does not allow for an understanding of the conflict; compare it, in the individual, to the level of self-preservation, the terrain, but also one of the stakes in the conflict. The political level of the state, with its borders, would correspond to the psychical topography; finally, the ethnic-ideologic-cultural forces present correspond to the psychical conflict in its reality. It is useless to try to contain the actual conflict within borders that it essentially overflows. Ethnic cleansing (creating borders corresponding to pure ethnic divisions) is a point of view . . .of the ego. But, fortunately, the ego can also have more flexible points of view: assimilation, intermarriage, coexistence . . .

collective and individual myths, whether archaic or more recent, or
even forged, restructured, or reinvigorated by psychoanalysis itself
(murder of the father). Far from being primordial elements of the id,
Oedipus and Castration are instruments for ordering in the service of
binding. The *castration complex* does not stimulate an anxiety (without an object), but a specific fear fixated on an object. Castration is
first of all an "infantile sexual theory" that received its canonical form
from its coauthors (Hans and Sigmund) and allows one to translate
anxieties and enigmatic messages into masterable form. The fact that
there exist less constraining forms of symbolization than the logic of
castration is something I have attempted to demonstrate in my book
Castration, symbolisations.[175]

To return to two aspects of binding, containing and symbolizing, it is important to perceive that they are *jointly* present in
every concrete process. Thus no casting of the individual history of
the subject into narrative, myth, or novel can be conceived without
the intervention of narcissistic elements, which precipitate, coagu-
late, from their presence in one place or another, into an "ego" or an
"ideal" within the fantasmatic structure. Inversely, however narcissistic they be, identifications take on a mobility and a dialectic through
their insertion into the scenarios, however rudimentary, that every
individual forges in order to give form to the enigmatic.

Concerning the opposition between binding and unbinding,
let us return for a moment to the primal situations of seduction. For
having insisted on the elements of instability, aggression, and unbinding included in the messages emanating from the other, for having
declared ironically that the mother, in order to generate the drive in
the child, would have to have been "sufficiently bad," we have run the
risk of neglecting the fact that the other, whether a parent or not, also
furnishes the child with the essential part of his arsenal for binding:
the other's love, care, and "holding" sustain the child's narcissism; in

---

175 *Problématiques II.*

addition, the other brings to the child the elements (verbal but also extraverbal) indispensable to his self-theorization, conveying to the child, by reorganizing them in the adult's own way, collective myths and scenarios. All this and much more make for the "good enough" parent.[176]

The Superego

I am reproached for my silence on the subject of the superego. I can only say a few words on the subject: the question should be sent back to the workshop. The opposition between a (Kleinian) drive-driven preoedipal superego and a legislating oedipal superego cannot satisfy us other than as an index of the difficulty of the question. Freud himself advances the most contradictory formulations, which make the superego at times the representative of reality and at other times an agency deriving all its force from drives. The primacy of the adult other in the genesis of the child's drives should at least allow us to take up the exogenous-endogenous question differently. The fact that the superego is discovered (in Freud and in every individual) in the form of pronouncements, messages of either interdiction or command, that those messages are most often immutable in a specific individual (that is, unable to be metabolized) allows us to surmise an origin in parental messages not having been subjected to primal repression. The comparison I advanced with a "psychotic" enclave is subject to debate and elaboration.

The paradox remains that the superego, even though originally emerging from the unbound, plays an important role in the processes of binding—notably in secondary repression, whose interdictions support and, as it were, *seal* the activation of oedipal and castrative structures.

---

176 I thank Silvia Bleichmar for having insisted on the parental contribution of elements that bind, restoring to the tableau of the adult-child relation its indispensable equilibrium.

Anxiety and Symptoms

To take a stance on the old opposition—debated by Freud in numerous texts without, despite appearances, finding a resolution in *The Problem of Anxiety*—anxiety, in our view, is anxiety of the drive, that is, the manifestation of the most primal affect in the ego, of an attack by the drive that unbinds.[177] This in no way means returning to the alchemy that Freud renounced concerning his "first theory," according to which libido would be "transformed into anxiety." Anxiety is a primal affect without an object which comes from the libidinal attack of the drive emanating from the id and occurs in the ego, as, moreover, does every affect. The series of negative affects—shame, guilt, fear—should be considered as a negative genealogy corresponding to different levels of elaboration and binding of anxiety. Real danger, far from being the origin of anxiety, is one way to master and stabilize it as fear. Notably this is the case for the fear of castration.

Symptoms in turn constitute various means, often quite costly and inappropriate, through which the drive is expressed and bound. Among the symptoms that lead to binding, we may recall acting out, concerning which the expression "criminals out of a feeling of guilt" remains quite eloquent and eminently true. To this I have added the idea that Oedipus himself can be considered as the most illustrious (if not the very first) of these criminals of guilt. That inverted formulation, willfully provocative of so-called oedipal guilt, tends to resituate the myth in its proper place, not as foundational and primordial but as an attempt at binding to be situated as secondary, in the higher layers of the apparatus of the soul.

The Forces in Play in Analytic Treatment

It would be simple to say that the forces in play in treatment are the

---

177 See Jean Laplanche, *Problématiques I: L'angoisse* (Paris: PUF, 1980) and "Une métapsychologie à l'épreuve de l'angoisse," in *La révolution copernicienne inachevée*, pp. 143–58.

same as those that confront one another in the soul-apparatus through the course of everyday life. "Simple," but allowing little hope for genuine change. In our view, therapy is one of the rare situations,[178] assuredly the privileged situation, for calling into question the Ptolemaic enclosure of the apparatus of the soul. Transference is to be considered as the possibility of reopening that apparatus, renewing and prioritizing the enigmatic address emanating from the other, instigating and even generating a neogenesis of libidinal energy.[179] The renewal, *mutatis mutandis*, of the primal situation of seduction, may indeed create an exception to the "constancy" principle concerning the sum total of psychical energies.

---

178 Alongside certain "cultural" constellations.
179 See "Transference: Its Provocation by the Analyst," in *Essays on Otherness*, pp. 214–33.

VI
Responsibility and Response

> You would wish to be responsible for everything except your dreams! What miserable weakness, what lack of logical courage! Nothing contains more of your own work than your dreams! Nothing belongs to you so much! Substance, form, duration, actor, spectator—in these comedies you act as your complete selves! And yet it is just here that you are afraid and ashamed of yourselves, and even Oedipus, the wise Oedipus, derived consolation from the thought that we cannot be blamed for what we dream. From this I must conclude that the great majority of men must have some dreadful dreams to reproach themselves with. If it were otherwise, to how great an extent would these nocturnal fictions have been exploited in the interests of man's pride! Need I add that the wise Oedipus was right, that we are really not responsible for our dreams any more than for our waking hours, and that the doctrine of free will has as its parents man's pride and sense of power! Perhaps I say this too often; but that does not prove that it is not true.

This quotation could well have been from Freud, with the extraordinary conjunction of a responsibility that is total and an irresponsibility no less total, which the man of science is called upon to proclaim and that bears the name of determinism, with the concluding exhortation to humility and the only courage possible, logical or

Cahiers de l'École des Sciences religieuses et philosophiques, 16 (1994; Brussels).

intellectual courage. The text is not from Freud, but from Nietzsche in *Dawn*.[180] But how is one to speak of responsibility in an era intent on revisiting the term in its every sense? How is one to avoid falling into homilies or commentary? It is out of a profound sympathy for these premises,[181] where I have already spoken a few years ago, that I have agreed to speak on a theme that I feared would, from the outset, trap me between those two perils. By taking a step backward, I have seized on this occasion (I might almost say this pretext) to address you on a number of matters revolving around the subject of *response*.

I will also be led to speak about Freud. I "have an interest," as one says, in Freudian thought, no doubt as a translator, but most frequently in order to take him to task. I willingly use the image of man's struggle with the angel: Freud's struggle with his object, which is the unconscious. But in that struggle I am more concerned with the object than with Freud himself. I am not a Freudologist; but the ways in which that great mind circles around his discovery—his paths of access, his wrong turns—seem eminently instructive, if one is willing to review them along with him and, when called for, to denounce his "going astray."

As for Freud's "morality," like this text of Nietzsche, it is to the highest degree one of prudence and humility; I would characterize it with the German term *Nüchternheit*, which means "cold-bloodedness," "coolheadedness," "prosaic bent," "sobriety." Among other passages, I will quote the following from *Civilization and Its Discontents*: "Ethics is thus to be regarded as a therapeutic attempt—as an endeavour to achieve, by means of a command of the super-ego, something which has so far not been achieved by means of any other cultural activities."[182]

---

180 Friedrich Nietzsche, "Dream and Responsibility," *The Dawn of Day*, trans. John McFarland Kennedy, (New York: The MacMillan Company, 1911), p. 128.
181 Delivered at the Facultés universitaires Saint-Louis, Brussels, March 9, 1994.
182 In *SE* 21: 142

124

This *Nüchternheit*, this coolheadedness, causes him to speak not of responsibility but of guilt, gravitating around the word *Schuld*, meaning both "fault" and "guilt," with a possible slippage toward "debt," which had already been anticipated in Nietzsche and poses some rather difficult problems for the translator in following the thread of *Schuld* in German. In any event, guilt is given priority over responsibility, which corresponds quite well to the intention not to unduly subjectivize the problem.

La culpabilité, axiome de la psychanalyse is a book written under my supervision by one of my students, Jacques Goldberg,[183] and, with him, I would say that one might articulate things as follows: "Whether there is a fault or not, in any event, you are guilty."

Is there a possible reversal leading from guilt to feeling guilty? To be sure, but it is not in order to strip us of guilt in the name of an illusion, in the name of a sentiment that would itself remain to be demystified. The path to "discharge" is not evident even when one speaks of a *feeling* of guilt. It is not enough to pay or even to renounce. I cite again: "[Renunciation of the drives] now no longer has a completely liberating effect."[184] We have used the commercial or monetary term *discharge* as a translation: the more one pays, Freud declares in that text, the more one owes.

Nüchternheit, coolheadedness, is also conveyed—and perhaps conveyed above all—by the choice of the appropriate word. In this sense, Freud frequently said, to speak of an unconscious feeling of guilt is not only inexact, but perhaps dishonest as well. I have found, in *Civilization and its Discontents*, in the middle of long pages in which Freud discusses the question of morality and the superego, all of a sudden, a strange aside. As if to rectify his terminology, precisely with reference to the unconscious, he tells us the following: "*Wenn wir ein reineres psychologisches Gewissen haben wollen*," which means

183 Jacques Goldberg, *La culpabilité, axiome de la psychanalyse* (Paris: PUF, 1985).
184 *Civilization and Its Discontents*, SE 21:127-128 [translation modified]

approximately this: "If we want to keep our moral conscience as a psychologist more pure."[185] In a text dealing with moral conscience, it is finally the conscience of the scientist, or the psychologist (as he says), that must be safeguarded, and that conscience (*Gewissen*) is manifested notably in the fact of calling a thing by its name, calling a cat a cat. You will recall that phrase, which is quoted, moreover, by Freud; it is, in fact, drawn from Boileau and ends as follows: "I call a cat a cat and Rollet a scoundrel." You will have observed that Boileau, long before Freud, establishes a bridge between the adequacy of a term (a cat is a cat) and rectitude of judgment: X . . . is a scoundrel and it is immoral not to say so.

It is still Freud's *Nüchternheit* that causes him to practically never speak of the subject, but of an agency cast in the nominal mode: whether *the* "ego" or *the* "I" matters little; it is not "I."

But since I have begun with this detour by way of Freud, I will recall the rare places in which he speaks of responsibility.

In a subsection of the bibliography of the "literature" on dreams (the first chapter of the *Traumdeutung*), which deals with "ethical sentiments," Freud questions the texts which were themselves already examining our responsibility in relation to all those immoral contents that had, of course, been discovered before Freud. Moreover, it is precisely at this point that Freud speaks of *Verantwortlichkeit*, "responsibility," which is one of two possible words in German (the other being *Verantwortung*, which is not quite the same thing, but I will pass over that point). In any event, Nietzsche is not quoted (you are aware that Freud's relation with Nietzsche consists of scotomization: "not wanting to know" that quite often Nietzsche had already said what he would rediscover). And then, as a counterpoint, there is a late addition (1925) to *The Interpretation of Dreams*, which is interesting, especially because it is situated in the framework of the "structural model," and thus of the division of the psychical appa-

---

185 Ibid.

ratus into "ego, id, and superego"—a division that, for some, might appear to be a comfortable way to solve the problem of responsibility. That addition is composed of three short essays of two or three pages, and the essay in question is titled "Die sittliche Verantwortung für den Inhalt der Traüme"—that is, moral responsibility (or the charge of moral responsibility) with regard to the content of dreams.[186]

In that short text, then, Freud, like Nietzsche and most authors, starts from the fact that our dreams often represent extremely immoral events in which we participate. What he adds at this point is a *supplementary* immorality: even in dreams that do not strike us as immoral, analysis often discovers immoral wishes lurking behind them. Psychoanalysis thus renders dreams even more immoral than such authors, who relied only on the manifest contents, had believed. To be sure, the conscious account of the dream may reflect immoral desires, but even when it does not reveal any overtly, very often— usually—there are some it conceals. That immorality, Freud reminds us, stems from "egotistical, sadistic, perverse, incestuous" impulses. On the basis of that important generalization, Freud would proceed along the same path as Nietzsche: how is one to say that they are not mine? "Must we," he tells us, "assume responsibility for the contents of the dream?" You have the word *assume*, which is interesting in Freud, and you have the "must we," which is *muss*: the verb of material obligation.[187] This is tantamount to saying that Freud is not speaking of a moral obligation; we are quite simply being forced. Along exactly along the same lines as Nietzsche, Freud is saying we can't do otherwise: we must affirm that the dream is us. Freud thus situates himself solely at the level of facts. He evades the objections of good conscience through the coolheadedness of objectivity.

---

186 In "A Metapsychological Supplement to the Theory of Dreams," in *SE* 14:222–35. Parenthetically, Freud offers no detectable distinction in his terminology between morality and ethics: *sittlich, moralisch, ethisch* are strictly synonymous in his work.
187 Ibid. p. 182; *müssen* and *sollen* indicate two types of "obligation," which German differentiates, whereas French conflates them.

I alluded a while ago to the distinction "ego, id, and super-ego" in order to emphasize that this distinction, which was new in 1925, does not get us out of difficulty. To be sure, the immorality of the dream stems from the id and the drives, but the ego cannot exculpate itself by arguing that it is on the side of condemnation. I quote: "It stems from the id and forms a 'biological unit' with it. It is perched [*aufsitzt*, a quite picturesque term] on the id."[188] Let us retain these formulae in order to grasp something of what will shortly emerge as *my divergence* concerning the relation between the ego and the id.

As for the superego, the agency that is moral by definition, it turns out that here, as in the last part of his work under the influence of Melanie Klein, Freud approaches it from the perspective most closely related to drives. The superego, which lays claim to issuing condemnations, is as cruel and sadistic as the drives it claims to judge and suppress. The law is a symptom of evil and equally sadistic; and so we are very far from the ethics or the moral doctrines that some have attempted to extract from psychoanalysis. "Ethics" versus "morality": might that distinction itself be a hypocritical way of claiming to be . . . better than one's superego?

An *ethics of the superego*? Well, there is no possibility of that, the superego is "ferocious and obscene," according to Lacan's colorful formulation, and in fact he was following the lead of Melanie Klein. An *ethics of the id*? The expression can be found in the same Lacan, with formulas such as "don't yield on one's desire." But has that ethic, which is that of the Marquis de Sade, ever been advocated except literarily?[189] And finally, with regard to what would be an ethics of the ego, it is swept away like an illusion issuing, according to Freud, from "ethical narcissism" and neglecting the evidence that the ego is seated, "perched," on a mount that it does not command. An

---

188 Ibid. p. 183.
189 The two ethics of Lacan, that of the Law and that of Desire, are conjoined: the Law is that of Desire and desire that of the Tyrant . . . and even of the Analyst.

ethics of the ego, he says in conclusion, would be headed toward inhibition and hypocrisy: "If anyone …would like to be 'better' than he was created, let him see whether he can attain anything more in life than hypocrisy or inhibition."[190]

The matter would thus appear to be settled. Freud, with other and deeper means, rejoins Nietzsche and his denunciation of idols. *Nüchternheit* tells me: in the name of what might I pretend to leap over my own shadow, leap beyond "what I am made of" (*geschaffen*; what Freud calls our *Beschaffenheit*)?

If, along with Freud, I have introduced dreams, it is not only to speak in praise of *Nüchternheit* but also, as I frequently do, to attempt to introduce a fissure somewhere in Freud.

> Un songe (me devrais-je inquiéter d'un songe?)
> Entretient dans mon coeur un chagrin qui le ronge…
> [A dream (should I be worried by a dream?)
> Sustains a worry in my heart that eats it away]

Athalie's dream is the most sadomasochistic dream in existence—and also the most Kleinian.

In order to attack Freud, as I often do, I will make use of something out of Freud'a method: detail and proximity. In a general way, as a path of association, metonymy is always more corrosive than metaphor. Metonymy is a strange detail in the syntagmatic sequence of the text. The detail in the text is this sentence: "If the content of the dream is not the result of the inspiration of foreign spirits, then it is a part of my being." And here we are in agreement with Nietzsche: the dream is me . . . except—a hypothesis presented as absurd—if the dream were the result of foreign spirits. Is it a rhetorical hypothesis simply touched on in passing by Freud, this *demoniacal hypothesis*? Well, as you know, but I will remind you of it, when Freud praises Charcot for his theorization of hysteria, it is for having spent some time on

---

190 *SE* 19:133

an explanation in terms of possession and having taken it seriously. And Freud emphasizes that he derived something from it on the order of a cleavage. As opposed to the simulationist theory, based on malingering, that prevailed and frequently still prevails with regard to hysteria—against the "first-person" explanation, which asserts that ultimately the hysteric's symptom conveys only the patient's will (whether to simulate or not)—there is in the notion of a cleavage or splitting something that brings us back to the hypothesis of possession in a way that is clearly more illuminating.

All this in 1893. But allow me to take a brief excursion. In 1906 Freud responded to a questionnaire on the ten best books he would have liked to take with him, say, to a desert island. He first specifies: one cannot answer that simply; there are literary books, on the one hand, and scientific books, on the other—so much so, that one would be forced to submit two lists of ten works each. But when he comes to the list of scientific books, he mentions only three: one would first of all have to take Copernicus and Darwin; these are, we should remember, the two discoverers of decentering, which Freud would later call the "humiliation" of the human being. There is, first of all, the humiliation that can be called cosmological: the fact that the human being is not at the center of his cosmos; that the earth is not at the center of the world, since it turns around the sun; and that, from that point on, our solar system itself cannot be considered as a center. There is thus, given the "Copernican revolution," something that moves toward an *absolute decentering* of the cosmological perspective. As for the second major scientist, Freud sees Darwin as the apostle of a biological decentering, since, following him, we no longer believe that man is the center of the animal realm: the honor and glory of that realm. But Freud later asserts that there is a third humiliation,[191] the psychoanalytic humiliation, which consists in showing that man is not at home in himself, in other words, that he is not master of himself and that

---

191 "A Difficulty in the Path of Psychoanalysis," in *SE* 17:135–44.

finally (and this is my term), he has been decentered.

Let us return to our list of the three best scientific authors and suggest that Freud might well have said: the three leading authors to be cited are Copernicus, Darwin, and . . . Freud, as the discoverer of the third mode of decentering. (On the subject of humiliation, it recalls the joke captured in the sentence "As to modesty, I am second to none.") Thus Freud might have said: as to modesty I am second to none and so, to understand that the human being is to be put back in his modest place, the best thing would be to take my complete works to that desert island.

All this is something of a joke. For Freud does not recommend classifying his work as third. Who is the third scientist Freud would take with him? An illustrious nobody (for us) named Johannes Weier, whose work—published in Basel in 1563—is titled (fittingly in Latin) *De praestigiis daemonum et incantantionibus de veneficiis* (On illusions of demons, spells, and poisoned beverages). The third scientific author, the one who comes in the place that Freud will occupy, the precursor of the third decentering, is an author concerned with demonic possession, the first to suggest to us that man is not at home even at home, and that the demoniacal hypothesis was but an extravagance elaborated on the basis of that *truth*.

There is an additional element I would point out to introduce a fissure in Freud's little article on responsibility for dreams. That text is part of three brief additions to the *Traumdeutung*, which we published in volume 17 of the French complete works. I will skip over the first, but the second is titled "The Occult Secret of the Dream." Historically, this title explains that three short passages that were supposed to be inserted in the edition of the *Traumdeutung* were not. They were published in a psychoanalytic journal but never added to Freud's volume on dreams. That was because Ernest Jones, Freud's rationalist guardian, was violently opposed to it. Everything Freud might fantasize on the subject of occultism and telepathy was a source of absolute horror for our Jones, and each time he was able to prevent it from appearing he did so. Jones, let us call him, the neopositivist.

Moreover, dating from the same period, in addition to that short text; we have three other articles and lectures by Freud, which are far more lengthy: "Dreams and Telepathy," "Psychoanalysis and Telepathy," and "Dreams and Occultism."

I will deal quite rapidly with the subjects of occultism and telepathy. Freud, as is known, includes telepathy among the so-called occult phenomena, with regard to which, he tells us, one should initially have a scientific impartiality. He even, in this respect, offers an encomium to prejudice as a way of approaching certain phenomena. It is preferable to have a favorable prejudice than to condemn at the outset. But in very short order unfavorable prejudice will make a return regarding occultism/telepathy. Occultism in general is to be separated from the circumscribed phenomenon of telepathy; in the face of prophesy, whether in dreams or outside them, he says, "my resolution in favour of impartiality deserts me."[192] I cannot accept (he does not say it in these terms) an inversion of time's arrow such that I can, in one way or another, perceive at time T what will transpire at time T+1. As for telepathic dreams or telepathy in general, he accepts, on the other hand, their possibility, by way of a term allowing a sort of pun or dissociation in translation, since it is a question of *Gedankenübertragung*: *Übertragung* is the term meaning transference; except, whether one likes it or not, it is also a term meaning transmission in current German parlance. So much so that *Gedankenübertragung* is simply the transmission of thought for anyone who speaks German, but, at the same time, for a Freudian, or for Freud himself, it is difficult to speak of *Übertragung* without thinking that the term *transference* lies behind it. Thus there is a dilemma for the translator, an issue I will not examine: we have opted to translate it as *transfert de pensée*, "thought transference," which is fairly inaccurate for current speech, but indicates to the reader, at least, that there is a problem relating to *Übertragung*.

---

192 "Some Additional Notes on Dream Interpretation as a Whole," in *SE* 19:136

Freud thus admits, concerning this transmission or transference of thought, that certain experiments performed with it are credible and, in particular, certain examples of dreams he reports are incomprehensible without transmission of thoughts.

But it is here that the point on which I personally am critical supervenes, without my taking a direct position on the question of telepathy. After having admitted that telepathy exists, Freud asserts brusquely that this is of no importance for dreams; telepathic content would be a perceptual content like any other; there are perceptions prior to the dream that are treated in the dream (the "day residues") and, similarly, there are perceptions during sleep: you can have the perception of a shock, of someone touching you, you perceive corporeal stimuli during sleep, etc., and they are taken up and elaborated in dreams. And such would as well be the fate of telepathic content: it is treated like any other perceptual content, without any priority and without any particularity. I quote: "The telepathic message is treated as a fragment of the material in relation to dream-formation, like another stimulus coming from within or without, such as a disturbing noise coming from the street, or an importunate sensation coming from one of the dreamer's organs." Telepathy, he concludes, "has nothing to do with the essence of dreams."

I am sketching here (and taking the time to do so) a collateral path—but barely so. *The Interpretation of Dreams*, the inaugural work of Freudian thought, contains, as everyone undoubtedly knows, seven chapters. A first chapter of bibliography, five chapters of analysis, of dream interpretations, in which Freud is intent on showing in innumerable examples that through his method one arrives at this universal thesis: "The dream is a wish-fulfillment." And then a seventh section, the notorious "chapter 7," titled "Psychology of the Dream Processes," which deals principally with the hallucinatory form assumed by our dreams; in these dreams, which are all equivalent to wish-fulfillments, why is the wish not conveyed discursively, or even by *imaginings*, but without hallucination or belief? It is here that the psychological problem of *hallucinations*, and particularly of hallucinations in dreams, surfaces. Thus, to resort to my own terms, five chapters to account for the strangeness of dreams, reduced to wish-fulfillments, one chapter on what I will call the strangerness of dreams, namely, their hallucinatory aspect. Now the chapters on that strangeness and the one on that strangerness are clearly independent of each other. Freud deals with the problem of hallucination almost in neuropsychophysiological terms; in order to explain the hallucinatory form, he largely detaches the strangerness of the form from the strangeness of the content. And he does so at the price (and I come back here to the example of telepathy) of treating so-called telepathic elements, whose *a priori strangerness* should be maximal, as simple stimuli.

My path is neither occultist nor telepathic. But my question is the following: might we not reenvisage the strangerness of dreams and that of hallucinations on the basis of the vector of strangerness present in every message?[193] Freud forgot in this seventh chapter, but also in the five others, that dreams do not deal with things or stimuli or perceptual traces, but with traces of interhuman messages.

Here then is an article on "responsibility" that is curiously squeezed between the short passage on demonic possession, on one side, and telepathy, on the other. Once again: I am not interested in telepathy, but in *messages*, with or without telepathy.[194] *It was in vain that Freud expanded to the occult what he took to be the realm of experience; that realm remains irremediably inaccessible to the entry of the other.* And inversely, I will say: if Freud had fully perceived the strangerness of the id and the strangerness of the message emanating from the other, he would not have been obsessed by the strangerness and the strangeness of telepathy.

My most recent work, which collected my articles over a certain number of years (and which Jean Florence recalled a while ago)

---

193 "Seduction, Persecution, Revelation," in this volume.
194 Whereas one might well say, on the contrary: Freud is interested only in perception, with telepathy as well as without telepathy.

is titled *La révolution copernicienne inachevée*. We thus return to Copernicus, about whom I was just speaking, and precisely to the question of knowing whether the "Copernican revolution," that decentering of man, is actually completed by Freud on the level of the psyche or the soul. In the text introducing the volume, I oppose a Ptolemaic vision and a Copernican vision. This to say that, Freud remains Ptolemaic despite everything. Despite a good start, he remains centered, and centered on the self. Everything he says about the ego perched on the id is situated in a perspective of recentering. Not, to be sure, a recentering in relation to consciousness, but a recentering in relation to our biological being, which allegedly would be the very foundation of the id.

How is one to achieve a perception of Copernicanism—as I call it—in philosophy, a universe of thought that, from Descartes to Kant, to Husserl, to Heidegger, and to Freud, is irremediably Ptolemaic? As a provocation of sorts and largely for its shock value, I enjoy posing the following question, which has the appearance of a sophism: the three grammatical persons are the following (by definition): the first person, the person who is speaking; the second person, the person to whom I am speaking; the third person, the person of whom I am speaking. *But* which then is . . . the person who speaks (to) me? For it is assuredly neither *I* nor *you* nor *he*.

My encounter with the thought of Levinas is recent and largely fortuitous. It is rather a matter of overlap. To be sure, as a young philosopher, one of my classics was his inaugural book of 1930: *Théorie de l'intuition dans la phénoménologie de Husserl*. It was an excellent book for a philosophy student, and, to be frank, Husserl was little known in the 1940s, when I was beginning my advanced preparatory classes. But that book is quite different from Levinas's other works, which I did not read as they were published, which I have only come to know quite recently, in the last few years, and which, I can say, did not influence my thinking. Well, I would say that, with the book on Husserl (that I just mentioned), Levinas had a very shaky start insofar as Copernicanism was concerned. As he himself put it: "The relation with others in Husserl remains representative. The relation with others can be sought as irreducible intentionality, even if one is obliged to finish by seeing [or acknowledging] that there is a breaking with intentionality."[195]

That being said, my overlap with Levinas takes place in the element of difference and with broad differences. The major difference being the following: the Copernican decentering is valid not only for the subject self-centered perceptually and for the cogito but for the *subject self-centered in time* as well; centered on its adult being, "perched" (to take up Freud's expression invoked above) on itself as a full-grown adult. Just as much as for Husserl, this critique is valid, in my opinion, for Heidegger.

To be sure, in the case of the latter, it is no longer the Kantian "I think," which should be able to accompany all my representations, but, let us say, the "I am situated," *Dasein*, which should accompany all my understandings and elucidations, but these are irremediably those of the adult philosopher, here and now. If one attempts to take it seriously, the primacy of childhood in Freud decenters us as irremediably—and as anti-reflexively—as the extraneous nature of the unconscious or the id.

I am aware that I am saying things here that seem to a philosopher non-philosophical or prephilosophical and that appear to be (to use Heidegger's vocabulary) ontic and not ontological. Is not the decision to start from childhood tantamount to starting from the constituted (and not constitutive) person, a person targeted, and even reconstituted in a manner of naive objectivism, and not apprehended from within as a "subject?" Accept, however, for an instant being affected by this sophism, on the same basis as the one evoked above: "Which is the person that speaks (to) me?"

---

195 Emmanuel Levinas, *Éthique et infini* (Paris: Fayard, 1985), p. 28.

The primacy of childhood (and even of the nursing infant) is only temporal in appearance, a pure "before" in chronology. When we speak of childhood, it is not essentially a question of *post hoc, ergo propter hoc*. That primacy brings us back to a situation that is not one of self-centering, not even one of reciprocity or, as is said, of inter-action, a situation that is not one of reciprocal communication, but rather an essentially asymmetrical situation in which I am passive and disarmed in relation to the message emanating from the other. A situation whose trace we refuse to recognize in the structure of strangerness or foreignness of persecution, of revelation, or of the dream, and also in the structure of the foreignness of the analytic session, *there, where it was rediscovered.*

I should speak here of something central to this presentation that obviously I can not develop for reasons of time and also out of respect for my audience, namely, what I call t*he general theory of seduction*. I shall all but ignore what is at stake in it, retaining the option of perhaps returning to it in the discussion: saying only that it begins with the confrontation of the small child with sexual messages said to be enigmatic—enigmatic *because* that is what they are for the other, the adult emitting them. But what is essential is the small child's "treatment" of the message with whatever (inevitably inadequate) means lie at hand. That treatment is an attempt at translation, an always inadequate *response* whose fallout is what I call "thing-representations," which are nothing other than unconscious signifiers. An imperfect translation, the failure of that translation, this is a way of giving content to what Freud calls "primal repression," i.e., the constitution of the unconscious and which, if one takes it seriously, implies that the unconscious has an individual origin in the human being and should not in any way be reduced to a preexisting biological id.[196]

---

196 Not any more than to a transindividual "treasure of signifiers" in the style of Lacan.

It will thus be seen that I have shifted the notion of response to refer to a response to a message emanating from the other, to which I have alluded in my title, a shift from a "respond for"—which would be "responsibility," and is declined, once again, on the basis of a Copernican subject—to a "respond to."

"Respond to": take the parable of Job. Job is addressed by an utterly enigmatic message. I was asked this morning[197] about what a nonverbal message might be. Well, God's persecution of Job initially takes place without a word: it begins by the killing of his herd; then he is overwhelmed by a series of fires and plagues . . . and that is it! Job is thus addressed by this message in a situation of absolute dissymmetry. The message is the address of an action (or successive actions) performed by the persecutor, who, in the Bible, is a kind of perfectly ambivalent character, a sort of God/Satan, since Satan and God are absolutely complicit in putting Job to the test. Now Job believes that he is being asked to "answer for"; that is: What is my responsibility in all of this? In point of fact, he is attempting to respond, to answer in the sense in which one says "answering back"—taken comprehensively—with regard to a child, a quite interesting situation. When one says (or said) of a child that he "answers back," that is precisely what he should not be doing; he is insolent, and his insolence is unacceptable. I quote the definition in the *Dictionnaire Robert*: "To argue, justifying oneself when respect demands silence."

Every bit as garrulous as Job, his companions Eliphaz, Bildad, Sophar, and Eliphon also do nothing but answer back, inadequately. Responding to unspeakable sadistic persecution, characterizable in our terms as anal-sadistic, once one thinks of the excremental stench rising from the dungheap, and of Job reduced to this pestilence.

I will break off here in order to return to Freud—and to my critique of Freud. Freud, in his long argument in *Civilization and Its Discontents*, attempts to bring into play two titanic, metabiological or

---

197 During a discussion session held the morning of this lecture.

metacosmological forces: a death drive and a life drive. For years now I have been criticizing this notion of a death drive, attempting to make it give up what might well be its truth. I have offered a critique of its assimilation to a tendency to pure destruction, which would allegedly be nonsexual, and that is why I have spoken of a "sexual death drive." In addition, I have been no less critical of the idea that it would be biological, endogenous, and more primal, as might be said, than man himself, finding its point of departure with the very emergence of life, in brief, an instinct and not a drive, and even the biological instinct par excellence.

In that text, *Civilization and Its Discontents*, Freud takes up rather unconvincingly the old adage: *homo homini lupus*. One might have hoped that psychoanalysis would have discredited this adage, but one could just as well have counted on animal psychology to address it. *Is the wolf a wolf for the wolf?* Nothing is less certain, even in the case of rivalry between males. In any event, in that case, it is certainly not a wolf in the sense of the adage. *Is the wolf a wolf for man?* Assuming that man is occasionally a prey for the wolf, there is nothing demonstrating a cruelty or ferocious destructiveness on the part of the wolf for its prey. That being the case, saying that "man is a wolf for man" can only be a kind of biological fiction, the invocation of a mythical animal, more animalistic than any other and crueler than any animal in the world. It is a matter of a biological alibi disguising something that ultimately has nothing to do with biology and is not found anywhere else in the realm of life. Man's cruelty toward man can in no way involve any "biological" dimension, even in the inmost depth of our being. The wolf of the adage, which comes from Hobbes, is a kind of *emblematic* figure for our own cruelty, but can in no way serve as an argument for invoking our so-called biological being and the so-called biological character of our destructiveness.

Freud thus wrote *Civilization and Its Discontents* in the 1930s under the influence of the war of 1914–1918. It was called a "butchering," and admittedly was a massacre of tens of millions of human beings, but with relatively little overt sadism. The "War of 14–18" (as in Georges Brassens's celebrated song, "Rien ne vaut la guerre de 14–18" [Nothing as good as the war of 14–18]) is perhaps the only episode in history in which what are called the laws of war took on some plausibility. Neither before nor after were those rules of war—respect for prisoners, respect for the Red Cross, and relative respect for civilian populations—heeded. The War of 14–18 would be a pure war of interests, without any consideration for humanity—without any concern for sparing men, to be sure, but without any pleasure in making them suffer. The War of 1914–18 is perhaps what gave birth to the myth (among others) of a pure instinct of destruction that would be nonsexual. How should we situate it in relation to the appalling episodes before and after: say, the Thirty Years War, on one side as point of reference, and then all that we have known since then, with Nazism, the Khmer Rouge, Bosnia, etc.? Would that "pure" war—however destructive, however pure a "death drive" it might appear to be—be a kind of "sublimation" of those sadistic horrors? Or would they be but the "blunders" of pure violence? Since then, in any event, we have witnessed the resurgence of cruelty, which is something other than war; and one would have to want to blindfold oneself not to recognize it as sadism (and even sadomasochism) that is *sexual*. In the Nazi camps and the extermination, have we forgotten, behind the apparent coldness of the term *Final Solution*, the deliberate and sexual cruelty of every instant? But in that case is the cruelty a perversion of the war of interests, or, to the contrary, might it not be what is most "human," that is, most sexual, whereas conflicts of interest could be understood at the simple animal level of the struggle for life? I do not separate the Nazi camps from what we have seen since them with Cambodia or Bosnia. The term *holocaust*, which has been added for the Nazi camps, seems to me a partially religious interpretation[198]—

---

198 And a sacrificial translation aiming to master what is most enigmatic and most radically alien. See Job above in Chapter 1.

respectable to be sure, but also, in turn and to a certain extent, a kind of sublimation.

Do we have the right to say, in all these cases, that the sexual-sadistic is added on or adventitious? That seems to me extremely dubious. And to return to the theoretical level, to Freud's theory, how are we to speak of an episodic or adventitious sexualization when elsewhere Freud had just converted the sexual into an "Eros" that is an entirely positive force for love and unity? Where is the sadism, which nonetheless leaps to the eye, in all that? What relation might there be between the Ninth Symphony, that great hymn to Eros, and the rapes of Bosnia and the cannibalism of the Khmer Rouge? As you will see, I have several axes of affirmation, but also many questions . . .

My philosophical axis is that human violence—insofar as it is human and not animal—is sexual. What may be called the sexual death drive is neither biological nor instinctual, contrary to what Freud thought. But it is linked to sexual fantasies inhabiting our unconscious, and to which our dreams every day bear witness, as we recalled at the outset with Freud and Nietzsche. I do not see how those cruel fantasies, causing the suffering of the other and the imagination of that suffering to intervene, could be situated on the side of nature and the innate.

I return, however, to the development of my subject: answering to and answering for. The tiny human being, who is in no position to do so, is expected to answer messages charged with sexuality. That answer, those answers, are his self-construction, his "Ptolemization," as we might call it. A self-construction with a fallout of untranslated residues, those uncoordinated, unbound elementary signifiers that we call unconscious. When we say "unconscious" with Freud, and beyond Freud, I think that we are not referring essentially to a reflexive consciousness, in the sense of a light illuminating contents in a flash. What is important in the term *unconscious* is to decompose it into three, that is, *in-con-scire*—what is not known together, what is not symbolized in a co-herent whole. It is what is heterogeneous to consciousness in the sense that the term implies a unity: think of what Hegel calls consciousness, "unhappy consciousness," for example. That un-con-scious, that unbound, or non-bound,[199] is what continues to attack us in the element of its strangerness. It is there that one finds the "pure culture" of the death drive, of unbinding, of strangerness to which we continue to be called on to respond, as we were called on to respond to the parental adult. The great question consists in asking oneself how those unbound residues turn, so to speak, to vinegar, how one passes from an unbinding of signifiers to a disarticulation of tortured bodies.

I have intervened in times past in debates on the subject of punishment to defend the rights of responsibility and penal retribution. It was at the time when the death penalty was being debated, and my plea for sanctions or consequences was assimilated—with utter bad faith—to a position taken in support of the death penalty. Since then, many have to some extent followed in my footsteps (which delights me),[200] in the idea that punishment is the criminal's *right*. Some even speak, somewhat hastily, of the "therapeutic function" of the sanction. "Therapeutic," if one likes, and on the condition of accepting the plurivocity of the term *treatment*, which ranges from the treatment of medical or psychiatric therapy to the treatment of objectives in war or even the treatment of a text.

In the debate, then, I said, in particular, the following: he who screams for death in the trial of a child murderer (punish him!) or even he who screams on the subject of Bosnia (Bomb it!) . . . is also he who, from childhood on, screams: "It's not fair!" In brief, he who thirsts for justice—and that means each of us—is also the person yelling out against what attacks him from within, against the torturer inside himself. Much has been said on the forcefulness of photos and the

---

199 As opposed to Lacan: not structured (and not "structured like a language") and without subject (as opposed to the "subject of the unconscious").

200 P. Poncela, "Se défendre de l'expertise psychiatrique, in *Psychanalystes*, no. 37 (1990): 35–39.

pregnancy of the image, specifically the one that provoked a reaction, at Sarajevo. Without wanting for all that (as one says) to make us feel guilty, how does one not see that such images are on a spectrum without any clear transition between those images and the ones displayed by scandal sheets and a literature dedicated to sadomasochism? The emotion is no more pure in one case than in the other; and who would dare analyze why the weeklies with photos of the massacre in Sarajevo have sold so well? Our demand to settle the question, to *treat* (I return to the term) certain targets, is also the demand to treat, or *take care of,* the same unconscious drives in ourselves—even to silence them.

I have not presented a theory of responsibility, and it has not been my intention to comment yet one more time on the celebrated "Wo Es war, soll Ich werden." A formula that can be translated, depending on the context, with a sense of *Schwärmerei,* a slightly delusional enthusiasm, or of *Nüchternheit.* In the sense of *Schwärmerei,* one can say: "a subject is to come to be"; but with a coldness or more Freudian *Nüchternheit*: "where id was, must ego be." That last translation (you will see that I often return to these questions of words, but they are quite important; if one yields on words, Freud used to say, one ends up yielding on things themselves) I owe to Conrad Stein, who quite rightly invited us to note that a noun like *Es* or *Ich,* without article, might be quite simply a partitive, and he quoted a sentence as an example: "Where there was wheat, we will put barley." "Where there had been sea (as Freud phrases it), there should be land, namely the reclamation of the Zuydersee." Which takes us in the direction of a slightly prosaic and flattened out translation: "There where there was (some) id, (some) ego should be." And, to continue, one might amuse oneself by pushing the polders as far as Candide's garden: there where there was raging sea, if you please, a bit of firm land on which eventually to plant some tulips . . .

In displacing responsibility onto the question of the answer or response, I have in no way intended to sketch an ethics or a morality of psychoanalysis. I have spoken of one or two things that I believe

143

I know as well as a few that puzzle me. One of the things I believe I know is that psychoanalysis, therapy, the analytic situation, as inaugurated by Freud, is the major locus, if not the only one, in which the human being can attempt to re-elaborate his answer, his answers, to the strangerness of the sexual first in him and then perhaps outside.

VII
Psychoanalysis in the Scientific Community

I want to recall and underline the topic proposed for this issue in order to contest its terms.[201] It reads in part: "Whether it be deplored or celebrated . . . the recurrent problem of the transmission of psycho-analysis through academic channels persists."

"Contest" them, since surreptitiously and even before posing the question of "academic channels," it is the notion of *transmission* that is posited as a sort of consensus, as a specific mode of communi-cation of psychoanalytic truths and knowledge.

My reservations with regard to transmission do not date from today. But they are reinforced by a quite searing incident, occurring quite recently and in which "the example is the thing itself"; as the title for this paper, I had proposed "Psychoanalysis in the Scientific Com-munity." But, as if such a title were quite simply inaudible, as if it were inconceivable that psychoanalysis might be part of the scientific uni-verse, all of a sudden I discovered that in the program my paper had been given the title "Psychoanalysis *and* the Scientific Community."

The notion of transmission, with its most precise German

Cliniques méditerranéennes 1995, nos. 45/46 (1995).

201 This issue stems from the colloquium organized January 22 and 23, 1994, in Paris and titled "La psychanalyse en tant que science ? Un mode universitaire de la transmission de la psychanalyse s'est-il constitué?" (Psychoanalysis as a Science? Has an academic mode of transmission for psychoanalysis been constituted?)

equivalent, *Übermittlung,* is barely present in Freud. The word *Über-tragung,* which might be invoked with that meaning, is reserved, as is known, for something quite different: transference. Where does the word—at least in French psychoanalysis—come from? In my view, from a double derivation best considered as illicit: the too eagerly transmissive and abusive practice linked to the "training analysis" (that monstrous *contradictio in terminis*) —and the impact of that conception of the psychoanalysis of the future analyst on the entire range of analytic communication.

The so-called training analysis, whatever the institutional and ideological framework sustaining it, is a *finalized* psychoanalysis— undertaken "on command"—and thus open to functionality (which makes it the very opposite of analysis). I have emphasized its functioning as power, indoctrination, and affiliation. And I have never stopped denouncing it—along with others, who are, finally, relatively few. The fact that it is occasionally decked out in more noble names (such as "transmission" or "filiation") changes nothing in what it proposes nor in where it ends up.

From where, in turn, does the word *filiation* come to us? It is a recent arrival in analysis and certainly even less Freudian a term than that of *transmission.* And that, even if Freud is inclined to invoke paternity, and did so more than once with students and/or analysands. But since then the realm of transmission/indoctrination in analysis has become extraordinarily broad. One has only to see candidates for a second analysis in order to perceive the conveyance, whether covert or overt, of one or another analytic doctrine. One candidate will speak rather hastily of transcending the depressive position, another of assuming castration or the law, and a third of an ideology of maturation, etc. I will come back to these ideological aspects of psychoanalytic thought.

But first I will briefly comment on the coalescence that has been established between teaching and the personal analysis. The term *my students* to designate one's analysands is characteristic of this. The fact that Lacan was a great promoter on this front—through the meshing of analysis and seminar—does not prevent it from having been the case before him or at the same time as him or after him. Little clans and large sects have proliferated, within the university and outside it, surrounding one or another grand or petty guru, presenting himself simultaneously as analyst, instructor, and transmitter.

It is a position, in my opinion, that is rigorously anti-analytic to the extent that—something I cannot develop here—the very essence of the analytic process is quite simply "analysis" and has as its correlate the divestment of any power on the part of the analyst, including the power stemming from any alleged ideological knowledge. A knowledge that has a meaning only to the extent that it is relegated to a state of suspension, "supposed to be known," as Lacan puts it so well. And if I refer to Lacan himself on more than one occasion—to "Variations on the Standard Treatment"[202]—it is in order to show the clear contrast between a specific text, one or another of whose formulations may lie at the heart of our practice: "What must the analyst know? How to ignore what he knows?" and certain practices of filiation and indoctrination that, although they advance under other banners than those of ego psychology, have no reason to envy it in this regard.

To conclude on this matter. I have been fighting, for years now, against the process of transmission-filiation known as the "training analysis," which is being renewed to varying degrees in almost all analytic societies, but not in order to transport something of that very process to the university!

***

I have also done battle on behalf of the presence of psychoanalysis, as a scientific and investigative discipline, within the University. I have said the following on certain occasions: the attacks

---

202 Jacques Lacan, *Écrits* (Paris: Seuil, 1966), pp. 323–62.

against a "doctorate in psychoanalysis," coming from analytic societies, were in fact projections. In pretending to see in the doctorate a diploma with professional implications, those societies or individuals revealed their aim of *retaining for themselves alone* a power of indoctrination and professional accreditation, which are too easily confused with the analytic process itself.

It is now almost thirty years that I have been claiming for psychoanalysis a fully legitimate place in the scientific community and thus, to that extent, in the University. It is not the error of transmission in the title of my paper that will prompt me to change my position.

A scientific place, alongside the physical sciences, among the human sciences or sciences of communication or even (the formulation, once again, is Lacan's) the sciences of intersubjectivity. At this juncture the pertinence of the opposition between "hard" and "soft" sciences might be questioned. For it leads to a misunderstanding. Its tools are certainly not mathematical; they tend to be more flexible, but its conceptual rigor is not necessarily any less. The assertion of truth or falsehood is not vulnerable to softness. To take an example from another human science, a linguistic theory such as that of "double articulation" is subject to refutation or falsification.[203] Before evoking the criterion of refutability for psychoanalysis, I shall assert what is for me the essential aspect of this presentation: the distinction, in psychoanalytic theory, of levels, and more precisely of two levels. On the one hand, metapsychological theory taken in the broadest sense; on the other, "psychoanalytic" ideologies (which circumstance obviously presupposes a metapsychological theory accounting for the function of the second level).

In defining psychoanalysis, I always insist on starting from

---

203 To continue the reference to Popper for a moment, I will recall what he says concerning the laws of statistics, laws that are allegedly approximate, indeterminate, and even soft: in point of fact, he shows that it is the instrument that is flexible, but the assertion is no less "hard" for all that; the statement that "a specific phenomenon takes place in 50 to 60 percent of cases" can perfectly well be refuted.

Freud's definition. Freud situated method as being of primary importance and theory or therapy as being of secondary or tertiary significance. Method thus comes first, but on the condition of considering it as something other than a collection of recipes.[204] It is directly related to a specific field of phenomena, a realm of being. I quote: "Psychoanalysis is first of all a procedure for the investigation of mental processes that are more or less inaccessible by other means."

This link between what is observed and the procedure for bringing it to light no doubt implies a certain circularity; but this is not unprecedented in science and does not invalidate the scientificity of the set constituted by the object *plus* the method—as the case of particle physics demonstrates . . .

What accounts for the scientificity is that the procedure is not isolated or restricted to the particularity of a single case. It is reproducible. The access to the unconscious that it affords is, to be sure, indirect, a situation that in no way implies it is unknowable . . . But that inseparability of the method and the object is not for nothing in the *urgency of a model* that accounts for the specificity of the one as a function of the singularity of the other. This explains why metapsychological considerations intervene very early on in Freud's thought, in the very first psychoanalytic experiments: *Studies in Hysteria*, the correspondence with Fliess, the "Project for a Scientific Psychology." There is thus, in the first place, in psychoanalytic science, metapsychology itself: a model attempting to account conjointly for the unconscious and the method allowing access to it. A theory encompassing coherent hypotheses on the genesis of the unconscious (specifically on repression), on unconscious contents and processes, on manifestations of the unconscious (symptom formation, dreams, etc.) and, on the other hand, hypotheses on the specificity of the situation apt to bring the unconscious into evidence: specificity of the

---

204 The distance between Descartes's *Discours de la méthode* and lame appeals to research "methodology" of the sort we are inundated with is positively intergalactic.

analytic situation and the transference.

Metapsychology is abstract, at a distance from experience (like every theory); it is not "inducted" from experience, as Popper well demonstrated with regard to all scientific theories. It is a construct that aims to be simple, elegant, and as rigorous as possible in the way in which it claims to account for the facts. It is thus subject to *criticism*, with regard to its simplicity, elegance, and pertinence; to *refutation*, with regard to its internal coherence; to *falsification*, that is, to an eventual establishment of contradictions between its consequences and the facts.

On more than one occasion I have developed the idea that the abandonment of the theory of seduction in September 1897 responded in part to this schema. One finds in it, to be sure, affective elements, notably the exclamation: "One would have to believe in the perversion of the father." But one also finds in it something interesting with respect to the very idea of falsifiability. Freud, at one point, says: this theory has to be abandoned, not only because it is false but because on one point it could not be falsified. This point is the "absence of an index of reality in the unconscious," which would forever preclude any decision regarding the reality of the seduction.

Despite the crossfire of arguments, I have attempted to show how that refutation might have led not to an abandonment but to a broadening of fundamental hypotheses.[205] But that is another question.

I come now to a *second level* of the theory. Not only does psychoanalysis construct a theory; it *discovers* theories in man, in the course of its own investigation. The very term *infantile sexual theories*, although restrictive, in fact explains what is at stake: systems or fragments of systems, scenarios, myths, that come to the aid of the child in his effort at self-theorization. The child is confronted with enigmas; he attempts to account for them for himself in scenarios that are not only "intellectual" but implicate his entire being.

---

205 See *New Foundations for Psychoanalysis*.

A historical remark. This discovery of theories by psychoanalysis, notably of infantile theories, does not appear at the outset. On the whole, up until 1900, the theory and practice of psychoanalysis do quite well without them. The *Studies in Hysteria* and even the *Traumdeutung* do quite well without thematizing the myth of Oedipus, not to mention the theory of castration, which was still totally absent. To be sure, psychoanalysis would not *merely* discover those theories. Much like an ethnologist discovering myths, psychoanalysis reconstitutes them rendering them explicit; it displays their variants and tries to explain their psychical genesis (and, if that should prove impossible, it has recourse to the *deus ex machina* of phylogeny); it shows how such theories may succeed each other, mesh with each other over time, "retranslate" each other (e.g., the genital theory that takes up and rearranges anal or oral elements). Psychoanalysis also shows their psychical function, which in my view is essential, and, finally, it makes more or less verifiable assertions regarding their universality.

These organizing theories or myths have the major function of answering anxiety-inducing enigmas by establishing an order, an understanding. A partial translation in which the myth takes on the function of a translator's code. Such theories are numerous. Their classical enumeration does not exhaust them: the cloacal theory, the sadistic theory of intercourse, combined parents, etc.

The most exemplary case no doubt remains the castration theory, which I have named, with an ironic insistence, the "theory of Hans and Sigmund," formulated, as it was, by Hans, and reformulated by Sigmund. In a word, the enigma to which this theory pretends to provide an answer is that of *genders*. The terms of the theory are that all beings begin by possessing a penis; some of them are subsequently castrated, the others remain under constant threat of castration, but in both cases one can have one "screwed back on." Freud's reflection was also concerned with studying the genesis of the theory, along with what I have called its individual "ingredients": perception, threat, etc. But Freud fails to formulate the fact that the theory preconditions the ingredients.[206] As for the *function of the theory*, which is to master the primal anxiety due to the attack of sexual excitation, that is explicitly formulated on more than one occasion.

Are these "theories" refutable? Freud makes absolutely no claim of this sort. Their "truth" is of the same order as that of myths, legends, and religious dogmas. It is plainly those theories at which Popper more or less confusedly takes aim when he accuses psychoanalytic assertions of not being falsifiable, this no doubt as a result of his poor knowledge of psychoanalysis and his ignorance of the metapsychological level. Finally, in the case of a number of critics,[207] there is frequently a confusion between "theories" as instruments of self-interpretation invented by the human being and the theories of psychoanalysis which should, among other things, account for the function of those spontaneous or ideological "theories".

But it should be admitted that Freud himself did not facilitate this distinction by forging, in his very terminology, a link between his *Three Essays on the **Theory of Sexuality*** and such "infantile *sexual theories*," and above all by giving the seal of his authority to certain psychoanalytic ideologies. This is patent precisely in the analysis of little Hans, in which he presents himself as "speaking with the good Lord" and being familiar for all eternity with the oedipal scenario. What more massive example of "transmission" is there than that of Freud with Hans? A transmission claiming to be primal, foundational, and quasi-religious. A transmission whose propelling force is overtly an argument from authority and covertly suggestion: "speaking with the good Lord." From there to a certain normativity there is but a small step, often quickly and cheerfully taken.

To remain with this example, castration will undergo transformation into a metaphysical dimension and be taken, a bit rapidly, as a synonym of "finitude." But for all that it remains no less funda-

---

206 See *Problématiques II*.
207 Even including Lévi-Strauss.

mentally ideological, neither more nor less respectable than so many others denounced in times past: free enterprise or the "American way of life."

What place is to be accorded to ideologies in psychoanalysis? The last of Freud's *New Introductory Lectures* on "the question of a *Weltanschauung*" is instructive in more than one respect. In it Freud pits psychoanalysis, which has no specific *Weltanschauung* other than science, precisely against "worldviews" that are essentially religious but also metaphysical, and even political. He sketches their analysis, or rather their function, which consists in "plugging gaps in the Universe" (according to Heine's formula) and sealing off anxiety. It is an insufficient (and often polemical) analysis in which several dimensions are poorly perceived. In brief: in wanting to replace religious ideology (and even ideologies in general) with science, the risk of transforming the latter into a *Weltanschauung* is clear. Despite the dimension of incompleteness and indefinite progress that characterize it, the scientific ideal was quick to make a leap toward the absolute and a dream of total mastery. Does not the positing of "neuronal man" correspond to this overtly metaphysical leap?

But *above all, at the very heart of what can be called the psychoanalytic corpus,* Freud does not seem to perceive the difficulty generated by the coexistence of these two levels: on the one hand, psychoanalytic theory and, on the other, the spontaneous theories that, for all the "infantile" aspect characterizing them, play no less of an essential role in psychical functioning. For failure to maintain this distinction, and for failure to appreciate the metapsychological function of the self-theorizations (and even the "illusions") of the subject, the psychoanalyst himself risks (more or less completely) taking those theorizations for truths. Whereupon he risks being tempted to transmit them—in analytic treatment and outside of it—as transcendent truths.

One of the major tasks of psychoanalytic thought and research at present appears to me to be to advance along these two tracks:

1. On the one hand, a new foundation and re-elaboration of metapsychological theory and models, such that they are to account for the unconscious in our experience and our practice;

2. On the other hand, a new appreciation of the myths and ideologies that help the human being, in Lévi-Strauss's words, to "soothe intellectual—and, as the case may be, existential—anxiety," and, in psychoanalytic terms, sexual anxiety.

On those two investigative tracks, psychoanalysis has nothing to fear from confrontation and/or collaboration with other fields in the human sciences; it has no grounds for invoking any more or less mystical privilege related to the nature of its experience, which, however private and idiosyncratic it may be for each individual, it is not ineffable; it is, in its legitimacy and its obligations, fully "within the scientific community."

***

I have not broached directly the problem known as that of "psychoanalysis in the university" (which, after all, is not the explicit theme of this issue). I have expressed myself publicly and in writing on this question on numerous occasions.[208] Only a reading of truly "malevolent inattentiveness" could claim to find "oscillations" in my positions. The two absolutely firm points in my position on the subject are:

1. the extraterritoriality of the practice of analysis (including the analysis of a future analyst) in relation to any institution—be it of the state or marginally affiliated with the state

208 "Psychanalyse à l'Université," an editorial in *Psychanalyse à l'Université*, no. 1 (1975): 5–10. *Problématiques I*, pp. 153–57; "Un doctorat en psychanalyse, editorial for *Psychanalyse à l'Université* 6, no. 21 (1980): 5–8; Problématiques V, pp. 135–43; "Une révolution sans cesse occultée," *Revue internationale d'histoire de la psychanalyse*, no. 2 (1989): 393–402; "A l'Université!," editorial in *Psychanalyse à l'Université* 16, no. 62 (1991): 364. See also chapter 4, in this volume.

(universities), but also private (analytic societies), and thus a fundamental critique of the "training analysis";

2. the assertion that the realm of psychoanalytic discovery and investigation is in its rightful place wherever there is an active scientific community—and thus, ultimately, in universities.

The rest, I would say, is a function of the times, and particularly of the university and what it is becoming. To be sure, the name implies an ideal of universality, a place of dialogue, but also of confrontation, and even conflict, of ideas, always in the context of a certain rigor. But a certain naïveté would be needed in order not to see that ideas also progress by other means than their inherent strength. On more than one occasion I have analyzed the "politics of ideas," for example, within the psychoanalytic movement, but also in Freud himself. That ideal, however unrealizable it may, by definition, be, has nonetheless been more or less on the horizon during certain periods. But today?

Does it make sense to talk of a scientific academic community when one university is the fiefdom of a specific doctrine or individual, and another one of another? I do not know whether one can maintain an ideal of the university as a place of research and progress, a place of rigorous confrontation in which knives are left in the cloakroom. After all, that is not my principal passion, and future generations will keep us apprised. In any event, in the idea of a scientific community, "community" manifestly transcends "university." If the university were to more or less definitively abandon the ideals that should serve as its compass, I am convinced that its place would in short order be taken up by others.

I will add one remark, concerning the current drift of the university, a drift that psychoanalysis cannot fail to take into account. One may regard the university as having three rather distinct functions: research, the communication and dissemination of culture, a certain professional training. The first two functions were long of a weight equivalent to that of the third and were even predominant. Thus the only professional "doctorate," an aberration amongst all the others, was the doctorate in medicine! Not long ago no one would be advocating that a diploma in classical letters (bac + 3 . . . bac + 5) should give access—or even the right—to exercise a profession such as that of writer or journalist!

But as soon as the professionalization of academic networks (*filière* or "network," a word that is already an entire program!) is established, the reservations of psychoanalysts should become more pronounced. Will we find them—those whose point of honor is (or should be) always to question the "functionality" of their function, the "professionality" of their profession—will we find them plunging into a university become more technologized by the day, as it is summoned to respond with ever more *well-adapted* forms of professional training to the social problem of employment.

There is thus, between psychoanalysis and the university, many a "misunderstanding," stemming, on the part of the analysts, from the absence of precise points of reference and, on the part of the university, from the rapidity of its excesses. I have set forth, all too succinctly, certain of my own points of reference as an analyst. As for the excesses of the university, they are quite beyond our power; let us be satisfied with the vigilance with which we take them into account.

SUMMARY

The presence of psychoanalysis in the university is but a consequence of this major imperative: the acknowledgment of its fully legitimate place within the scientific community as a theory of the unconscious. Such a theory (metapsychology) should not be exempted from possible confrontation, refutation, and falsification.

The problem of so-called transmission (and even professional networks) is entirely different. Along with those two dubious terms, there has been an attempt to impose, on pretext of analytic training, the influence exercised by allegedly analytic ideologies—of which Castration, the Father, or the Law are the most recently fashionable versions.

As for the personal analysis, which is indispensable for anyone intent on practicing psychoanalysis, it should not be subordinated to any psychoanalytic institution. If we, in the Association psychanalytique de France, have definitively eradicated the "training analysis," it is not in order to accept its reappearance in the framework of state-run institutions!

VIII
The So-called Death Drive: A Sexual Drive

This lecture[209] will assume three successive forms:

 • A *historical or historico-critical* form: the way in which I understand the appearance and the function of the death drive in the development of Freud's thought.

 • A *metapsychological* form: in a metapsychology of the human being and the unconscious, what position ought we to assign to the forces that Freud inappropriately characterizes as death drives / life drives?

 • The third part will offer several suggestions concerning a question of *general psychology*: by what factors might one explain the major affective phenomena of love and hatred, and do so without precisely adhering to the Freudian conception?

 In anticipation, I will clarify my procedure by way of several core assertions. These theses are expressed here in a rather radical form.[210]

Adolescence 15, no. 2 (1997): 205–24.

209 Lecture delivered November 3, 1995, at the Sigmund Freud Stiftung, Frankfurt.
210 My ideas on drives in general, and on the death drive in particular, have been continuously developing since 1967. My most recent effort has been *Problématiques VII: Le fourvoiement biologisant de la sexualité chez Freud*. English translation by Donald Nicholson-Smith, *The Temptation of Biology: Freud's Theories of Sexuality* (New York, The Unconscious in Translation, 2015)

1. The so-called primal struggle between life drives and death drives is absolutely not a biological opposition existing in the living being, and consequently it is not pertinent to biological science.

2. This opposition finds its place uniquely and entirely in the domain of the human being—and does so not as a difference between sexuality and a nonsexual aggressiveness, but within sexuality itself. If one were to retain Freud's terms, one would be obliged to insert the adjective *sexual*. That is: *sexual* death drives versus *sexual* life drives.

3. Far more than two hypothetical biological forces, this opposition concerns two distinct types of functioning in the fantasy life of humans, the bound (secondary) process and the unbound (primary) process, or, better put, two principles: the principle of binding which would regulate the sexual life drives and the principle of unbinding, which would have authority over the sexual death drives.

4. It is only in a crude sense that these two principles correspond to the topographical difference between the ego and the id. In the ego there is much that is extremely bound, but also some that is less bound, just as in the deepest layers of the id one finds more that is unbound, but, as one approaches the surface, urges that are better bound.

I. OUR FIRST CONSIDERATIONS WILL THUS BE OF A HISTORIC ORDER

In Freud, as in the case of every great thinker, the "history of ideas" is not purely anecdotal, but is closely correlated with content.

As important as the discoveries are the paths and structures of thought used in the attempt to account for results. The paths can also be false leads emerging under pressure of prior constructs or prejudices. Certain prejudices may even manifest their action from the outset.

How then can a genuine and significant discovery nevertheless find its place in the context of an initial straying off course?

Which discovery? But first of all, which *straying?* As you already know, in my view, the beginning of Freud's going astray is the so-called abandonment of the seduction theory.[211] By the words *so-called*, I mean that my interpretation of this important turning point in the theory is as distant from Freud's understanding of it as from that of his adversaries. Much like those wanting to return to the material factuality of the seduction, Freud remains the captive of a single opposition: specifically the opposition between material reality and subjective reality, between what are called facts and what are called fantasies, the latter understood as purely subjective imaginings.

Here I can only assert, without being able to demonstrate, that Freud failed to generalize his theory into a theory of "generalized seduction" because he lacked a major category, a third category of reality, namely the reality of address, or message, as emanating primarily from the other.

Let us pause for a moment to consider the consequences of this failure for the conception of the life of drives. But to do that we must first clarify and emphasize the opposition between *drive* and *instinct* as being perhaps the most important opposition in psychoanalytic theory. In French psychoanalytic thought, that opposition has been known and fully elaborated for more than forty years. It was Lacan who first brought it into relief even as he falsely asserted that the word *instinct* was never to be found in Freud. And yet the specialist in and translator of Freud's works can affirm that Freud did indeed make use of the two concepts, and did so in ways that can be differentiated with precision.

Instinct, in Freud's language, always means incitement to a specific behavior (or to a mechanism) that *in the individual* is organized in a more or less fixed way, *in the species* is preformed in a stable and stereotyped way, and that, *insofar as its aims are concerned*, is adapted

---

211 S. Freud, Letter to W. Fliess (September 21, 1897) in *The Complete Letters of Sigmund Freud to Wilhelm Fliess*, p. 264.

to or structured in relation to its goal. For example, in his *Introductory Lectures* Freud emphasizes that man, as opposed to most animals, is lacking instincts that would allow him to survive.[212]

In bringing to light what we are to understand by the concept of *drive*, there is no better explanation than that of *Three Essays on the Theory of Sexuality*.[213] I am referring here to the first edition of the book, that of 1905, since the later editions include many addenda: both discoveries and a number of generalities are apt to lead us astray.

The *Three Essays on the Theory of Sexuality* of 1905 presents what I am inclined to call an "odyssey of the instinct." First, the sexual instinct *disfigured* ("The Sexual Aberrations"); second, the instinct *lost* ("Infantile Sexuality"); and, third . . . might one speak of the instinct "regained"? But what, then, is rediscovered or regained with "The Transformations of Puberty"? Assuredly, in the best case, something akin to a normal genitality, and, by way of the Oedipus complex, a heterosexual object. And yet it is impossible to detect here a return to a genuine and clearly defined instinct: what is rediscovered is but a *false instinct*, hesitant and, as it were, imitated, inhabited by all the childhood perversions that in the course of this process have necessarily been repressed.

The object remains contingent, linked to chance; the aim is removed from any natural conformity: for instance, the paths of procreation are multiple, for men as for women, and they are prepared with the most complicated fantasies. One can no longer find here anything of what is accepted by the "popular" conception. Consider the first lines of the *Three Essays*:

> Popular opinion has quite definite ideas about the nature and characteristics of this sexual drive[214] {instinct}. It is generally understood to be absent in

212 *Introductory Lectures on Psychoanalysis*, in *SE* 16:413.
213 *Three Essays on the Theory of Sexuality*, in *SE* 7.
214 See Editorial Note page xx.

childhood, to set in at the time of puberty in connection with the process of coming to maturity, and to be revealed in the manifestations of an irresistible attraction exercised by one sex on the other; while its aim is presumed to be sexual union . . . The popular view of the sexual drive is beautifully reflected in the poetic fable [ascribed to Aristophanes] that tells how the original human beings were cut up into two halves—man and woman—and how these are always striving to unite again in love. . . .We have every reason to believe, however, that these views give a very false picture of the true situation.

Thus, against the preformed *instinct* described by Aristophanes, Freudian investigation pits a sexuality whose characteristics are *perversion* (polymorphism) in relation to the aim and the object; *autoerotism*, that is, obedience with regard to unconscious fantasies; and finally *the absence of binding* and, in that sense, anarchy and even destruction.

And yet already in 1905, in the trajectory of Freud's thought, the drive cannot quite manage to maintain its positions in the face of an Aristophano-instinctual conception.

This point is directly linked to an uncertainty concerning the origin and genesis of unconscious sexual fantasies. Either they arise from the heart of the relation with the adult other, or else, being preformed, they in a certain way precede that relation. Concerning that point, we are once again obliged to refer to the abandonment of the seduction theory. As soon as the relation to the other is no longer maintained as the fundamental factor, endogeny is left as the only possible source for the fantasy. And that, according to two variants that Freud and the Freudians have never stopped developing, either one after the other or simultaneously: a purely biological endogeny and/or a phylogenetic-historical or, more precisely, a phylogenetic-mythological endogeny: that is, either the metabiological and metacosmological speculation of *Beyond the Pleasure Principle* or the mythology of the murder of the father in *Totem and Taboo*.[215]

At the core of that initial incertitude, a retrograde path remained open for a return to the preanalytic conception of a sexual *instinct* in man. Which means this: Freud's genuinely foundational discovery is endlessly endangered by an inappropriate theorization in which a biological determinism—which is more invoked than proved—relegates interindividual communication to secondary status.

We shall now take a big chronological leap from 1905 to 1919. In passing, we can only mention a concept to which I have devoted a number of attentive elaborations, that of *leaning on*: something that I am inclined to characterize as a latent concept or a cryptoconcept in Freud's work. By saying this, I want to convey that such a concept— although it does not serve as the object of any particular article nor of any special presentation—plays an important role in the structure of the system, even if that role is only provisional. The role of leaning on (namely the sexual drive leaning on the self-preservative instincts) is an attempt to rediscover a certain autonomy of the sexual drives in relation to the biological. To cut short that question, which would be too long in the framework of this contribution, I will propose a *Witz*: in the development of Freud's thought, the fate of the concept of leaning on is to remain . . . a concept for leaning on.

1919—Beyond the Pleasure Principle

A highly speculative essay and, in many respects, a text in shreds for which the imperatives are: to tease out what the text says explicitly (quite often things that are contradictory), the function the text fulfills in the economy of Freud's thought (which is, in my view, what is most important), and, finally, what subsequent interpretations the text will occasion after the fact—Freud's interpretations as well as those of his adepts.

---

215 *Beyond the Pleasure Principle*, in SE 18; *Totem and Taboo*, in *SE* 13.

The most general interpretation is that the great discovery that finds expression in the text is that of aggression (as Freud says as well as Melanie Klein) or aggressivity. A pure, savage, nonsexual aggressivity is what the "death drive" will come to mark with its seal, while claiming to be a major concept of a biological nature. We shall merely mention at this juncture that very few adepts and subsequent invokers of the so-called aggressive drive will still recall that what Freud initially had in mind was a primal *self*-destruction and only secondarily an aggressiveness deflected toward the exterior.

Among the most radical successors one would have to count the Kleinians, and here I would like to quote a few words of Paula Heimann (in her Kleinian period). In her article "Notes on the Theory of the Life and Death Instincts," she asserts that what drew attention to the death instinct was the experience of a destructiveness that would be, so to speak, chemically pure and was only erroneously called sexual:

> It is unnecessary to give instances. From time to time the world is shocked by reports of savagely cruel, "bestial" murders committed by an individual or a group . . . in such case the cruel acts are so calculated and worked out in detail that nothing but an instinctual urge for savage cruelty can be regarded as the motive and the purpose. . . . Strangely enough, such behavior is usually regarded as perverse sexuality and often such crimes are called "sexual crimes." . . . The murdered victim of so-called sexual crime does not die from a sexual experience, however infantile it may be, but from the infliction of maximally cruel violence. The sexual aspect of the murderer's behavior may possibly only be introduced in order to deceive the victim and so to provide the opportunity for the aim of the urge to cruelty.[216]

---

216 P. Heimann, "Notes on the Theory of Life and Death Instincts" in M. Klein, P. Heimann, S. Isaacs, and J. Riviere, *Developments in Psychoanalysis* (London: Hogarth, 1952), pp. 328–29.

Here the Kleinian reversal is remarkable in that it is pressed to the extreme. With Freud, until now, one was obliged to insist on the fact that people refuse to notice what is sexual in their behavior; here, on the contrary, the sexual would be no more than a false pretext for allowing pure aggression to be unleashed!

We may note that when, après-coup, Freud would understand his death drive as an aggressive drive, he claims to establish a relation between his discovery and clinical observations of sadism and masochism. Yet this assertion of Freud could not be more dubious: on the one hand, he had previously called attention to and extensively examined manifestations of sadism and masochism without appealing to a special drive, and, on the other hand, if we examine *Beyond the Pleasure Principle*, we perceive that the observation of sadism and masochism is never invoked as an initial reason for introducing the death drive—and even less the observation of that pure and nonsexual cruelty advanced by Paula Heimann.

What then, essentially, is *Beyond the Pleasure Principle* about?

1. It is about the repetition compulsion, which is characteristic of the way in which unconscious processes function. This compulsion of "unconscious prototypes" is characteristic of the entire range of drives and is not at all the exclusive prerogative of the death drive.

2. It is about a biological or metabiological speculation linked to the repetition compulsion: what then does life, in its generality, repeat? To help with an answer, abstract arguments as well as biological experiments are called to the rescue—all on the presupposition that the thesis to prove is the following: the living comes after the nonliving and, as a consequence, the living organism can only tend toward death, since that is what preceded it. And when experiments seem to prove that the living organism, using its own forces, tends toward only one thing—to keep itself alive—Freud, with a gesture, sweeps away all the experimental biology he had just called to his assistance and does so to the benefit of latent, hypothetical, and ultimately purely metaphysical forces: "The instinctual forces which seek

to conduct life into death may also be operating in protozoa from the first, and yet their effects may be so completely concealed by the life-preserving forces that it may be very hard to find any direct evidence of their presence."[217]

3. What is it, in *Beyond the Pleasure Principle*, that is ultimately posited by way of this speculation? It is not exactly the death drive, but the opposition of the life and death drives. Thus, *two types of drive*. And yet . . . are those forces truly drives, in the psychoanalytic sense assigned to them above? With their grandiose aspect, would they not be, rather, *instincts*: that is, general types of behavior that are as prede-termined in relation to their past as with regard to their aims?[218]

We are well aware of what is allegedly aimed at by the death drive: the primordial state of matter without life, a state in which all forces tend toward a terminal leveling. What is far more interesting to us is the final aim—and simultaneously the prototype—of the life drives. It was only on two occasions in his entire work that Freud made use of Aristophanes' myth. And it is here that we find ourselves confronted with the second occurrence: "The original human nature was not like the present, but different. . . . Everything about these pri-meval men was double: they had four hands and four feet, two faces, two privy parts, and so on. Eventually Zeus decided to cut these men in two, 'like a sorb-apple which is halved for pickling.' After the divi-sion had been made, 'the two parts of man, each desiring his other

---

217 *Beyond the Pleasure Principle*, in *SE* 18:49. This is an argument that Freud himself had rejected in "On Narcissism" as being without application and speculative. "It may turn out that, most basically and on the longest view, sexual energy—libido—is only the product of a differentiation in the energy at work generally in the mind. But such an assertion has no relevance. It relates to matters which are so remote from the problems of our observation, and of which we have so little cognizance, that it is as idle to dispute it as to affirm it. . . . All these speculations take us nowhere." "On Narcissism: An Introduction," in *SE* 14
218 I do not mean that these two drives can be conceived (as Freud would have it) only as biological mechanisms. Each of them is based on a fantasy: the fantasy of interstellar and inanimate matter, on the one hand, and, on the other, Aristophanes' mythological scenario.

half, came together, and threw their arms about one another eager to grow into one'."[219]

What a magnificent model: illustrative of both preformation and of a harmonious, complete, and well-adapted love life! Each is by nature slated to rediscover his sister-soul or, to put things more precisely, his "brother-body."

But what is troubling for the attentive reader is this: in the *Three Essays on the Theory of Sexuality* Freud had used Aristophanes' myth, specifically the concise expression of "popular opinion," as a foil, in order to underscore the value of his own conception of sexual life.[220] And here, in *Beyond the Pleasure Principle*, this very same myth is given as the primordial model, the very prototype of Eros! It is, however, beyond doubt that between the sexual activity described in the *Three Essays* and the life instinct understood as Eros in *Beyond the Pleasure Principle* the discrepancies are not mere details. They are opposed to each other at every point. The first is autoerotic, fragmented and fragmenting, its sole aim being satisfaction by the shortest path; it has no consideration for the independence of the object, which is, to a large extent, exchangeable. Eros, on the contrary, is synthesis and an aspiration to synthesis; it is totally oriented toward the object—the total object; its aim is to maintain that object, to improve it, and to expand it: it loves the object much in the way that it loves the ego itself, as a first object.

It would thus be an error to think that Eros adopts as its own Freud's former conception of sexuality, since it so precisely contradicts it. But on the other hand it would be altogether frivolous to assert that Freud had quite simply changed his mind with regard to sexuality in its entirety, returning to "popular opinion" and thereafter adopting the preformationist and instinctual views proposed by Aristophanes' myth; views he had definitively refuted in the *Three Essays*.

---

219 Plato's *Symposium*, quoted by Freud in *Beyond the Pleasure Principle*, in *SE* 18:57–58.
220 See above, p. 163.

In our opinion, the only fruitful point of view is to consider the entirety of the modification as structural, that is, to remember that a change at one point of a system of thought cannot occur without changes at other points intervening.

Within the context of an error—such was our hypothesis—*an authentic discovery* may find its point of insertion. We have insisted on the error. But, in that case, what is the grandiose discovery that imposed such a reconfiguration? It is not aggressivity since that had already been discussed in depth by Freud.

The discovery, we maintain, is that of *narcissism*, as Freud developed it in the article of 1914, "On Narcissism: An Introduction."[221] According to this profoundly new thesis, it was necessary to accept that alongside an anarchical, autoerotic, and unbound sexuality, there exists another solidly bound to the love of an object.

One step further: the first object in which one can encounter that binding, the first whole object . . . is the ego itself: the ego constituted as a totality and through whose action component drives can converge in a more or less complete unit.

"On Narcissism: An Introduction" is the first great text on love, and even on love as a passion. Which means it is a text about Eros *and not* about the erotic. The ego unifies the sexual drives and is itself the prototype of a unitary object. In large measure, it also adopts as its own the interests of the self-preservative functions: I no longer eat, says the little human being, with an eye to survival, but for love of love—out of love for my mother, but also out of love for the ego, which is itself a love object for the mother.

This, then, is where the great discovery is situated. But it is produced on the basis of an erotics that is fundamentally insecure in its foundations. It is insecure with regard to the origin and essence of the world of fantasy, which is its essential support. So much so that a danger surfaces, namely that love, Eros, might become everything,

221 "On Narcissism: An Introduction," in *SE* 14:67–102.

the sole drive, unjustifiably absorbing the erotic.

In his dispute with C. G. Jung, who wanted the term *libido* to designate nothing more than vital energy, Freud did not have a solid position to the extent that he himself had contributed to just such a hegemony.

This Eros, as narcissistic as it is object-driven, is on the path to incorporate everything: it conceals, even as it supplants them, the persistent presence of biological mechanisms of self-preservation,[222] but worse still, it no longer permits an acknowledgment of the destructive and destabilizing aspects of the sexual per se. The proposition from which Freud never retreated—that there was in the essence of sexuality something contrary and hostile to the ego—could no longer be heard once the psychoanalytic sexual found itself reduced to the eternal paean of universal love which is, precisely, correlative with the ego.

In the face of the threat of victory by a narcissistic and hegemonic Eros, there irrupts—in real life as much as in Freudian thought—an imperious need to reassert the drive in its most radical form: in its "demonic" form, obeying only the primary process and the compulsions of fantasy. In this perspective, the so-called death drive would be nothing other than the reestablishment of the undomesticated pole of sexuality; and if one were still obliged to speak of a polarity, it would be that of the *sexual drives* of death and the *sexual drives* of life. This, however, not without precautions, and remembering that the words *life* and *death* do not here designate biological death or biological life, but their counterparts in the life of the soul and in psychical conflict. This, then, is the ultimate meaning I wanted to give to the title of one of my first books: *Life and Death in Psychoanalysis.*[223]

The "death drive" is thus a concept that can be correctly situated only at a specific moment in the drama of Freudian discovery. Outside of that context, it becomes an empty formula . . .

---

222 Even if it is true that those mechanisms as such are not party to psychical conflict.
223 Jean Laplanche, *Vie et mort en psychanalyse* (Paris: Flammarion, 1970).

Yet the emptier it is, the more attractive it is! In fact, everyone can make of it what suits him. In the Kleinian system the death drive marks an extreme of destructive fury—one that is found, for example, in the paranoid position. In Freud, however, one eventually finds the exact opposite: the death drive as a tendency to Nirvana. No longer death by the drive, but the death of the drive, non-desire. This is the direction in which we are led by an expression such as "the silence of the death drive," which evokes, once again, the silence of the galaxies. But what is there in common between the demonism of Melanie Klein and the image of inanimate matter, with its eternal peace?

I have evoked only what transpires within the intellectual circle of psychoanalysts. But what about outside of it? In current cultivated opinion the death drive has become a convenient intellectual theme. Think, for instance, of the allegedly psychological interpretation of fatal illnesses, cancer or AIDS. But, even more, remember the case of philosophy, in which the death drive finds an all too facile echo in Heidegger's "being-toward-death" or in Hegelian dialectics. In this, to be frank, I fail to find any genuine consonance, but a heterogeneity that profits neither psychoanalysis nor philosophy.

As you will have understood, my intention is not to lend a helping hand to any metaphysical speculation, nor is it to salvage every moment of Freud's thought, down to the slightest word. "To work Freud" (and to put him to work) means "to do him justice" in his discoveries, but also in his errors and, even more, in the way in which his thought proceeds. But once the shell is cracked and the kernel has become accessible, need we persist in safeguarding the fragments of that defensive shell, which has benefited so many misinterpretations?

Once one has located the real opposition, that of bound and unbound forms of libido at work in psychical conflict, can one not attempt to express things in a renewed metapsychology? And then, as is familiarly said, simply "toss out" the death drive?

II. METAPSYCHOLOGICAL INDICATIONS

The origin of the unbinding/binding opposition is to be found nowhere else than in the process of repression itself.

It is indeed repression that creates the unconscious, and by way of the specific nature of that process we may explain the particularities of the agency of the id as Freud describes them: absence of contradiction, no community or coordination of urges, absence of negation—including, it should be emphasized, of negative representations such as those of death or castration—and absence of temporality.

In my way of conceiving things, all those specific features of the unconscious are to be explained by the attempts at translation and temporalization ceaselessly undertaken by the child in the face of the messages coming to him from the adult other: an initially embryonic translation, so to speak, to be exercised first on nonverbal forms of address (gestures, for example). Translation is an "ordering," a "novelization," an "insertion into time," and, ultimately, an "insertion into the ego." But it must be asserted that repression is not a translation but (to use Freud's terms) a failure (*Versagen*), refusal, or denial (*Versagung*)[224] of translation, which is expected to transcribe (*umschreiben*) the message into a language of a higher level, another code. It is not arbitrarily that I adapted and excerpted the translational model from a few lines of the Freud-Fliess correspondence, but did so in order to account for the particularities of the process of repression.

Taken as a whole, the process of translation can be understood either as a specialized task, the passage from one verbal language to another or as a more general operation that effects a transition from any mode of expression to any other. As soon as there is an address, there is also, on the part of the receiver, an attempt at translation, that is, a determined mode of appropriation. Among those different

---

224 Freud to Fliess: December 6, 1896. In *The complete letters of Sigmund Freud to Wilhelm Fliess, 1887-1904*. Trans. J.M. Masson. (Cambridge: The Belknap Press of Harvard University Press, 1985), p. 212.

"languages," I place the principal accent on gestural language in the dispensing of maternal or parental care.

Let us return to repression. It always proceeds, says Freud, in a "highly individual" manner, that is, piece by piece, or, better put, it is repression that fragments into pieces what it is treating, without taking into consideration the preexisting links, whether of context, grammar, or meaning. Now that is precisely the effect of the process of translation regarding what it *neglects*. Translation endeavors to convey (that is the root of *tra-duire*: *trans-ducere*) a coherent message into something that is no less coherent. But what is not "conveyed," what is "dropped out" is not a second message—an unconscious message from the emitter as has been claimed—that would be directly rediscovered in the unconscious of the receiver. The waste products or residues of translation are isolated, distorted remainders, reminiscences of the addresses of adults dispensing various modes of care to the child, apparently arbitrary elements stripped of meaning and extracted from their context.

In order to clarify what I mean, allow me to introduce a comparison drawn from the domain of specialized (verbal) translation. Suppose that I were to translate into German the following French sentence "*L'étalon court dans la ferme.*" (The stallion is running on the farm.) For any decent translator, this would give in German: "*Der Zuchthengst läuft im Hofe.*" But you are no doubt aware that *ferme* and *etalon* have also, in other contexts, other meanings. *Etalon* (standard) is also a measure of reference, as in *etalon-or* (gold standard); and *ferme* (truss), in the technical languages of carpenters signifies a corner piece, which holds the construction "firm."

Thus our interpreter, spontaneously and naturally, will have allowed other meanings—or, better put, other aspects of those two words, aspects that are nonetheless inherent in the potentialities of the French language, and which would make possible puns—to drop out.

This is but an example, or model, that could easily lend itself to confusion, if one were to take it for the thing itself and neglect the differences. The differences are of two sorts. First of all, specialized translation, which presupposes the fixed codes of natural languages, is not identical to the procedure of generalized translation, which is situated for the most part beyond the verbal level. Second, what is latent in the messages addressed to the child and emanating from the adult is not of the same sort as what is latent in a natural language; the former is in fact of the nature of the repressed sexual unconscious.

The messages emanating from adults do not maintain themselves at a single and sole level, that of cares dispensed and tenderness. Most particularly in this situation, the sexual fantasies of the parents are reawakened and rushed or insinuated into the heart of the relation of self-preservation. Messages are "compromised"—in the psychoanalytic sense of the word—and this in a manner that is unconscious for the emitter herself. The child attempting to dominate these enigmatic messages will receive them in the codes of which he disposes. Codes and nothing else, which is indeed what Freud designates as "infantile sexual theories": myths, short tales, novels—even without words—that the small child uses for his own self-theorization and self-temporalization.

A consciousness—in this sense (and perhaps in Hegel's sense)—far more than who knows what beam of light, would be nothing other than a coherent ego temporalizing itself. What we designate as repression—and first of all as primal repression—is nothing other than an active exclusion from this continuous process of unification, theorization, and temporalization that is initially at work with regard to messages from without, and then with regard to what emanates from the inner "other." It is precisely such an exclusion that accounts for the particularities of the unconscious: "non-coherence," the "non-bound" or "unbound," the timeless.

In this sense, the so-called death drive is effectively a "pure culture" of alterity, that we find in the deepest layers of the unconscious. Doubtless these deepest residues are intimately related to sadomasochism. Here (exceptionally) we should adhere to the Kleinian notion according to which the partial—such as what, coming from the object, is not bound or is even reduced to ruins—goes together with attack, destruction, and persecution.

This, to be sure, holds for the most inaccessible layers of the id. For very early on, under the influence of the ego and with the help of the cultural world, there appear fragments of scenarios, bits of fantasmatic sequences, that will eventually fit themselves into the grand organizers known as complexes: Oedipus and castration.

The psychical forces of binding are no less sexual than the others. Nevertheless, they always draw their source from certain totalities: totality of one's fellow creature as a unified being, totality of the ego, of its form and also of its ideals, not to say of its ideologies.

Thus, in the grandiose opposition of the life and death drives, there is nothing either mysterious or metaphysical. It is a matter of two principles, binding and unbinding, whose opposition is ongoing within the psychical apparatus.

For the nursling, it was first a matter of mastering by translating the enigmatic seductive messages emanating from the adult, without allowing too much unbinding of stimuli. Subsequently, the struggle over binding is pursued against an internal alterity, that is, against the unconscious and its derivatives.

III

For my final development, I would like to broach a question of concrete psychology, which can find direct application in clinical observation. A point of general psychology, discussed, one has no hesitation in saying, ever since man has engaged in reflection, but on which psychoanalysis owes it to itself to cast decisive light. I am referring to the psychology of the passions, specifically of love and hate, from which Empedocles forged a fundamental opposition.

Freud frequently took up this question, both before and after 1919. For example in *Triebe und Triebschicksale*,[225] he studies what is

---

225 "Instincts and Their Vicissitudes," in *SE* 14:109–40.

called the "material" love-hate opposition at length. To summarize in a phrase, he sees these passions as phenomena dependent on the ego (a drive cannot be said to "love": only the ego can experience love) and, in addition, he refuses to consider the frequently observed reversal of love into hatred as anything other than an appearance.[226] This polarity forbidding any genuine transition from one to the other is further reinforced with the appearance of the life drive / death drive duality, which clarifies matters to the point of rendering them purely abstract. In the lineage of Melanie Klein, the psychology of the passions is simplified since the opposition of the two great instincts is discovered at every level. Once that is established, concrete phenomena are explained by simple combinations or dialectics in a kind of Manichaean logomachy. Here, how can one not emphasize the sheer boredom exuded by the texts of the Kleinians, concerning which a comparison with the extremely nuanced and perspicacious works of such great *Menschenkenner* as Stendhal and Proust would be rather uncharitable.

In my view, only a "genetic" and metapsychological conception of the complex forces at play will allow us to sketch solutions that give a better account of lived experience.

In my metapsychological approach, at the level of the sexual unconscious, I posit the existence of an opposition that is also a superimposition:

• unbound sexuality (which is erotic);

• bound sexuality (which is narcissistic or bound to an object).

I should emphasize the following: this opposition is purely human, that is, it is completely informed and oriented by fantasy life. As such, it is the only one with which psychoanalytic practice, which has no other point of impact than fantasy, is concerned.

But we cannot fail to acknowledge that this opposition happens to cover up, and simultaneously to supplant or take over as its own—

---

226 It would be incumbent at this juncture to take into account the Schreber case, with its famous reversals of the formula "I love him" (in the case of homosexual love).

elevating it to the level of fantasy—a more *instinctual* (i.e., preformed) level, which is that of self-preservation. Even if it is imperative to firmly maintain the idea that biological mechanisms in the human infant are extremely feeble and incapable of ensuring survival, one should not deny the preexistence of certain psychophysiological settings. But the specificity of the human being is precisely that those settings are, from the outset, invaded by the enigmatic messages emanating from the other.

There would thus be a triple level of factors:
- self-preservation (tenderness and natural aggressivity);
- the erotic
- bound sexuality.

The second and third levels constitute the psychical conflict, properly speaking, with which psychoanalysis is concerned par excellence.

I will not at this point broach the description and trifactorial analysis of love and hate.

As a stimulus, I will merely propose a critical commentary on the famous adage *Homo homini lupus*, which Freud borrowed from Hobbes and Plautus in order to explicitly stigmatize human cruelty: "to satisfy their aggressiveness on him, to exploit his capacity for work without compensation, to use him sexually without his consent, to seize his possessions, to humiliate him, to cause him pain, to torture and to kill him."[227] And, quite imprudently, Freud advances the idea that the "atrocities" of human history "reveal men to be savage beasts."

Consider the question simply, as a function of what is known to us through both casual and scientific observation of animal life.

Wolves—the animal that has almost disappeared from Western Europe: is the actual wolf truly "a wolf for man"—and if so, in what sense? Let us consider man here for what he simply is for the wolf: an animal of a different species—to respect or flee if he is stronger, to attack and devour if he is a potential prey . . . and then only if the wolf

---

227 *Civilization and Its Discontents*, in *SE* 21:111.

is hungry. There is very little destructiveness and no sadism in the behavior of the animal toward his prey. The cheetah chooses a young antelope from the herd, bleeds it with its fangs, and calmly devours it along with its cubs. No pleasure in causing suffering; no inclination to massacre the entire herd in a holocaust! Such is—schematically, and despite a few exceptions—natural, animal, self-preservative aggressiveness. No, the wolf is not a "wolf," in the sense of Hobbes's hideous monster, neither for man nor for other species.

Might the wolf, however, be a cruel "wolf" for wolves? Cases of aggressive behavior within species have been studied by ethologists. A wolf does not kill another wolf in order to nourish himself. On occasion, two animals—two males from a pack—confront each other in behavior linked to rituals of courtship,[228] a struggle that ensues according to relatively stereotypical rites and that rarely ends in death, but more likely in the extreme discomfort of the defeated: humiliation and flight.

If, then, I call *Lupus* the emblematic figure of Hobbes, I can only conclude: no, the wolf, in relation to the other wolf, does not behave as a *Lupus*.

In the biology on which Freud would like to ground himself, there thus remains nothing of that cruel, sadistic behavior, destructive for the sheer pleasure of destruction, that characterizes the human being. It is man alone who is a *Lupus* for man. A conclusion that does away with any biologizing—or even zoological—deduction of the sexual death drive or, for that matter, of any drive in general.[229]

---

228 This would be the juncture at which to correct the notion that specular narcissistic behavior is present only in human beings.

229 Among numerous examples, see André Green pitting "what might be called the *natural dimension* of the human subject—the human animal, that is, the subject of drives" against the pole of "socialization," the other pole of primordial conflict. "Le mythe: Un objet transitionnel collectif," in *Le Temps de la réflexion*, 1 (Paris: Gallimard, 1980), pp. 99–131. Where I depart from Freud's thinking, which is well represented here by Green, is in the notion that the drive is not an originally "natural" reality, but an actual "*second* nature" deposited in man through the effects of his relation to the adult *socius*.

My apparent digression on wolves has two objectives: first and foremost, to indicate the absolute heterogeneity of sadistic aggression in humans in relation to any animality: no, neither the Thirty Years War nor Auschwitz nor Cambodia can be attributed to the "biological animal" in us. We must persuade ourselves that

The theme of the wolf and his mythical and fantasmatic double is immense. Groundwork on the subject has been famously done in a number of well-documented investigations. Freud's "wolf man" constitutes no more than an infinitesimal part of the archive.

In order not to overburden my argument, I will append briefly several other promising developments:

a) Is man not a wolf (or rather a *lupus*) to his fellow animals? The denunciation of human cruelty toward animals is based on observations that, until the contemporary era, had been willfully ignored. The "beast," in point of fact, was not to be situated on the side that one had assumed!

b) Experts on prehistory appear to agree that the domestication of the wolf into the dog is to be dated to approximately the fortieth millennium. Might we not then conclude that an extraordinary break occurred around then? On the one hand, the *good* wolf, the dog, the companion to whom man is connected in an eminently narcissistic bond (which is specular to the point of issuing in French in echoing syllables: *chien/chien* to its *mère/mere* . . .) And on the other hand, consigned to the shadows of alterity, the *bad* wolf, the beast of the Carpathians or the Gévaudan, the werewolf, etc. We find here, in the evolution of humanity, a remarkable parallel to what I am describing as a process of translation-repression: the wolf is *translated* into a dog, and the discarded residue of the translation is the *lupus*.

c) Is the case of the wolf unique? A quick examination of man's "second great conquest," the horse, is instructive: is not the prototype of the animal that haunts our nights (in a number of languages) the "nightmare," concerning which Ernest Jones has opened so many paths of inquiry (*On the Nightmare* [London: Hogarth, 1931])? The wild horse, exactly like the wolf, has undergone a split, with an overtly sexual residue (an incubus) and, what is more, a residue that is feminine. This would in turn serve to corroborate the idea of a "feminine" essence of the drive and of sexuality at its most primal; see Jacques André, *Aux origines féminines de la sexualité* (Paris: PUF 1995).

Many years ago (in my first analytic paper), I proposed (without being understood) that a distinction should be made, in the case of animal phobias, regarding those cases in which the anguishing animal was an emblematic or culturally marked figure from the outset. That idea returns here, but with a more compelling argument behind it: the *lupus* or *night-mare* is, as it were, culturally prepared to depict the internal attack of the drive: the cultural process of its genesis (domestication of the good/fantasmatization of the bad) has an affinity with the individual genesis of the source-object of the drive.

the *intraspecies* cannibalism of Pol Pot's soldiers is entirely human. "Human, all too human!"

My second aim was to orient us in a trifactorial analysis of forms of behavior said to be aggressive. There would be, first of all, the level of plain self-affirmation of the living and acting being. This is, if one likes, what the language and civilization of America call healthy aggressivity,[230] a quality that might be required as a factor in success. It is claimed that this level is without fantasy—in any event without either the imagination or the appreciation of the suffering of the other, without either useless violence or cruelty.

But mention of this level should not mean adhering to the ideological alibi according to which it might persist autonomously: it is, in fact, observable only in animals. In humans it can only be postulated, since psychoanalysis demonstrates, on the contrary, that self-preservation is supplanted and replaced very early on, and in an extensive manner, by sexual motivations.

The second level is the one characterized, on the contrary, by the deployment of the sexual death drive. The intrinsic aim of inflicting pain on the other (and on oneself) cannot be denied, even if it is camouflaged. It is even this appreciation of the suffering of the other that characterizes, according to Freud, sexual sadomasochism.[231] How can one fail to see, in this taking into consideration of the subjectivity of the other, the inverse of the origin of the drive in the enigmatic message emanating from the other?

The third level, finally, that of the specular narcissistic relation, has been emphasized by Lacan. It is that of the rivalry over identity, the rage in the face of "my other self." Lacan here reclaims as his own the specular dialectic of master and slave in Hegel. He also quotes an exemplary passage from Saint Augustine: "I saw with my own eyes

---

230 Or *combativity*, in the term advanced by Denise van Caneighem, *Agressivité et combativité* (Paris: PUF, 1978).
231 See "Instincts and Their Vicissitudes," in *SE* 14, and my analysis of that text in chapter 5 of *Vie et mort en psychanalyse.*

and knew very well an infant in the grip of jealousy; he could not yet speak, and already he observed his foster brother, pale and with an envenomed look."[232]

On the other slope, that of *love* and *being-in-love*, the problem would also profit from being rid of the ambiguities into which Freud dragged it by specifically superimposing, without distinguishing, a theory of sexuality and a mythology of Eros.

The three levels in play are the same as those invoked as evidence for aggressivity: at the level of self-preservative functioning we would situate tenderness (Freud) or, to use the more inclusive term of modern psychologists, attachment;[233] the second level is that of the erotic, described since the *Three Essays*; the third, finally, is that of love of the whole object, an Eros indissociably narcissistic and object-driven.

Here, I will content myself with noting that such a multifactorial psychology of love and hatred should allow for a more concrete approach to the notorious "reversal into the opposite." A problem that Freud never stopped raising, but concerning which he always denied that it was a question of a genuine inversion at the level of drives.

I will restrict myself to the following assertions: at the level of self-preservation and in animal psychology in which modes and aims of behavior are fixed there is, so to speak, no possibility of reversal; on the other hand, at the level of the erotic aggression and pleasure are mixed from the outset, as may be seen perfectly in sadomasochism. Finally, the specular relation is the realm in which genuine reversal finds its place par excellence. Of a sudden and, as it were, immediately, specular love for the "other ego" can be transformed into specular hatred, and fascination into exclusion. "He and I" are, in the mirror, one and the same thing, a proposition that can also be phrased as: "it's either him or me."

---

232 Quoted by Lacan in *Écrits*, p. 114.
233 Here, too, this level can be well observed only in animals, since in human beings it is invaded by sexuality, conveyed by the adult *socius*, from the outset.

To conclude, I will summarize the manner in which I have tried to clear the terrain:

• by liquidating the all too facile metaphysical opposition between Eros and Thanatos;

• by proposing a theory of the unconscious and drives that takes into account the genesis of forces in conflict in the human being, a genesis in which the primordial relation is the relation to the adult *other*, the emitter of messages;

• by proposing a theory of psychical conflict in which it is the relation to the external other that is pursued in an endless attempt to contain the other within.

IX
Goals of the Psychoanalytic Process

The topic proposed for this colloquium, "Goals of the Psychoanalytic Process," displays considerable perspicacity.[234] It allows us to posit from the outset an essential distinction between the goals one might want to assign to analysis from the outside, so to speak, and the goals that can be derived from the process itself. A distinction all the more important in that in recent years it has been increasingly obscured.

In a way, psychoanalysis, which is constantly called into question about is results, has never stopped taking its own measure in comparison with other techniques (psychological or not) with regard to effectiveness, which also might be called "conformity to a goal."

Let us recall Platonic (and above all Aristotelian) distinctions, which have not aged on this point: technical knowledge, the province of the artisan, is one that subordinates its means and its rules to the achievement of a precise goal, but a goal proposed from without. To be sure, the fabrication of a shoe, the construction of a ship or of a temple obey "rules of art" that are themselves fixed by the science of nature, but it is not the architect who decides where the temple will be placed, which divinity will be worshiped there, and by whom the necessary funds will be contributed.

---

234 This lecture was delivered on November 22, 1996, at the Deutsche Psychanalytische Vereinigung (Wiesbaden).

The current interest in this question inspires us to linger a bit on this situation in which the analyst is considered a specialist to whom one addresses oneself by proposing a precise purpose extrinsic to the process itself.

Freud described just this sort of contingency in his comments on a "case of feminine homosexuality." The patient was sent to Freud by her father in the hope of ridding her of her perversion. If the analysis did not produce the desired result—which the father scarcely expected—"a speedy marriage was to awaken the natural instincts of the girl and stifle her unnatural tendencies."[235] Whereupon Freud takes up what might be called the ancient Platonic description: "[certain situations are] to a greater or lesser degree unfavorable for analysis and add fresh difficulties to the internal ones already present. Situations like that of a prospective house-owner who orders an architect to build him a villa according to his own tastes and requirements, or of a pious donor who commissions an artist to paint a sacred picture in the corner of which is to be a portrait of himself in adoration, are at bottom incompatible with the conditions necessary for psychoanalysis."[236]

And Freud cites two possible cases: the husband who sends his irascible wife into analysis, with the goal of restoring peace to the household, or the parents who "demand that their high-strung and unruly child be restored to health."

We are quite familiar with the difficulties of such cases: analyses initiated by families or judicial authorities: children, psychotics, delinquents, etc.

Freud's perspective, moreover, is not purely negative. The analysis may, on occasion, take place, but the result risks going against the wishes of the sponsor: additional proof that the goals intrinsic to

---

235 *SE* 18:150. Once again, when Freud uses the word *Instinkt* (and not *Trieb*), it is in order to characterize—and even mock—the popular conception of a "natural" sexuality.
236 Ibid., p. 151.

the process are on an entirely different level from the goals assigned to the psychoanalyst from outside the analysis.

The crude (and even grotesque) aspect of the situations just evoked runs the risk of concealing this contemporary fact: the danger of a generalization of what may be called "psychoanalysis on command."[237] The social demand for psychotherapy, which has become virtually universal, is reinforced, on the one hand by the physician colleague sending his patient to the analyst from whom he hopes for the cure for a specific "illness" and, on the other hand, and above all, by the constant involvement of health-care bureaucracies. Not satisfied with paying for therapy, they have the "poor taste" to demand precise results. And with this, the permanent presence of a third party is introduced into analysis bringing with it the require-ment of periodic reports, accounting for the number of sessions, and the menace of an interruption in reimbursements.

It would be interesting to study the evolution of this social demand throughout the modern world. It is increasingly subject to objective and pragmatic criteria of the sort found in the *DSM III* or *IV*. But, simultaneously, under pressure from a sector of public opin-ion, it banishes from its indications anything that might appear to be a residue of Freudian "sexism": who, in the United States, would dare claim that homosexuality is a disturbance relevant to analysis? Inversely, another sector of public opinion will be astonished that psychoanalysis has not eradicated delinquency, particularly sexual delinquency, obviously without taking into account the existence or absence of subjective suffering on the part of such subjects.

These contradictory developments demonstrate how much the demands referred to are impregnated with pragmatism and ide-ology. Like the husband just referred to, who effectively asked that his marriage be cured, society asks that it be cured of its neuroses.

But before moving on from this all too vast realm of psy-

237 See chapter 4, in this volume.

choanalysis on command, I cannot leave in silence one of its most pernicious forms: what is currently known as the training analysis. The radical critique formulated by Anna Freud has not prevented analytic institutions from making the demand that a personality conforming to their wishes be produced through psychoanalysis. I shall not engage in a detailed examination of the contradictions entailed by this practice, and of the situation it generates, in relation to an authentic analytic process. To define the situation of the training analysis in the briefest of terms, we may say that in child analysis the mother occasionally waits in the waiting room, and genuine analysis only begins when—symbolically, but even actually—one closes the door on her. In a training analysis the mother institution remains present, symbolically with its full weight, in the waiting room, and no denial can prevent this from being the case.

Freud prefers—as do we—that the subject come to us "out of his own motivation." The situation, which he characterizes as ideal, is that the subject be suffering from a conflict he cannot resolve and that he ask for our "assistance." A part of him—his ego, clearly—would be considered an ally in the process.

From the perspective of our theme, we should add the following: such apparent spontaneity does not at all mean that we should adhere to the patient's goals, as he expresses them in his request. We have an obligation to be skeptical about their manifest content. The ego, as we will make explicit further on in our metapsychological section, is an agent of misprision. Its autonomy is an illusion. Quite often, in its heteronomy, the ego is no more than the vehicle and reflection of those social aims evoked above, which are no less present when internalized. We also know that the ego, while claiming to represent the interests of the whole, is in fact but one of the parties in the conflict and thus a party with a bias.

For its part, the symptom, which occasionally occupies the foreground in the subject's request, can not be understood solely in terms of its manifest content. Unlike the classical medical symptom, it is not a simple discrete sign. Moreover, it is a common experience that as soon as the process is engaged the symptom quickly assumes secondary importance.

The dismissal of the conscious representations of a goal—or at least leaving them in the background—is an integral part of the fundamental rule, even though that rule is but an imperfectly observed ideal. Analysis requires, on the part of the *analyst* himself, the same sort of asceticism or distancing in relation to the goals that he may glimpse. And this from the first session until the last. Not that he should be indifferent to suffering. Here we might contrast the two neighboring German words *Indifferenz* and *Gleichgültigkeit*. The analyst demonstrates *Gleichgültigkeit* in the precise sense that he is to *gleichmässig gelten lassen* (accord equal value to) all the elements proposed to him by the analysand.[238] Leading the list of repudiations he must impose on himself is skepticism toward any concrete adaptive goals he might imagine. He must also be distrustful of the idea of a cure, an idea physicians themselves have relativized, abandoning the aim of a *restitutio ad integrum* in favor of a new relation among the existing forces.

The psychoanalyst is benevolent; he *wants* the *good* of his patient, but without giving the good a precise shape, without deceiving himself as to what would constitute a regained autonomy.

Recall the concluding passage in *Studies in Hysteria*: "you will be able to convince yourself that much will be gained if we succeed in transforming your hysterical misery into common unhappiness."[239] It is a passage that finds echoes not only in the Stoics but once again in Plato when he distinguishes the good of the soul from limitless pleasure or unjust power. The illness of the soul is precisely that *misery* from which it suffers, the misery of an obscure and devastating conflict.

I fear that we cannot advance much further so long as we

---

238 German possesses two words, one rather negative, *Indifferenz* (indifference), the other with a more positive connotation, *Gleichgültigkeit*, which means "according equal value."
239 *SE* 2:342.

envisage the goals independently of the *process*. But what can we say about the process? We know that Freud constantly connects it to meta-psychology. His wording varies. The earliest versions—"rendering the unconscious conscious," even "removing infantile amnesia"—seem to retain something of the old illusion, perhaps stemming from hypnosis, that the unconscious is like a second personality, a second ego that has to be liberated, so that it can supplant a "repressive" ego. A debatable idea that gave birth to many illusions, as can been seen for example, within some "Freudo-Marxism" or, inversely, in the significant hostility against psychoanalysis, which—when it is not dismissed as ineffective—is accused of unleashing hidden per-verted instincts.

The final formula, and the most inspiring in its openness, is surely the *"Wo Es war, soll Ich werden,"* to which we should add Freud's comment: "it is a cultural labor akin to draining the Zuyderzee."[240]

To be sure, for this phrase, important questions arise about each word. What is this *id* if it is to take root, as all too often Freud seems to believe, in a set of forces of biological origin? In what could the hope of "civilizing" it consist?

And what is this ego (*Ich*)? If it is the agency of repression, misprision, and negation, what possibility does it have truly to appropriate the id? But, inversely, if the *Ich* of the formula—as Lacan, somewhat idealistically, would have it—is not the ego as agency, but the eternal subject of the "philosophy of the subject," what "labor" would it be capable of accomplishing?

Finally, what is this civilizing process? The comparison with the draining of the Zuyderzee is not exactly encouraging: it refers us to Freud's definitively pessimistic views on the renunciation of drives.

Ultimately Freud's sentence has the merit of positing an "imperative" intrinsic to the process itself. But it is incumbent on us to take up the question anew—with our own means.

---

240 *SE* 22:80.

Our thesis will be twofold:

1. The goal of the process can only be conceived by starting with an explication of the nature of the treatment; in no case can the process be subordinated to a goal proposed from without. The principal elements to be clarified here are, on the one hand, the analytic *situation*, which generates the transference, and, on the other, the *method*—with its two dimensions: associative-dissociative and interpretative.

2. The treatment is not secondary or subordinate to metapsychology. In other words, we reject a sequence in which the first element is clinical observation, allegedly neutral and objective, on the basis of which a metapsychological theory is inferred, and then, in turn, technique or praxis are a set of precepts, instruments, deduced from that theory. This argument goes on: given that our psyche is standardized in one or another manner, what are the best means for making it develop. Which then poses, once again, the question of an alien goal, the goal implicit in and assigned by that notion to development.

We think, on the contrary, that therapeutic practice occupies the lead position in relation to metapsychology. Not because of a pragmatism, whose motto would be "First do, then justify what one has done," but because therapeutic practice (situation + method) is an invention, Freud's contribution of something radically new—an innovation concerning which we claim to show that it finds its source in a distant past, in the primordial order of the human being himself.

That invention was certainly not instantaneous, but it can be dated historically in a short period, between *Studies in Hysteria* and the analysis of the *Rat Man*.

It may be said of this practice that, in a certain way, the successive theories "limp behind it": "What cannot be attained by flying must be attained by limping."[241]

---

241 *"Was man nicht erfliegen kann das soll man erhinken,"* quoted by Freud in *Gesammelte Werke* 13:69.

Such is the case for the various theories of the psychical apparatus or the theories of drives: their progress is always motivated by problems encountered in practice.

However, what I have just asserted concerning the fact that theory "limped" along behind is partially false. For in fact the invention of analytic practice went together with the invention of a first theory: the seduction theory; and it can even be asserted that Freud was not far from making a single and selfsame advance in both domains simultaneously. The abandonment of the seduction theory prevented him from allowing the tight relation between the two inventions to progress, leaving to us the task of establishing a relation between what is primal in therapy and what is found at the origin of human existence.

This leads us back to Freud's *theory of seduction*, while taking into account a number of concepts that for decades have offered new dimensions for thinking about the analytic process. We will attempt to give full weight to terms such as language, message, translation, symbolization and, finally, hermeneutics. We can scarcely do without these terms to describe the treatment, but we must also assert that they are no less indispensable for describing the genesis of the psychical apparatus and of conflict—on the condition that they be situated in the place where they belong.

Today we will start with the term *hermeneutics*. A word frequently used—in a manner deserving criticism—to describe the analytic process. Most hermeneutic activities currently described are related to secondary situations. Beyond those derivative hermeneutics, we postulate a foundational hermeneutic: the fundamental situation of someone obliged to interpret, to give meaning to "what is happening to him."

But what happens to him is not on the order of brute reality. It is not even, as Heidegger would have it, a "being-there" (*Dasein*) or a "thrownness" (*Geworfenheit*). It consists in messages emanating from the adult and addressed to the human child.

Instead of invoking a so-called hermeneutic activity of the analyst, we must assert that the first hermeneut, the primal hermeneut, is the human being. What he has to translate are messages, the question being: what is happening to me? How might it be mastered by appropriating it through an act of "translation"?

For that point of departure we can refer to the beginning of "On the Sexual Theories of Children." Freud mentions two great enigmas of the adult world with which the child is confronted: sexual difference and the arrival of a baby brother or sister. But there are many other messages that are more primal: those conveyed by the breast as well as the early experience of bodily care and attention.

I should clarify here what I mean by the adult-baby dissymmetry, which I introduced with the words: "what is happening to me." It is a dissymmetry that contradicts current ideas regarding interaction and reciprocity. I do not deny the idea of reciprocity, but on the condition that the extent of its validity be precisely specified. There is no question of denying the reciprocal attachment between the child and the parent who feeds, protects, and cares for him. The messages from each member of that couple receive more or less appropriate responses from the other; from the outset, the baby is open to receiving more or less appropriate responses from the other; from the outset, the baby is open to the world—above all to the adult human world. The first relation between the human infant and his mother is a relation in the full sense of the word, composed of the most varied communications and affects. It is a rich relation, partly programmed genetically, which psychoanalysts, following Freud, long made the error of reducing to the provision of nourishment. *Self-preservation*, the term advanced by Freud, is not imprecise in characterizing this domain, except that it mistakenly leads to a denial of the affective dimension.

I now come to dissymmetry, which is no less essential than reciprocity. Psychoanalysis has taught us that the adult is inhabited by an unconscious Id, that the latter is sexual (or sexual-aggressive, a dimension I will not discuss here) and is constituted by representations and fantasies that infiltrate behavior. But as far as the nursling is concerned, nothing allows us to assert that in the beginning it has fantasies and an unconscious (or, for that matter, an ego).

In the course of the adult-child relationship, experience shows us that the earliest sexual fantasies are reactivated in the adult by the appearance of this little being, my other self, such as I myself once was, exposed to the most delightful (and perhaps the most perverse) bodily attentions.

The relationship is thus established at a twofold level; the reciprocal level of self-preservation constitutes the basis of the communication. But in the human being that self-preserving foundation is immediately inhabited, infested, interfered with by a communication that occurs in a single direction: from the adult toward the child. What we call "enigmatic messages" are all the messages directed from the adult toward the child, messages that are intended to be purely self-preserving—I want to feed you, to care for you, etc. —but that are "compromised" (in the Freudian sense of the term) by the impingement of sexual fantasies. I feed you, but—unconsciously—I cram you with food, in the sexual sense of intromission (*Nahrungszu-fuhr* becomes *Nahrungseinfuhr*—as it appears in a significant slip by Freud in his "Entwurf einer Psychologie").[242]

Faced with these enigmatic messages, the child is initially passive: he lacks the appropriate instinctual response. He is in a traumatic situation he must attempt to master by actively making it his own, by understanding it, which is to say by translating it.

We thus say that the human being is originally in a situation of passivity—and in the position of a hermeneut. But that fundamental hermeneutical position is not a hermeneutic of situation or facticity, but a hermeneutic of the message.

We are intent on emphasizing the radicality of this situation:

---

242 In *Gesammelte Werke*, Nachtragsband, p. 410; and *La révolution copernicienne inachevée*, p. xxvii, note 52.

the human being, from the sexual point of view, is centered on the other from the outset; he gravitates around the other: this is what I call a fundamental *Copernicanism*. On the other hand, the child continues to find himself in a position of mastery, or pseudomastery, in which he might consider himself as center and origin: this *Ptolemaic* movement is no less important than the initial Copernicanism against which it constitutes a defense. Thus the psychical apparatus is constituted in a movement of self-appropriation, which can be equated with a translation. But the crucial point is that this translation is always necessarily imperfect and a failure. This is precisely because, at the outset, the child does not possess sufficient means to integrate, understand, and bind the sexual elements concealed in the messages coming from the adult other.

In a schematic way we can therefore say that the constitution of the psychical apparatus—above all the division between an id and an ego—is essentially a result of this process of translation. The ego integrates what, in the sexual messages emanating from the other, can be translated and given form. What cannot be translated, the residue of translation, constitutes the unconscious id;[243] the id escapes from the constraints of binding and thereafter becomes a pole of unbinding.

Primary repression and, thereafter, secondary repressions are nothing other than the (obligatory) result of that partial failure of binding.

We should not lose sight of the initial formula of our *sollen*: "*Wo Es war, soll Ich werden.*" We can henceforth add this crucial point: the ego and the id under discussion are not two entities of different

---

243 Freud almost arrives at this formulation in *Moses and Monotheism* (*SE* 23:96) "At that time a portion of the contents of the id is taken into the ego and raised to the preconscious state; another portion is not affected by this translation and remains behind in the id as the unconscious proper." With the reservation that Freud remains captive of the conception of a primordial biological id and is unaware of the category of the message, which is the only element actually subject to translation.

origin: one that allegedly would be biological, and the other rational or cultural. The *ego* and the *id* are initially constituted in a single movement: the ego englobes what, in the sexual message emanating from the other, is amenable to translation and can be integrated into a more or less coherent story. The id is what remains refractory to translation. In addition, we should insist on the following: the unconscious id is not like a second "ego," as unified as the first is. The process of repression, working, as Freud says, in a "highly individual" manner, results in an "agency," which is not comparable to that of the ego and barely deserves the name of agency: it is made of representations that are not coordinated, are timeless, do not contradict each other, and that exercise a quasi-mechanical attraction (the primary process) on any representation, which, so to speak, passes within its reach.

Through the process of repression, psychical alterity has radically changed place: in the initial Copernican relation it is the relationship with the other person (*der Andere*) that is at stake. Once the psychical system closes in on itself, with the constitution of ego as an agency, the alterity or otherness becomes internal: the id becomes *das Andere*, the other par excellence, but an internal other.

How are we to conceive of psychical conflict once the ego-id system has been founded? Certainly it can be defined as a conflict of drives: between what we call the sexual death drives—sexuality in its most unrestrained form—and the sexual life drives, oriented by an aim of totality: the totality of the object and the totality of the ego taken as an object.

It can also be defined as a conflict between the two agencies, the ego as a center of binding, dominated by Eros, and the id, in which are found various levels of unbinding, as deep as the sexual death drive which is akin to a central abyss.

Finally, it can be defined more abstractly (even philosophically[244])

---

244 Freud, as is known, makes reference to Empedocles' opposition between *philia* and *neikos*.

as a struggle between two principles: binding and unbinding—principles that partially overlap with the topographical distinction between agencies but are also to be found at work within each agency.

It is outside the scope of this communication to detail the modalities of conflict, whether normal or neurotic. I would only like to insist on the following point. The conflict occurs on Ptolemaic terrain, that of the apparatus of the soul described by Freud. The binding/unbinding opposition, or that between Eros and the sexual death drive, or between ego and id, confronts the ego with a pole of otherness that is thereafter internal. In addition, unlike the primal situation, the ego is no longer in the presence of messages "to be translated," but of reified residues.[245]

Unconscious fantasies do not present themselves as demanding "to be translated" (*zu übersetzen*), but rather as "to be accomplished" or "fulfilled" (*zu erfüllen*). The alterity of the external other . . . presents itself within the forms of communication by the paths of language, even if the latter was at first merely gestural. The alterity of the internal other, the unconscious id, manifests itself as substitute formation by way of displacement and condensation, which are alien to any communicative intention.

The same opposition is found at the level of defense. In both cases the defense aims at binding in the face of the danger posed by unbinding. But the primal binding, in the face of an external enigmatic message, was above all on the order of connections of meaning. It is a *translational* binding. In contrast, in the face of the unconscious id—once it has been constituted—the ego uses far more "mechanical" defense mechanisms, the very ones described by Anna Freud, following Sigmund Freud. To be sure, it might be said that an intent to translate occasionally subsists in the defense mechanism. One could say that a phobia "translates" the danger of the drive into a real, exter-

---

245 What Freud calls *Sachvorstellungen*, and which I interpret not as *Vorstellungen einer Sache* (representations of a thing), but as *Vorstellungen als Sachen* (representations as things).

nal danger. In point of fact, rather than translating, phobia transposes from one location to another but without the labor of integration and without taking context into consideration, which are two features of a genuine translation. This is due to the fact that the repressed id is not constituted by messages, nor even by sequences possessing a meaning, but, on the contrary, by elements that precisely have escaped from the primal attribution of meaning.

In conclusion, it must be admitted that psychical conflict, once constituted, offers only the slightest perspective of genuine resolution, or even of progress toward resolution. Even when disguised, psychical conflict is usually devoted to the repetition compulsion: repetition of modes of substitute satisfaction—repetition of defense mechanisms.

This entire trajectory was necessary in order to arrive at the analytic process. Let's start with this observation: if analytic treatment merely brings into play the same forces spontaneously at work in the human subject, who already has constituted a psychical apparatus in which binding is at work between an ego and an id within the "Ptolemaic" enclosure of the ego, it is hard to see the means treatment might dispose of to initiate a genuine change. The early translations, life plans (whether chaotic or rigid), myths, and ideologies of each of us bear down with all their weight on an already constituted existence.

To return to the metaphor of translation, what we believe to be a new translation is, alas, all too often no more than a translation of a translation. Ernst Kris has shown quite well how an entire analysis might progress without the mythical idealization of an individual being even minimally called into question.[246]

Let us return to the question: what mad, utopian hope allows us to imagine that analysis might accomplish anything more than a local reconfiguration of the play of forces established by the first repressions as early as the constitution of the ego-id opposition? By what means

---

246 "The Personal Myth—a Problem in Psychoanalytic Technique" (1956) *Journal of the American Psychoanalytic Association* 4: 653-681

might "ego" become there where "id" was if, as we have said, the constitution of the two agencies is complementary and if the unconscious is what, from the outset, eludes mythologization by the ego?

My idea is that the practice inaugurated by Freud has as its latent meaning, and consequently as its aim, a reactivation of the primal Copernican conflict, the one that gave birth to the secondary play of forces and the derivative conflict that is subsequently played out between the ego and the internal other.

That reinstitution of the primal situation takes place by way of two principal means: 1) the analytic situation and the transference it provokes; 2) analysis as a method of detranslation.

Our point of view with regard to the *transference* is that it cannot be reduced to a pure and simple repetition of relations with one or another infantile object—a repetition, moreover, that is constantly observed in everyday life.

Opposed to this transference, which is occluded, so to speak, or blocked precisely by what it is repeating—what we call "filled-in transference"—we posit a reinstatement of the relation not to any particular object but to a relation to the enigmatic itself. What is called—rather banally—"neutrality" is to be conceived as the capacity of the analyst to provoke and sustain a situation in which the other (the analyst) is *assumed* to possess the truth of the subject. This is a reiteration of the adult-child situation, but with the major difference that the analyst must take care that he does not, in his turn, fill up or occlude the transference through messages compromised by his unconscious. What is called—quite controversially—the countertransference, and mastery of the countertransference, cannot be anything other than a strikingly idiosyncratic relation of the analyst to his own unconscious, *his own* alterity. Not an integration—both impossible and undesirable—of that otherness into his ego, but an acknowledgment that is at the same time an acceptance of distance, a kind of reserve or respect.

What I call *hollowed-out transference*—a transference that is not filled by one or another encumbering and immovable imago—

is thus a reinstitution of what might be called primal transference; if the transference is indeed characterized by a duplication of the other, and, if one may express it this way, by the presence of alterity in the other, the primordial child-adult situation can, in that sense, already be said to be transferential.

What remains to be discussed is the second element, namely, in addition to the analytic situation, *analysis*. For if the situation is the locus of a reactivation of the relation to enigmas emanating from the other, that effort can only be accomplished by way of a deconstruction, a detranslation of the myths and ideologies through which the ego constructed itself in order to master those enigmas. This is a properly analytic labor, linked to the method of free association which can also be called free dissociation. I cannot enter into detail except to underline three points:

1. This joint labor of analyst and analysand should not be pressed into the service of preestablished conceptions, even if these form part of the arsenal of psychoanalytic theories (castration, Oedipus, depressive position, etc.).

2. The labor chiefly targets the self-theorizations specific to the analysand's ego. It is only by inference that the unconscious elements (not integrated by the ego) can be detected. The "constructions in analysis" discussed by Freud are above all reconstructions of earlier occurrences of repression, that is: *reconstructions of defensive constructions* forged in the past by the subject. In this sense they are stages that are to be analyzed in turn up until the primal messages have been approached as closely as possible (without ever being reached).

3. This labor of progressive detranslation, proceeding by successive layers, is constantly accompanied by an inverse movement. For it must never be neglected that the ego itself is, to use Freud's term, motivated by a compulsion to *synthesize* precisely as a function of the danger of unbinding reactivated by *analysis*. It can even be said that this force of synthesis constitutes the reparative tendency proper to what is specifically "psychotherapeutic."

The analyst—except in clinical cases in which spontaneous synthesis is manifestly deficient—should not propose schemata or scenarios for retranslation—classical psychoanalytic schemata no more than any others. In that sense psychoanalysis in its essence does indeed remain an "antihermeneutic," the only hermeneut—who gives a more or less adequate (but always inadequate) meaning to his experience of being exposed to the other—always remains the human individual himself.

At this turn in our presentation, let us again take up Freud's formula *Wo Es war, soll Ich werden*. We will subject it to the following modifications:

The ego is not a definitive agency. It is constructed against a fundamental alterity using attributions of meaning (translation) and identifications. But the id itself is not an innate agency. On the contrary, it is the residue of a process that lets untranslated bits fall away.

Consequently, the *werden soll* that constitutes the aim of analysis is not the conquest of an antediluvian id by an autonomous ego. It is an attempt to put the primal process back on track, a process in which the other "to be conquered" was not the unconscious internal other, but the external other as source of enigmatic messages. That other was, in earlier times, the origin of a genuine "drive to translate" (*Trieb zur Übersetzung*, a term invented by the German Romantics).

We said earlier that if the psychoanalytic treatment did no more than reactivate forces already present within the apparatus, there would be little chance that it would come to a better end than the spontaneous psychical conflict. Now we can add that the new motivating force generated by the transferential situation and by the relation to the enigma is precisely that renewed "drive to translate."

Ultimately, one might define the aim of the process as a new attempt at structuring the ego, a new translation attempting to better take into account and to reappropriate, in a new form, elements until then excluded. But one should not forget the difference between the aim of the analysand and that of the analyst. The former, subjected to the trauma of the treatment, keeps working in an attempt to heal as quickly as possible. The analyst, on the contrary, cannot and should not lend his assistance to these repeated attempts at binding. He is primarily an artisan of unbinding and must never stop leading the analysand back onto the path of *analysis*.

My final point, however, will be this: however ambitious the aim defined in this way—reactivation of a primordial process—it cannot be ignored that that aim ultimately takes on a "Ptolemaic" aspect. However comprehensive it may be, the new unity of the ego necessarily closes in on a new version of the id as internal other.

Need we think that a "Ptolemaic"—and ultimately narcissistic—closure constitutes the final aim, in relation to which treatment itself would constitute no more than a fertile, but transitory, episode in restructuration?

Experience shows us that this is not always the case. The dimension of the transference, once stripped of its purely projective and illusory aspect, appeared to us in its truth as "hollowed out," a reiteration of the relation to the other as conveyor of enigmas. In certain cases that opening—that wound—of the transference may in turn be found, transferred outside of treatment, in a relation of address to the other and of vulnerability through the *inspiration* of the other, which is the specificity of creators, whatever their field of creation may be. That eventuality would in turn necessitate lengthy explanations.

1. The continuation of analysis as self-analysis has frequently been recommended, notably in the exercise of the profession of analyst. What I am speaking about here can be considered to be a modality, but a limited one, of that prolongation. It is a matter, we should say, of maintaining the wounding by the other. If Ferenczi was able to reproach Freud with not having immunized him against *new* traumatic experiences, it was because he failed to see the full fecundity of the "new" coming from the other. It is indeed a matter

of unending analysis, but one quite different from that rehashing of "psychoanalytic" schemata and their application in daily life, which can be observed in former analysands who have become technicians of psychoanalysis.

2. In the end of analysis, the movement of such a *transference of transference* is to be perceived by the analyst, and possibly to be grasped—and accepted. A justified mistrust with regard to "lateral transference" —when it comes to impede analytic work—should be articulated with an attitude of lucid acceptance concerning the transposition and pursuit, outside, of the Copernican relation.

3. The definition of the cultural realm, taken in the broad sense, cannot make do without the notions of message, address, and enigma. The message of the "creator," even when modest, is defined by the fact that his address is not directed at a single individual in whom he must produce a specific "effect": it is potentially infinite, open to the enigmatic reception by a public "scattered in the future" (Mallarmé).

4. Finally, it would be the entire notion of sublimation that would have to be reconceptualized. In the customary perspective, in Freud as in Melanie Klein, that notion remains a construct that is above all Ptolemaic, secondary, destined to domesticate the foreignness of the relation to the other.

It is at this juncture that an old notion such as that of "inspiration" would deserve to be given prominence as corresponding to an intuition of the Copernican character of cultural creation. It appears to us that the practice inaugurated by Freud has contributed something new not to the concept of sublimation but to *sublimation itself*, by introducing into it its "Copernican revolution."

X
Psychoanalysis as Antihermeneutics

For Serge Leclaire

For the majority of its readers, the title of this paper may include, a paradoxical—and even provocative—aspect.[247] How could psychoanalysis—if only through its foundational work, titled *The Interpretation of Dreams*—*not* quite naturally encounter the hermeneutic movement, which arose at the end of the eighteenth century precisely as a theory, method, and practice of interpretation?

From there to enrolling psychoanalysis within hermeneutics only a single step need be taken, and it has been taken quite cheerfully: psychoanalysis would be a special case, a "regional hermeneutics," either because one agrees to take it into consideration, as does Paul Ricoeur, or because one rejects it as poorly grounded and arbitrary, as, for example, Hans-Georg Gadamer, Jean Grondin, and numerous others would have it.[248]

---

247 Delivered on September 15, 1994, at the Cerisy colloquium "Herméneutique, textes, sciences."

248 [Editor's note: "Hans-Georg Gadamer (1900-2002) is the decisive figure in the development of twentieth century hermeneutics—almost certainly eclipsing, in terms of influence and reputation, the other leading figures, including Paul Ricoeur, and also Gianni Vattimo (Vattimo was himself one of Gadamer's students)." Stanford Encyclopedia of Philosophy. Jean Grondin is a Canadian philosopher, whose work focuses on hermeneutics, phenomenology, German classical philosophy and the history of metaphysics.]

I have been following a different path for quite a long time now—since 1968[249]—specifically in a confrontation with Ricoeur's positions on Freud, which I criticize, for not taking into account the method of Freud himself.

Today I will simply raise the question in these terms: it appears self-evident, especially given recent developments in hermeneutics, that there is no interpretation without a code or key for translation. Hermeneutics defines itself as a reception, transposition, or reading (of a text, a destiny, a *Dasein*), a reading based on a prior precomprehension or protocomprehension. In this context, psychoanalysis could be assimilable to a reading, which presupposes that from the outset it would suggest one of several codes.

It is against this seemingly straightforward evidence that my paper will be directed. In the first section, I draw on Freud. In the second, I propose the foundation of psychoanalytic antihermeneutics, which I call the general theory of seduction.

WITH FREUD

A number of Freud's assertions run counter to the inclusion of psychoanalysis in hermeneutics.

I have long insisted on the absolute priority accorded to the method. Before identifying itself as a variety of clinical practice or as a theory, psychoanalysis initially defined itself as "a procedure for the investigation of psychical processes, which are otherwise hardly accessible."[250] Now that method is consistently defined as *analytic*, associative-dissociative, "free association" (*freie Assoziation*) or "freely occurring ideas" (*freie Einfälle*), simply being the path used to dissociate every consciously proposed meaning.

The analytic method is allegedly suited to its postulated object:

---

249 "Interpréter [avec] Freud," republished in *La Révolution copernicienne inachevée*. See also "La psychanalyse entre déterminisme et herméneutique," ibid., pp. 385–41.
250 "Two Encyclopaedia Articles" *SE* 18:235-259

so-called unconscious representation. We are justified, as a function of the very method required to observe it, in positing the absence of any synthetic sense in the object under consideration.

Now, in a complementary way, Freud never stopped issuing declarations opposed to all synthesis: on one hand, there is no synthesis in the "id" where co-existence without coherence reigns; on the other hand, the analyst must be satisfied with analyzing without proposing any sort of "psychosynthesis" to the patient.

This question was the object of a late and important clarification in the article of 1937, "Constructions in Analysis." Freud no longer denied the fact that analysis might lead, layer by layer, to partial and provisional constructions; and, in any case, these are only brief *reconstructions* of sequences of historically well-defined meanings. But the place granted to *Konstruktion* allowed Freud to legitimize *Deutung*, interpretation, which, in complete contrast to reconstructive synthesis, is defined as proceeding element by element, that is, restoring missing links in the associative-dissociative chain. This quasi-mechanistic, associationist definition spurns any search for meaning, any preexistent understanding. In this regard I will note that Freud uses only the term *Deutung*, whereas hermeneuts speak of *Auslegung* or *Interpretation*. Although aware of the etymological roots of *deuten*,[251] I tend to perceive in Freudian *Deutung* the trace of the form *deuten auf*: to indicate, to point out a separate element. Which is still analysis!

Beyond these terminological considerations, I would like to bring a different variety of support to the notion that psychoanalysis is not that system of stereotyped interpretations to which it is too often reduced by certain of its adepts, much to the satisfaction of its detractors, who then have the upper hand.

My argument will be historical. I would like to show that psychoanalysis, in the first decade of the twentieth century, underwent a

---

251 "To show *coram populo*": the same root as *deutsch*.

change that was as important as it was disastrous, with the appearance of the codes for reading known as *symbolism* and *typicality*.

The main evidence for this first period and its antihermeneutic methodology are the *Studies on Hysteria* (1895) and *The Interpretation of Dreams*, the latter in its 1900 edition, before the additions in subsequent editions, which are characterized precisely by the arrival of codes for reading.

It is interesting to follow, from the methodological point of view, one of the psychoanalyses of the *Studies*, or even the celebrated dream of Irma's injection, which serves as a paradigm in *The Interpretation of Dreams*. Freud presents us with twenty pages of associations, decipherings, but decipherings that are not coded, and even less biunivocal: twenty pages of unbinding (*Entbindung*) in relation to the more or less coherent narrative of the dream. Associative paths are followed, points of intersection are noted, but no synthesis is proposed. The chapter ends abruptly—even disappointingly: "I have now achieved the interpretation of the dream. . . . It leaps to the eyes, the dream is the fulfillment of a wish."[252]

Let us insist on this historical point: in 1900 the analytic method was already complete, yet it was in no way a translation, a comprehension, or a reading. The method was one of *detranslation*, tracking down elements said to be unconscious (at the time Freud spoke of memories, or, better still, of reminiscences).

This is not to say that no synthesis occurred, but it was purely spontaneous and above all individual: as in chemistry, analyzed elements tend to recombine. But there are no preestablished codes for a retranslation.

To be sure, this primal stage of the method would soon be hidden. Very soon codes, which are called psychoanalytic, would intervene, and do so under two banners: *symbolism* and *typicality*.

---

252 See *Gesammelte Werke* 2–3:123, *SE* 4–5:120–121. We have insisted more than once on the expression (to which Freud adhered obstinately) "The dream *is* a wish-fulfillment" and not "The dream expresses a wish."

Symbolism, the fixed binding of symbol with symbolized, would be developed only in subsequent editions of the *Traumdeutung*. But then, as to symbols, Freud would go so far as to speak of a "fundamental language."

Typicality. What was initially at stake were dreams whose manifest content would correspond to a quasi-universal scenario. Although they were to undergo considerable development, in 1900 typical dreams occupied a limited place: dreams of nudity, examination dreams, dreams of the death of beloved persons, which would lead, as is known, to the Oedipus complex. Later would come the major typical schemata: the major "complexes," most prominently the "castration complex." This would be followed by the mythology of the two great instincts—of Life and of Death. And after Freud these synthesizing organizing schemata would continue to proliferate, for example: the schema of the depressive position according to Melanie Klein or, still later, the function of the Law and Castration in Lacan.

Let us pause at those years during which typicality and symbolism make their appearance. Freud believes he has made a fundamental discovery, perhaps the only genuine addition to his doctrine. And that discovery bears simultaneously on matters of content (which would be universalized) and of method. Alongside the step-by-step procedure of individual free associations, Freud proposes a kind of open-book reading or translation under the name *symbolic method*. So, symbolism versus associations: my question is are we dealing with parallel, even complementary, methods, as Freud would have it, or are they two antagonistic vectors, precisely those of anti-hermeneutics and hermeneutics?

The opposition between the two is clear:

1) The symbolic method offers a freewheeling open-book translation of the manifest discourse of the dream, retaining its coherence and, ultimately, *trusting* it; it transposes one narrative into another. Whereas the associative method dissociates the manifest narrative without evincing the slightest belief in it.

2) The methods are not in a relation of cooperation since, according to Freud, *when symbolism speaks, associations are silent.* It was even the obstacle constituted by what he called mute elements that obliges one to resort to symbolism. This is something that Freud underlines without attempting to explain it.

In order to make myself better understood, I will refer to a dream, present in the 1900 edition: the "man with the hatchet."

A twenty-seven-year-old man, who had been seriously ill for a year, reported that when he was between eleven and thirteen he had repeatedly dreamt (to the accompaniment of severe anxiety) that *a man with a hatchet was pursuing him; he tried to run away, but seemed to be paralysed and could not move from the spot.*[253]

It is not my intention to summarize the interpretation of this dream, only to emphasize the paradox it offers. Here—and this is before 1900—Freud takes up the narrative element by element, without concern for the scenario, and in accordance with the classical technique of unbinding or dissociation. The associative paths finally lead him to childhood scenes, the observation of a violent act of intercourse between the parents.

Not for a moment does Freud read "castration," the typicality of castration, which may seem striking to a contemporary psychoanalyst, beginning with the reading of the manifest dream. Such castration, moreover, would fit well with the extreme anxiety that accompanies the dream. But it was precisely during this period that Freud did not understand anxiety as a threat in the external world (castration), but as the result of an internal attack on the subject by the unconscious sexual drive.

To summarize my inquiry: here we have a dream that should be regarded as typical and read according to the key of "castration." Yet Freud deliberately ignores that key. Moreover, he does not observe that alleged silence of associations that ought to strike the subject

---

253 *SE* 5:584.

when his dream is governed by symbolism. And, to conclude, reading in terms of symbolism and typicality is not an aid to the associative method. When one is present, the other is absent, and *vice versa*.

All this to arrive at the following hypothesis: it is symbolism that *silences* associations. To take things further, synthesis or encoded thought is on the side of *repression*. In the analysis of the "hatchet man," it is because Freud refuses to discover castration as a synthetic scenario or "complex" that he is able to pursue the analytic method.

The *discovery of castration*, however, would continue in the history of psychoanalysis, to the point, perhaps, of invading it and obscuring everything.

The major step was the analysis of "little Hans," 1906–1909. I have ironically designated the theory elaborated in that analysis as the "joint theory of Hans and Sigmund." It is Hans who launches the fable that is an "infantile sexual theory," and it is Sigmund who will adopt it, giving it its form, to the point of, little by little, asserting its universality.

A few words on that infantile sexual theory that will become, allegedly, a psychoanalytic theory.

A theory, in order to do what? To master an *enigma* proposed to the child by the world of adults.

Initially, that enigma is not the difference of sexes, but the difference of *genders*. The baby does not perceive an anatomical differentiation. But, quite quickly, he perceives that the human species is divided into two genders, according to habitus, presentation, behavior, function, etc.

There must be, lurking behind it all, an enigmatic difference proffered by the adult as a message to be deciphered. The theory of castration attempts to account for that enigma, and does so by symbolizing it in a coded system. The code, for its part, is based on anatomy and functions like a binary myth, +/-. In a word: in the beginning, all humans had a penis. Then it was cut off in the case of some and not of others, but the latter are still under the threat.

Incidentally, this theory is the inverse of the biological theory, in which the basic sex is female, whereas masculinity is due to the action of a supplementary hormone. It is a phantasmagorical and contingent theory. As late as 1915, Freud would consider it to be far from universal. For their part, ethnologists, and even psychoanalysts like Roheim and Bettelheim, would show that there were far more complex and far richer ways of symbolizing gender difference.

Only later did Freud claim universality for the "castration complex," with all the difficulties posed by that application, notably for girls.

It is Lacan who first posits universality for castration as *a priori*, and it is done in the name of a metaphysical turn that desexualized the entire configuration. For Lacan, castration becomes the signifier of human finitude, a finitude whose burden each subject is expected to assume, which then becomes the aim of psychoanalysis . . .

To insist on the ethnological contingency of the myth of Hans and Sigmund is not to neglect its importance. It introduces what I have called phallic logic, a binary logic—via "plus" and "minus." The allegedly glorious assumption of castration is not a grandiose *amor fati*; it is directly tied to the rise of binary thinking, on which the modern Western world is entirely based.

But despite the irresistible conquest of the world by binary thought, it is worthwhile recalling that that triumph remains contingent in relation to numerous civilizations whose foundational myths are not binary, but pluralist, accepting ambivalence instead of wagering everything on difference.

In *concluding* this brief Freudian (and anti-Freudian) trajectory, I will again stress the fact that Freud's original discovery was a method. An unprecedented method, linked to the equally unprecedented foundation of the psychoanalytic situation. For where in the world, prior to and outside of psychoanalysis, is it proposed and permitted to say everything, even one's most secret thoughts of carnage, racism, and rape? A strictly individual method, favoring individual connections, from element to element, "associations" established to the detriment of any self-construction or self-theorization. The method is analytic in the literal sense of the term: associative-dissociative, unbinding. One would be inclined to call it "deconstructive"—and the term *Rückbildung* is indeed present in Freud—had the word not been subsequently monopolized by and acclimated within an exogenous philosophy.

The refusal of synthesis, before being a quasi-moral rule for Freud (refusal of suggestion, refusal to impose one's own ideals, even if they are psychoanalytic), is a methodological abstention. The principle underlying it is that where one follows the path of synthesis, one silences the unconscious.

But that discovery is masked, covered over by the return of synthesis, "reading," and hermeneutics. Hermeneutics initially assumed the names of typicality and symbolism and would flourish shortly thereafter as major "complexes." And then as the allegedly psychoanalytic myths that encumber us.

It is true that these complexes and myths are partly psychoanalytic, but those discoveries are poorly situated: concealing the unconscious in psychoanalytic theory, exactly as they conceal it in the human being. An imposition of form used by humans to master enigmas.

THE PROBLEM OF HERMENEUTICS IN THE FRAMEWORK OF THE GENERAL THEORY OF SEDUCTION

A few preliminary remarks

1. The preceding clarification (and correction), however radical in relation to a conception that alleges psychoanalysis to be hermeneutic, appears to remain "regional": circumscribed within a specific sector of our knowledge of man. A claim to the universal and the foundational cannot be asserted on the basis of merely scouring Freudian psycho-

analysis clean from a methodological point of view. It can be grounded only in a theory of the human being, one plainly elaborated on the basis of Freud's discoveries, but also on that of their concealment.

2. The elaboration of what I am calling the "general theory of seduction" is intent on pursuing that path:

- a rediscovery of the "theory of seduction" formulated by Freud around 1895;
- a deepening of the concealment to which it was subjected around 1897.

What is called, a bit rapidly, the "abandonment of the theory of seduction" cannot be restricted to a simple empirical confrontation with the facts, from which the theory would emerge defeated. There was, in that theory of Freud's, a kernel of truth, but one that was insufficiently elaborated and that consequently entailed weaknesses, failings to be generalized and channeled toward something essential.

Here there can be no question of pursuing that elucidation, which led me to a generalization in the epistemological sense of the term.

3. The concomitance of those two concealments—of the theory of seduction and of the individual method—which favors a return of hermeneutics, via symbolism, typicality, and complexes, plainly should be related to connections that run deep. I cannot develop them here, but they are easy to locate.

4. In the presentation of the general theory of seduction, I am more inclined to speak of translation than of reading, interpretation, or even comprehension. The reasons for this are several.

First of all, our starting point is always a meaning that has been expressed, and expressed to an *other*: a message. This message is expressed in a "language," if one is willing to give to that term its general meaning of semiological system—and not of verbal language in the restricted sense.

Subsequently, it struck me that the hermeneutic movement, when it rewrote its history in the eighteenth, nineteenth, and twentieth centuries—and it knows no end of doing so—all too frequently neglected a second history, which is, nonetheless, intimately linked to that of interpretation: namely, the history of translation and of the theory of translation as it has been retraced by Antoine Berman in *L'Epreuve de l'étranger*.[254] No doubt the node joining translation and hermeneutics is apparent in a Schleiermacher. What remains to be determined is whether reading and interpretation constitute a larger category than that of translation or whether they might not best be subsumed in a general theory of translation.

Finally, I have privileged the notion of translation, since it is apt for the elaboration of what I call the "translational model" in a theory of the message emanating from the other, a theory that is also a theory of repression.

Hermeneut, translator, theorizer: such are the facets of a single activity, that of receiving the message emanating from the other.

I return then to the general problem of hermeneutics and do so in order to assert, within the framework of the general theory of seduction, this fundamental proposition: *the sole genuine and primal hermeneut is the human being*. Every human being.

In this respect I come closer to Heidegger's point of view: fundamental hermeneutics cannot be introduced from without, as a specialized discipline. It can only be a hermeneutic of the human condition, practiced by a human individual. But my explanation of that thesis will be profoundly different:

1. What serves as the object of a protocomprehension, proto-translation, is not the situation but the message. How indeed might a situation serve as the object of a translation? There is no inquiry into the human situation that does not have as its vehicle the message emanating from the other. The great fundamental questions—Where do we come from? Where are we going? Why are there genders? etc.—come to the individual only as posed by the other.

---

254 Antoine Berman, *L'Epreuve de l'étranger* (Paris: Gallimard, 1984).

Which individual? Which other?

2. The individual engaged in this prototranslation is not the adult, situated as he is in terms of a *cogito*—or even a *Dasein*. Heideggerianism, indeed the entire gamut of hermeneutic thought, remains imprinted with the seal of reflexive thinking, what I have called Ptolemaic thought, which is par excellence the thought of the adult closed in on himself. The one who translates primordially is thus the small child, the nursling. And, for good measure, we may complete his portrait: the nursling infant who does not have an unconscious.

I run the risk, in saying this, of seeing the adepts of a philosophy of the subject, whatever it may be, close their ears to me forever. "Having an unconscious": what indeed might such a naive psychological realism mean? Does one have an unconscious the way in which one has a bag of walnuts or a stack of firewood?[255] But still graver from their perspective would be the centering of things on the nursing infant, or on the infant-adult situation. And indeed, if we had access to it only through an external procedure, a reconstruction based on memories or empirical observations, how would that effort escape the reproach of being ontic in nature, purely worldly, and its disqualification for consideration as a fundamental situation? Simple Cartesian doubt would suffice!

Without wanting at this point to develop my justification, I will give the principle behind it: the situation of primal translation communicates, as if from within, with the singular experience inaugurated by Freud: the analytic situation. What bears witness to infantile "seduction" is analytic "seduction," which we call the "transference."[256]

The primal situation (renewed in analytic treatment) is thus

---

255 "Und vieles / Wie auf des Schultern eine / Last von Scheitern ist / Zu behalten" (And much like a burden of firewood on the shoulders is to be kept). Citation from Hölderlin's "Mnemosyne."

256 See "Du transfert: sa provocation par l'analyste," in *La Révolution copernicienne inachevée*, pp. 417–37.

not: I am here, in situation, interpreting, but: the other is addressing me, enigmatically, and I (infant and analysand) am translating.

A few words, then, concerning those "enigmatic messages" of the adult, addressed to the child. I call them "enigmatic" in a quite precise sense—not mysterious or difficult of access or unexplained, but twofold, to the extent that the adult, for his part, "has" an unconscious, which is awakened in particular by the relation to the very small child he once was. Messages that are for the most part non-verbal—the dispensing of care, mimicry, gestures—but occasionally verbal as well. Messages that I call compromised insofar as they convey not only their manifest meaning but the way in which they are compromised by unconscious signifiers: "compromised" exactly as Freud demonstrated in the case of parapraxes, confusions in speaking (*Versprechen*), in writing (*Verschreiben*), etc. They are enigmatic for the receiver only because they are enigmatic for the emitter.

I can find no better model to represent the reception of such acts of address than that of translation. Translation occurs according to more or less elementary codes, initially furnished by the cultural sphere, but also by physiology and even by anatomy.[257] Moreover, and this is essential, primal translation not only has a luminous aspect (of elucidation and mastery); it also has a negative aspect, translation being always simultaneously a failure of translation, that is, repression, the constitution of the unconscious as the waste matter or refuse of translation.[258]

What would it be to practice hermeneutical psychoanalysis? In applying a new code to an earlier one, focusing on the manifest in order to "reread" it, it could only reduplicate repression. I am not referring principally to so-called anagogic or Jungian interpretation—too easy an adversary and one whose critique can serve as an alibi for more subtle exercises in hermeneutics endorsed by the master, Freud himself.

---

257 See above, chapter 10. The enigma of gender is translated in a "castratory" code, which is simultaneously anatomical and cultural.
258 See chapter 3, "A Brief Treatise on the Unconscious," in this volume.

But in the great tide of secondary, allegedly psychoanalytic theorizations, the analytic method and situation remain like a rock, reminding us of the heterogeneity of the unconscious in relation to every system. What does that method do? Animated by the field of the transference and the reactivation of the relation to the enigma (that of the analyst), it *de*translates, by way of association-dissociation and by *Deutung*, manifest translations. In the course of which, it often comes upon and permits itself to reconstruct early strata of translation, but only in order to press on in the detection of unconscious residues.

Recall the use of the metaphor of the "key" in hermeneutics. Recall as well Freud's examination and critique of the classical and popular interpretation of dreams using a book of keys, a "dream book" like Artemidorus's *Oneirocritica*. For the key that is used to open is also, and above all, used to close. Psychoanalytic method, in its origins, makes use not of keys but of a screwdriver. It dismantles locks and does not open them. It is only in that manner, like a burglar breaking and entering, that it attempts to approach the terrible and ludicrous treasure of unconscious signifiers.

The only practitioner of hermeneutics is the child, and then the analysand. We have no need to turn him into a Freudian, Kleinian, or Lacanian hermeneut. He will always be enough of a hermeneut on his own, given his ineradicable aspiration to synthesis, and that despite all analysis.

I will conclude with a rapid reflection on what *theory* is in psychoanalysis. In this case it appears indispensable to distinguish *two levels* that are nicely indicated by the titles of two of Freud's works: "Infantile Sexual Theories" and *Three Essays on the Theory of Sexuality*.

The first level, designated for convenience as level I, is that of the theories discovered in the human being by psychoanalysis. These are the ideologies, myths, and formal elaborations that, as such, can be neither refuted nor proven by psychoanalysis. It is these that critics of psychoanalysis are most eager to attack, and not without reason, since most psychoanalysts have made them into *their* theories. One might just as well claim to be refuting the ethnologist by showing the phantasmagorical and random nature of an Amerindian myth… My analogy with ethnology, moreover, is not in itself random: psychoanalytic "discoveries" concerning mythical theories intersect at a number of points with ethnological discoveries. As for the function of such theories, we find ourselves largely in agreement with Lévi-Strauss when he assigns them the function of "relieving intellectual uneasiness and even existential anxiety."[259] To which we would add only that this existential anxiety is correlated with the attack by the message emanating from the other: first the adult human other (*das Andere*), then the other thing in us (*der Andere*: the unconscious).

To this level I, I oppose a level II, the level of psychoanalytic theory properly speaking, known as *metapsychology*. Like all theory, it can only be constructed in an attempt to account for an experience; in the foreground would be the experience of psychoanalytic treatment: as situation, method, and object. Psychoanalytic theory is the theory of repression, of the genesis of the unconscious and its manifestations. Can psychoanalytic theory, as described at level II, lay claim to being refutable and falsifiable? The fact that it does not make use of physical-mathematical models does not prevent it from having to submit to logical argument and confrontation with experience.

However different (and even heterogeneous) those two levels of theory may be, there exists between them an essential *practical* relation: level II theory is intent on accounting for an experience and a praxis, and, inversely, it proposes itself as a guide for that praxis. Now one of the achievements of theory of level II is to account for the function of theory (myths and ideologies) in the human being, and specifically in the process of repression. In this sense, and if therapy proposes an (at least partial) lifting of repressions, its underlying maxim can only be

---

259 Claude Lévi-Strauss, *La Potière jalouse* (Paris: Plon, 1985), p. 227; English translation by Bénédicte Chorier: *The Jealous Potter* (Chicago: University of Chicago Press, 1988), p. 171.

"Hands off!" in reaction to the infiltration of "psychoanalytic" theories (or, rather, ideologies) into analytic practice. A stay-out-of-it—"Stay out of the treatment!"—addressed to hermeneutics and to *our* hermeneutics! A regulatory maxim that can only be observed asymptotically and might otherwise be formulated in terms of a "rejection of knowing" (*Versagung des Wissens*) on the part of the analyst.

XI
Psychoanalysis: Myths and Theory

Is it vain to assert that the exigency of truth lies at the heart of our practice, that it is present on a daily basis for any psychoanalyst worthy of the name? One would think so to observe that, from the outset until recently, illustrious and rigorous thinkers have allowed themselves, with consummate offhandedness, to forge ill-informed, composite images of "psychoanalysis," which they then have little trouble discrediting.

One remains sensitive to Marie Moscovici's cry of protest almost ten years ago on the subject of Lévi-Strauss's *The Jealous Potter*: "Psychoanalysis is a myth, which Lévi-Strauss has summarized."[260] However severe it be, the formula is not unfounded: Lévi-Strauss is surely within his rights in raising the possibility that psychoanalysis might be a "myth," and we too intend to do so in our own way. But it cannot be contested that the image of our discipline he proposes for discussion is a kind of "abstract," a makeshift assemblage of unilaterally selected passages, cobbled together without that reference to the history of the body of thought that is indispensable, above all when the subject is Freud.

Lévi-Strauss is certainly not alone in thinking that imprecise

---

Revue philosophique (1997) and *Revue française de psychanalyse* (1998): 3. First presented to a meeting of the APF on January 23 1996.
260 In Marie Moscovici, *Il est arrivé quelque chose* (Paris: Ramsay, 1989), p. 205.

information is authorized by the very nature of our discipline. One could easily cite Heidegger and probably Wittgenstein as well.

But it is Popper on whom I would like to linger, a reflection of the respect I have for his epistemology, his critique of inductive reasoning, and his notion of falsification. Popper, as is known, takes Marxism and psychoanalysis—those two idols of the intelligentsia between the two wars—for the very model of pseudosciences, alleging that their arguments and conclusions could be applied flawlessly to any state of the evidence and that one could not even imagine a situation amenable to "falsification," that is: one in which their falsity could be tested.

Psychoanalysis thus finds itself associated simultaneously with metaphysics and mythical thinking, two accusations that are often paired: "Insofar as the Freudian epic of the ego, the superego, and the id are concerned, such stories describe certain facts, but in the manner of myths, not in a testable form."[261]

Now, when one looks for the kind of "psychoanalytic" assertion against which Popper launches his attack,[262] one comes upon a fable entirely of Popper's invention and repeated several times, as though what were at stake were a great find: "A man pushes a child into the river with the intention of drowning him; a man sacrifices his life to try to save a child. Each of these two cases can be explained with equal facility in Freudian terms: according to Freud, the former suffered from repression (let us say: a component of his Oedipus complex) while the latter succeeded in his sublimation."[263]

One is almost ashamed to reproduce such nonsense, in which terms like *repression* or *sublimation* are used without any scruples in an argument of a metaphysical sort (in the sense of Auguste Comte), i.e.,

---

261 Karl Popper, *Conjectures and Refutations* (New York: Harper and Row, 1968), p. 38.
262 Popper is unhindered by considerations of embarrassment or inexactitude in his sources. "Psychoanalysis" is, with one fell swoop, "Freud, Jung, and Adler."
263 Popper (1957), quoted in A. Grünbaum, "Precis of the Foundations of Psychoanalysis" in *The Behavioral and Brain Sciences* 9 (1986): 254.

as abstractions concealing, in their mere names, their entire explanatory power. What would one think of an epistemologist attempting to show the pseudoscientific character of the theory of gravity through the following "argument": "Whether a building collapses or continues standing, each case might be explained just as easily in terms of gravity." This is an assertion in which, plainly, the word gravity is advanced in mythologico-metaphysical manner, stripped of any scientific content.[264]

It is not enough to wax indignant. "Neither laugh nor cry, understand!" as Spinoza put it. What then is the fate that causes psychoanalysis to be reduced, by its most illustrious adversaries, to such perfunctory fables?

No doubt, one will recall here those moments in which Freud seems to be on the brink of giving up his scientific (and even positivist) ideal, with formulations such as the "witch of metapsychology," "the theory of drives is our mythology," and even the scantly elaborated notion of "scientific myth." This is in contradiction with virtually the entirety of his work—with its relentless debates over proofs and counterproofs.

At this point, Popper and his successors would object in vain that an accumulation of confirmations never validated a theory in absolute terms, because Freud, on numerous occasions, and precisely in the context of an epistemology that is Popperian *avant la lettre* (whose sources it would be interesting to discover) invokes the possibility of what he calls, in quotation marks, the "negative case"— for example, as the possibility of falsification of his theory of sexual etiology.[265] And it is in the same way, through an exposure to falsification, that he proceeds, both in his "abandonment of the seduction theory" and in the text proposing to examine "a case of paranoia contradicting the psychoanalytic theory of that affection."[266] We may also recall the manner in which Freud welcomes the falsification,

---

264 [These two sentences were put in a footnote in the French text.]
265 *SE* 3:259–85; 12, part 1.
266 *SE* 14:261–72.

by Melanie Klein, of the theory according to which internal interdictions (the "superego") inherit parental interdictions—along with their severity. Melanie Klein objects that quite often individuals feel all the more guilty to the degree that their upbringing has been more permissive. One can be circumspect in appreciating Freud's capacity to integrate the objection theoretically; but at least he does not attempt to outfox it!

Finally, to conclude this all too brief review, I will mention the well-known beginning of "Constructions in Analysis" in which Freud discusses at length the assertion of a "thinker of merit" according to which psychoanalytic interpretation, pursuing a logic of "heads I win, tails you lose," would by definition be impervious to contradiction. Freud confronts that objection directly without seeking to circumvent it. The core of his response, which no epistemologist would contest, is ultimately that there is no basis for conflating the "no" or "yes" uttered by the analysand with the "no" or "yes" emergent from the experience of treatment and reflection on it.[267]

By virtue of what curse, then, does Freud, who never yielded in his allegiance to the demands of positivism, find himself repeatedly confronted with the accusation of having himself done no more than forge one more myth? A curse? The hidden vice of psychoanalytic theory? Or rather *theory's erroneous assessment of the mythical function itself*? It is thus something *between myth and theory* that I am advancing here. But a third term is on the horizon and should be taken into consideration—that of the *narrative*. For ever since Freud's "family romance of neurotics," and Lacan's "individual myth of the neurotic,"[268] what can be called narrativization has never stopped making advances in psychoanalysis. Narrativity—a term in frequent

---

267 *SE* 13:255–69.

268 There is an interesting crisscross between the formulae "family romance" (Freud) and "individual myth" (Lacan). But in both cases it is a question of showing how the individual (the "neurotic") forges a personal version of scenarios bearing on the "family" and proposed by myth.

use since Spence, but that also derives from Ricoeur, Viderman, and other less significant authors—has become, as it were, the slogan in the name of which an old but vigorous hermeneutics has staged a return within psychoanalysis.[269]

Between myth, theory, and story. Between the narrativization of the subject and the mythification of theory, a position need be taken. It should consider the question I have tried to anticipate previously: why and how is it that mythosymbolic thought, a major discovery of psychoanalysis, has wrongly tended to become the whole of psychoanalysis, for its adversaries, and also perhaps at times for itself?

Freud's discoveries, by which I mean his essential discoveries, can be counted on the fingers of a single hand—which is already enormous. Each of them poses, quite obviously, the problem of its integration, whether successful or more or less abortive. On each occasion it is possible to go astray. And no doubt such going astray was already more or less predictable as a function of earlier options.

I have tried to show how the discovery of *narcissism* (1910–1915) led, in a structural and quasi-kaleidoscopic way, to the hypothesis of the life and death drives.[270] In this paper I propose to situate us at an earlier stage of Freud's progress. Anzieu, in *Freud's Self Analysis*, describes the two major, initial discoveries of Freud under the headings of, on the one hand, the "meaning of dreams" and, on the other, the "Oedipus complex."[271] I will accept that double rubric while giving it a far broader extension. For what is at play is not only two kinds of *content*, but what is designated as two *methods* (asso-

---

269 The fact that this dispensation recruited the Freudian term *Nachträglichkeit* only to find in it the meaning of a retroactive bestowal of meaning is not without worrisome implications with regard to the more complex conception of temporality that the concept allowed one to hope for (see chapter 2, in this volume).

[Editor's note: Donald P. Spence (1926-2007) and Serge Viderman (1916-1991) were psychoanalysts (Canadian and French respectively) whose work affirmed psychoanalysis as a hermeneutic discipline.]

270 See, for example, *Problématiques IV*, p. 222.

271 Didier Anzieu, *Freud's Self-Analysis* (Connecticut: IUP, 1986), p. 122 and p. 175.

ciative versus symbolic) and two *fields of application*—and even two different origins: the individual versus the cultural domain.

This second great area of excavation opening up for psychoanalysis—Freud liked to emphasize that he was neither the only nor perhaps the first explorer—is situated in the years 1906–1911. What is at stake is not, in the strict sense, a turning point, but the opening of a new domain. To place it solely under the sign of the Oedipus complex is far too restrictive. In my view there developed at that time, in a single selfsame movement, the establishment of the major complexes (Oedipus and castration), the proliferation of so-called typical scenarios discovered in dreams, the efflorescence of symbolism, and, last but not least, the relation to myth. The principal disciples involved—but they were not the only ones—are Stekel, Jung, and Rank. Freud did not hesitate to add two essays written by Rank, including one on myth, to the fourth edition of *Traumdeutung*. It is, moreover, the complex development of the successive editions of *Traumdeutung* that offers the best evidence of the difficulty entailed in integrating this new domain into the original design.

It would be difficult, and perhaps in part futile, to portray Freud's first discovery *before* this somewhat incoherent (and in any event disturbing) invasion by the *typical* and the *symbolic*. It should be recalled that the first discovery was in fact correlated with a genuine invention: that of the analytic situation and the associative method; it was as a function of the establishment of that unprecedented instrument that the object that became its target or its umbilicus took shape: namely, the unconscious.

How might one reconstitute that "proto-analysis" at the moment when it fundamentally rejected any "key to dreams," and, in so doing, any *key* at all, that is, any preestablished knowledge of structures that might be discovered. No doubt such an image is itself ambiguous since, despite everything, it reveals a Freud who seemed to know more than he was prepared to say. And yet the analyses in the *Studien* and, beyond that, the dream of Irma's injection, are impressive for what one might call a way of casting off the moorings of discourse guided by an aim in order fully to give themselves over to chains of associations, their divergences and intersections, in sum: to a process of *unbinding*, without proposing, even on the horizon, any possible rebinding. No regrouping under the heading of a grand theme of understanding. Wish-fulfillment itself, considered to be the motor force of the dream, is unhesitatingly declined in the plural; much like scenes or reminiscences that are unmasked one after the other, as in a procession.

But rather than force those features that make of analysis essentially a mode of unbinding, I would like to offer as a test the analysis of a dream that strikes me as particularly significant for what it proposes and above all for what it omits.

"A man," Freud reports—this in the first edition of *Traum-deutung* and thus before 1900—"a twenty-seven-year-old man, who had been seriously ill for a year, reported that when he was between eleven and thirteen he had repeatedly dreamt (to the accompaniment of severe anxiety) that a man with a hatchet was pursuing him; he tried to run away, but seemed to be paralysed and could not move from the spot."[272]

On the basis of this dream Freud presents in a page or two the series of associations collected from the dreamer. These associations lead, by way of bifurcating paths, to notions of violence, aggression, fraternal rivalry, etc. Until there finally and suddenly emerges, as a detached and incidental idea, memories of having perceived parental intercourse;[273] anxiety, according to the conception that Freud at the time was developing, is linked to the sexual excitation provoked by the scene, which has not been mastered by an adequate understanding.

What is important, however, from my perspective, is the following: in this dream, even though it is presented as repetitive, Freud

---

272 *SE* 5:584.
273 Not yet designated at the time by the mythical term *primal scene*.

does not for a moment read what today seems to leap to the eye: namely, "castration"; which would, moreover, be in perfect agreement with the fact that we are dealing with an anxiety dream. It is a blindness or a paradox that will continue in the course of successive editions of *Traumdeutung*, since this dream will never be taken as a reference when the focus is on symbolism or on typical dreams of castration.[274] I will come back to what indeed seems to be a reciprocal exclusion of the associative work and symbolic reading

The emergence of symbolism and the extension of what Freud calls typical dreams brought with them, in the very publication of *Traumdeutung*, not only additions (as would be the case for the *Three Essays*), but rather complex attempts at reorganization, of which the preface to the Standard Edition gives a partial account. The difficulty is tied to the fact that symbolism (or symbolics) and typicality are *closely connected*. Freud, moreover, would insist on the fact that "dream *symbolism* reveals itself to be indispensable in understanding the so-called *typical* dreams of human beings, and the *recurrent* dreams of the individual."[275]

One cannot object that symbolism and typicality are two different things, symbolism bringing into evidence term-to-term relations between symbol and symbolized, whereas typicality would bring to the fore fixed scenarios. We are, in fact, well aware that a term-to-term equivalence of a signifier and a signified is an illusion and conceivable only in the framework of a context. "Analogy," which Freud quite rightly makes the major motivating device of symbolism, is always an analogy of relations; to read the hatchet as a cutting instrument is at the same time to read the context, the scenario: castration.

---

274 To even things out, we can add that the analysis of this dream ends with a violently ironic caricature of the explanation of infantile anxiety proposed by certain pediatricians in terms of "medical mythology." Need we, as a matter of course, adopt one mythology—that of castration—after having rejected another? (*SE* 5:598–609).
275 It should be recalled that the dream of the "hatchet man" is a *recurrent* dream that can be considered simultaneously as *typical* and as *symbolic*

But as we know, in Freud typicality is what directly serves to introduce the "complexes": in *Traumdutung* the Oedipus complex is developed entirely within chapter V section D in the sub-section on "Dreams of the Death of Persons of Whom the Dreamer Is Fond."

Symbolism, typicality, complexes: what remains to be added is a fourth element, which is myth. In the section "Dreams of the Death of Persons of Whom the Dreamer Is Fond" it is indeed the myth of Oedipus, as staged by Sophocles, that constitutes the major reference, serving as the catalyst that makes the ingredients "take" or merge into a coherent whole. It is not merely a matter of the complex being confirmed in the myth. The reading of myths is thereafter regarded as primary, as the locus and test for the truth of symbolism. Thus Freud express himself in the note of 10 November 1909: "Dream symbols that are not based on myths, fairy tales, and popular usage, etc., should be considered dubious."[276]

I will also mention Freud's enthusiasm when Oppenheim, a physician he did not know, sent him ethnographic documents dealing with the "dream in folklore": "For a certain time now I have been pursued by the idea that our studies on the content of neuroses might well have the vocation of clarifying the enigma of the formation of myths, and that the core of mythology is nothing other than what we call the 'nuclear complex of neurosis,' such as I have been able to lay it bare in the analysis of the phobia of a five year old boy."[277]

Those documents of Oppenheim, as is known, would be the subject of a joint publication, titled "Dreams in Folklore," in which the interpretative commentary is by Freud.[278] I will emphasize in relation to that work only that it is not a matter of dreamed dreams, but dreams inserted in folklore, so that the method of interpretation, entirely symbolic, is, *by definition non-associative* since there is *no*

---

276 Ernest Jones, *The Life and Work of Sigmund Freud* (New York: Basic Books, 1974), p. 443.
277 Letter to Oppenheim (October 28, 1909). OCF-P XI, p. 85. [No English translation.]
278 "Dreams in Folklore" (1911), in SE 12:175–203.

dreamer other than the one invented by the folkloric narrative.[279]

A final element in this cluster, and not the least significant, is the "infantile sexual theories" to which, in the letter to Oppenheim, we are introduced by the allusion to the analysis of Little Hans. Those theories are themselves, at least partially, based on mythology or fables. But it remains no less the case that the theory of castration, expressed by Hans and formalized by Sigmund, subsequently had an independent mythological fate that was considerable. In this case what is at stake is a myth of the genesis of sexual difference starting from a human race that was initially comprised of a single sex, the male. A "theory" for which little basis was sought (or found) in the myths consigned by the ethnographic corpus. It was the "theory of Hans and Sigmund" that would, so to speak, be transmuted into a psychoanalytic myth whose fate we know: from a theory of the genesis of the sexes, it is transfigured into the idea of a "castration" effected between the mother and her child; and, more generally still, "castration" would become, in an entirely metaphysical manner, a simple manner of speech to say "finitude."

But whereas Freud and, after him, Lacan would erect the castration complex into a Universal of psychoanalysis—perhaps more universal than the Oedipus complex—the research of ethnologists has consistently shown that myths and rituals of amputation, excision, and circumcision have a more ambiguous meaning than the binary phallic logic to which the modern psychoanalytic (and post-psychoanalytic) versions have confined themselves. With Roheim, Bettelheim, and also with Groddeck, what emerges is a path to symbolizations that are less fixed and ultimately are ambivalent and even contradictory. In *Problématiques II: Castration-Symbolisations*, it was precisely the opposition between an unambiguous symbolization ("castration" in the singular) and plural symbolizations that I attempted to bring to the fore.

---

279 A situation quite different from that in which one interprets *in absentia* the dream of an actual dreamer. In the latter case, the "symbolic" option is chosen *for lack of individual associations*.

How are we to situate that immense domain, by which Freud, far from minimizing its importance, appears to be stunned? Let us follow a few ideas from lecture 10 of *Introductory Lectures on Psychoanalysis*.

Initially, Freud was intent on emphasizing that symbolism was an *exogenous contribution* to psychoanalysis, and was so in several senses: historically, it was a reasoned return to the "key to dreams" (or "dream books") of the ancients, which *Traumdeutung* had originally criticized because they proposed fixed meanings, independent of the person and history of the dreamer. In a more modern context, Freud expresses his agreement with the philosopher Scherner[280], to whom he explicitly attributes the discovery of dream symbolism.

Symbolism was also exogenous in another way, by which I mean exogenous in relation to the original locus of analytic activity: the interpretation of dreams or symptoms. Its origin—as Freud never stopped emphasizing—was first of all the reading of collective cultural productions: "we learn it from very different sources—from fairy tales and myths, from buffoonery and jokes, from folklore (that is, from knowledge about popular manners and customs, sayings and songs) and from poetic and colloquial linguistic usage."[281] "Dream symbolism does not belong, properly speaking, to the dream."[282] "The field of symbolism is immensely wide, and dream-symbolism is only a small part of it: indeed, it serves no useful purpose to attack the whole problem from the direction of dreams."[283]

---

280 [Editor's note: Karl Albert Scherner (1825–1889) was a German philosopher and psychologist whose one published book, *Das Leben des Traums* (The Life of the Dream) discussed symbolism in dreams.]

281 *SE* 15:158–59, *Gesammelte Werke* 11:160.

282 Translation of Laplanche's translation of *Gesammelte Werke* 2–3:699. In the *SE*, in volume 5, on p. 685, the passage is rendered: "Dream-symbolism extends far beyond dreams: it is not peculiar to dreams, but exercises a similar dominating influence on representation in fairy-tales, myths and legends, in jokes and in folk-lore. It enables us to trace the intimate connections between dreams and these latter productions. We must not suppose that dream-symbolism is a creation of the dream-work."

283 *SE* 15:166, *Gesammelte Werke* 11:168–69.

The *second point*, which is no less essential, is that symbolism allows for a coherent *reading* of the *impromptu variety*: "we are often in a position to interpret a dream straightaway—to translate it at sight, as it were."[284]

I will open a parenthesis here. We occasionally take the trouble to reject the idea that a given psychoanalytic reading is conducted, so to speak, using an "open book." For instance, André Green undertakes just such a refutation concerning myth or ritual in his preface to an extremely interesting book by the ethnologist Juillerat, *Oedipe chasseur*: "The interpretation of a mytheme," he tells us, "does not risk being deciphered in the manner of simultaneous translation: this meaning that."[285] Yet it is just such a simultaneous translation that Freud invokes as a model for his symbolic reading, the one that, for instance, he undertakes in the book published with Oppenheim.

Ultimately, and still following Freud, such a one-level reading entails a crucial theoretical consequence. The discovery of the symbolic shows that distortion can occur without censorship:[286] it is precisely what we encounter in myths and in the symbolic aspect of dreams.[287] And it is the very idea of a distortion linked solely to the process of symbolization, to expression in a different code, that brings Freud to create the hypothesis of a "fundamental language."[288]

At this point, the major problem was articulating this new dis-

---

284 *SE* 15:151, *Gesammelte Werke* 11:152.

285 Bernard Juillerat, *Oedipe chasseur* (Paris: PUF, 1991), p. 16.

286 Although the censorship can, if only secondarily, make use of symbolic distortion, according to Freud that distortion is in no way the work of the censorship. From the start, Jones's virtuous effort to associate symbolism with repression was in contradiction with that assertion of Freud's. Jones's effort is "virtuous" in that he was trying to salvage both sexuality and defensive conflict, but he was unable to take the step of saying that in defensive conflict the symbolic is entirely on the side of defense. See E. Jones, "The Theory of Symbolism," Chapter VII in Papers on Psychoanalysis.

287 Once again, this contradicts Green's idea that the "unconscious" of myths "cannot be conceived of independently of drives, repression, and censorship," in Juillerat, *Oedipe chasseur*, p. 16.

288 Depending, in particular, on the hypotheses of Sperber.

covery, simultaneously *content* and *method*, with what until then had been considered the core of the Freudian discovery.

As *content*, first, since, Freud tells us, psychoanalytic investigation, until then, led to the discovery of "unconscious tendencies."[289] Let us say, in slightly different terms: to drives and their unconscious representations. "But now," he adds, "we are dealing with something more; indeed, with unknown knowledge, with thought relationships, comparisons between unlike objects . . . ," etc. To the point that, when what is at stake is a knowledge of symbolism, Freud asks himself whether the designation "unconscious . . . is taking us very far indeed."[290] With regard to the situation and nature of the kind of unconsciousness characterizing mythosymbolic knowledge, we can sense the emergence of an inquiry that Freud would not press much further, but that would not cease haunting the debate between mythologists and psychoanalysts. Thus, in the case of the ethnologist Juillerat, whom I have already cited and who raises the question of the nature of that specific unconscious—only to take refuge, perhaps a bit hastily, in an allegation of incompetence: "We will not attempt to distinguish the unconscious from the pre- or subconscious and prefer to declare from the outset our incompetence in assigning them a precise function in the production of myths."[291] Let us retain that question about the nature of the so-called unconscious of myth in order to come back to it when we conclude our journey.

The second opposition, which is *methodological*, between psychoanalysis before and after symbolism, is even more important.

The associative-dissociative method, as we know, was not intended to reveal a latent unconscious meaning directly. By way of multiple, diffluent paths, intersecting in some points only to diverge anew, it aimed to discern or postulate unconscious *elements*, which

---

289 *Gesammelte Werke* 11:168. In the *SE* Strachey has "unconscious endeavors" (SE 15:165).
290 Ibid.
291 Juillerat, *Oedipe chasseur*, pp. 35–36.

in the best of cases might be reinserted into conscious discourse in order to produce a more complete and satisfying meaning. It is in this—and I have had occasion to insist on this for a long time[292] —that the original analytic method does not aim at a *second meaning*, coextensive with conscious meaning, but at signifying elements that were originally excluded, repressed, and, for all that, without having been organized into a second discourse. In a word, the id is not a second ego, one that might possibly be truer than the first.

Now the symbolic method, as described by Freud—and he does not beat around the bush—is opposed to the associative analytic method in that it is precisely the *reading of a hidden meaning*. Perhaps not always a simultaneous translation or open-book translation, but nonetheless always a clarification aimed at restoring a latent sequence deemed to be truer, more fundamental. Freud does not speak of a clarification (*Auslegung*),[293] but that term, which I borrow from hermeneutics, offers a perfect account of his procedure concerning typical dreams or the dreams of folklore. It is also the current recognized procedure of mythologists, whose successes are not to be challenged.

That being said, the problem for Freud (and for us) is indeed to ask how those two methods, different as they are, might be articulated with each other. He makes use of the term *complementarity* (*Ergänzung*). But one should certainly not understand complementarity as collaboration or reciprocal assistance. I will quote at some length the passage that opens lecture 10 of the *Introductory Lectures*, since it is crucial for our purposes:

> I have already admitted to you that it does some-
> times really happen that nothing occurs to a person
> under analysis in response to particular elements of
> his dreams. . . . There remain cases in which an asso-

292 J. Laplanche and S. Leclaire, "L'inconscient: une étude psychanalytique" (1959), in *Problématiques IV*, pp. 261–74.
293 Hermeneutics is opposed to analysis as *Auslegung* is to *Zerlegung*.

ciation fails to emerge . . . If we convince ourselves that in such cases no amount of pressure is of any use, we eventually discover that this unwished-for event regularly occurs in connection with particular dream-elements . . .

In this way we are tempted to interpret these "mute" dream-elements ourselves, to set about translating them with our own resources. We are then forced to recognize that whenever we venture on making a replacement of this sort we arrive at a satisfactory sense for the dream, whereas it remains senseless and the chain of thought is interrupted so long as we refrain from an intrusive intervention of this sort [*Eingriff*].[294]

I note the term *Eingriff*, "encroachment" or "intrusion," and also the words *translation* and *replacement* to characterize the analytic method. But what is most significant for me is the reference to "mute" dream-elements (*stumme Traum-elemente*): *where symbolism speaks, free association is silent.* It is a circumstance that one cannot fail to link to its inverse, observed in the analysis of the hatchet man: the associations spoke while the symbolic reading remained curiously mute. Between the two methods, there is thus, apart from a seeming complementarity, a relation of reciprocal exclusion. When one speaks, the other is silent. So much so that a pressing question comes to be: does symbolism cause associations to be silent? If Freud had read castration in the hatchet man dream, it may be suspected that the associations would have remained mute!

Given this new discovery of an as yet unexplored field, *one must look at how things would be organized thereafter.* Pure and simple juxtaposition of the two methods is minimally possible and scarcely (solely) exists in a realm that has not been thought through. On the

---

294 *SE* 15:149–50, *Gesammelte Werke* 11:150–51.

other hand, what one does perceive in psychoanalysis is the extraordinary expansion of the method and style of thought that can be called "mytho-symbolic." It is an expansion that takes as its launching pad nonclinical psychoanalysis. Freud has convinced us, no doubt quite rightly, of the fact that such thought is at home, as in the place of its discovery and efflorescence, in approaching collective phenomena.

But psychoanalysis outside of treatment is not restricted to collective phenomena; there are also individual cases. And in such cases it is rare for the analyst to have at hand artifacts (e.g., Leonardo's notebooks) that can be compared to the associations that emerge in therapy.[295] Such being the case, we might say, the analysis of individual cases outside of therapy presents, as if by necessity, the paradigm of an object in which individual associations are silenced, leaving the entire field open to the mytho-symbolic and its hermeneutics. With regard to the Schreber case, for example, this is the crucial reproach formulated both by Zvi Lothane and by Edmond Ortigues (in his review of Lothane's work): "Applied psychoanalysis [. . .] can degenerate, as Freud himself showed, into "wild" psychoanalysis and give rise to hermeneutical myths. Hermeneutical readings of Schreber have given birth to myths, which have become legends."[296]

This is an objection that is not always fatal, but solely on the condition that the analyst (in this case, Freud) shows himself able to detect, as if *between the lines of an overly accessible and hegemonic symbolism*, what the latter did not quite succeed in silencing.

As for what occurs in analytic treatment, I believe that mytho-symbolic thinking is far more present these days than one might suppose. One observes, to be sure, that specific symbols, the "dream keys" described by Freud, are hardly in fashion, nor are they taught

---

295 See J.-P. Maïdani-Gerard, *Léonard de Vinci: Mythologie ou théologie* (Paris: PUF, 1994), pp. 23–36 (ellipses by Laplanche).
296 Zvi Lothane, *In Defense of Schreber: Soul Murder and Psychiatry* (Hillsdale, NJ: Analytic, 1992), p. 438, quoted by Edmond Ortigues, "Schreber revisité," in *Psychanalystes*, no. 48 (1993–1994): 215.

at school. But mytho-symbolic thinking cannot be reduced to a battery of symbols. It primarily resides in the system, the relations—or binding—of those symbols. To speak openly, what Lacan calls "the symbolic (*le symbolique*)" is not so far from "symbolics (*la symbolique*)." It matters little what imaginary figures turn up and assume their place in a card game, Lacan used to say; what counts are the places and the rules governing the game. But that rule itself, alas, has become depressing in its uniformity! When the associative method is considered obsolete, or when one quite simply *silences* the associations by cutting them off after five minutes, the intrusive encroachment, the *Eingriff* of the symbolic, risks uttering the words: "Associations, keep silent! I, Castration, am speaking!"

Before delving into personal perspectives, I would like to recall the theoretical solution ultimately adopted by Freud: it consists of establishing a hierarchy in which the mythosymbolic would be situated at a deeper, more archaic, more primordial level than what is individually repressed. In the last analysis, at the very core of the individual there is the original—non-repressed, structural, and structuring—unconscious that is posited as foundational. This is the hypothesis of "primal fantasies," which has brought with it considerable damage such as the unexpected return of the instinct as preformed pattern of behavior (damaging even if the instinctual schema is oedipal). And there is the risk of devaluing repression as the origin of the unconscious, an accomplished version of which is to be found in Kleinian thought. Finally, in the individual-society relation, this path leads to the phylogenetic hypothesis, in the strict sense of a biological inheritance, the only way to "stuff," if the word be permitted, atavistic experience into the center of the individual.[297]

---

297 A centering whose principle I have criticized in *La révolution copernicienne inachevée*, pp. xxxii–xxxiii and in "Essays on Otherness" pp 80-81. As for "phylogenesis," who among its advocates would dare risk asking a biologist to situate the gene for the "murder of the father" on the chromosome chain?

In my opinion, we are obliged to look for a different type of articulation. The first, preliminary move would be a necessary disengagement, the taking of distance that psychoanalysis must establish in relation to the myths and theories it has contributed to clarifying. However fascinating these structures for understanding—and to be sure, the Oedipus complex most of all—it is not for analysis to engage (and even less to compromise) *its truths* as if coinciding with *their "truths."*

Doubtless not even a Lévi-Strauss quite escapes the temptation of considering his own thought as being virtually part of the set that it describes. "We have constructed"—he says in the vertiginous finale of *L'homme nu*—*"a myth out of myths."*[298] And he wonders: are we dealing with a scientific model or might our own myth itself be rediscovered, concretely, in some distant population of America, in the "Oregonian singularity" or "umbilicus of North American cultures," a "once promised land."[299]

As can be seen, the vertigo of a "fundamental language" as the original version of scientific thought can be found in other disciplines. What is advocated, we may say, is the homogeneity of our theory of facts about humans with theories discovered in—and spontaneously created by—human beings. I cannot enter into the absorbing and poetic movement of this drift, in which the ethnologist seems to have cast off the moorings of his position as a scientist, a veritable "drunken boat," as in the poem by Rimbaud, sensing it is no longer being "guided by its haulers." As for me, and at the risk of reaffirming my prosaic bent (and even my positivism), while "regretting the Europe of ancient parapets," I definitely refuse to see myself committed to the truth of the "theory of castration," or even in the grips of the shibboleth of an Oedipus complex that is scarcely canonical any longer and whose variants may well constitute its major interest. An "Oedipus complex" such as that of the Yafars, in which the murder of

---

298 Paris: Plon, 1971, p. 504.
299 Ibid p. 541–542.

the father is absent and castration barely mentioned, and in which the major danger, as a punishment for incest, is precisely a return to the maternal breast, strikes me as eminently instructive without my having to accept it as truth, even if what is involved may be a privileged "organizing" schema.[300]

Psychoanalysis, as Freud had the wisdom to say with regard to symbolic interpretation, should remember that its great complexes, like many another myth, have been explored and clarified by many disciplines other than its own. All the more reason for it not to lay it on too thick when it comes to the mythic, forging its own allegedly canonical schemes, such as the death-of-the-father-of-the-primitive-horde.

But, above all, psychoanalysis must demonstrate its difference from mytho-symbolic thought by elaborating a model capable of *situating that thought and accounting for its function.*

Models in psychoanalytic thought are above all *metapsychological constructs*. As all of Freud's thought demonstrates, those models are elaborated at a distance from experience; and, while imposing a change of register, they occasionally make use of notions drawn from other disciplines. The importance of physicalist models in Freud is well known. They are not without their convenience, but they have the disadvantage of perennially encouraging a return to their field of origin. For example, and this even though Freud consistently asserted the opposite, localizing libidinal energy in a particular "instance" or agency (the "id") constantly and fallaciously encourages a return to neurophysiology.

Rallying, with all due prudence, to the grand agencies of Freud's topographical model—ego, unconscious id, superego, and ideal instances—I have, for my part, principally concerned myself with attempting to account for the genesis of the apparatus of the soul, notably through the process of repression. The model from which I

---

300 [This paragraph and the one just before were placed in a footnote in the French edition.]

work is a so-called translational model. Inspired by a few lines from letter 52 to Fliess, it offers the advantage, in my view, of a greater proximity between metaphorizing (translation) and its result (repression). A proximity, but also a distance, allowing one to perceive the differences with translation *stricto sensu*. But the translational model presents another interest that is still greater. If it is true one never translates anything other than a text already possessing a meaning, this model reminds us that no conferral of meaning can bear on raw data. The human being, from his very first seconds, is *not* confronted with a world of *objects* to be interpreted (even if those objects are human, such as what is called a breast). No! From the outset he has the task of translating *messages* addressed to him by the adult world. It is precisely to that extent that, in my opinion, the debate between material truth and psychological truth ought to be transcended: the original locus of truth and error, and consequently of *psychical truth*, can be conceived only in terms of this tertiary domain: that of the message.[301]

Let us return to myth. It is clear that for mythologists the notion of code has become increasingly important. In Lévi-Strauss in particular, myth acts by proposing a code, or rather a plurality of codes, that are simultaneously different and convertible into each other. Lévi-Strauss's assertion that Freud merely *rediscovered* these codes in the

---

301 To this extent, I thus see nothing but inconvenience in continuing to speak, as Freud does, of representation. The term *representation* necessarily refers to a subject-object problematic, which is—perhaps—that of a "theory of knowledge." The latter is situated in a perspective I have called Ptolemaic. Psychoanalysis must assume as its starting point the fact of interpersonal communication as well as the priority within it of the sexual message emanating from the other. The messages "I love you," and even "eat to make me happy," convey neither information about the world nor a problem concerning the congruence of a "representation" and what is "represented." My distortion of Freud's formula *Sachvorstellung* through the skewed translation "representation-thing" is but a pedagogical way of suggesting that the problem, in the unconscious, is not one of the intentional relation between a representation and its object (the representation of a thing), but the fact that a part of the message becomes "designified," i.e., a kind of "thing" (and a "cause"). Concerning this point, see chapter 3, "A Brief Treatise on the Unconscious," in this volume.

human being need in no way perturb us and does not at all contradict what Freud says about the original locus of myths in the realm of culture. To be sure, Lévi-Strauss, in distinguishing, amid the plurality of codes, their logical armature, is all too often led to privilege abstract structure at the expense of the "flesh" of myths, which nonetheless is the essential dimension of his studies.

"The exigency of order," he tells us, "is at the root of all thought."[302]

The problem, of course, remains of determining precisely what it is that must be ordered. If the function of mythical thought is to encode, what is to be put into code? Lévi-Strauss vacillated or evolved on this point, from the time when he was inclined to reduce totemism, quite coldly, to being no more than a system devoted to classifying human groups. I will cite as an emendation a few lines of *La Potière jalouse*, reflecting an entirely new phase of his thought: "A solution that is not a real solution to a specific problem is a way of relieving intellectual uneasiness and even existential anxiety when an anomaly, contradiction, or scandal is presented as the manifestation of a structure of order that can be perceived more clearly in [other] aspects of reality . . ."[303]

To put things differently, in my own terms, the myth proposes a scheme for a new translation with the purpose of confronting the "existential" anxiety aroused by enigmatic elements that figure as "anomaly, contradiction, or scandal."

For there is no question of annexing, without reservation, the reflections of mythologists,[304] since I would willingly underscore the points in which their thinking strikes me as inadequate: first, because in considering only the mythical thought elaborated in the myths or

---

302 Claude Lévi-Strauss, *La pensée sauvage* (Paris: Plon, 1962), p. 17.
303 Lévi-Strauss, *La potière jalouse*, pp. 227–28.
304 Even if some, like Juillerat, adopt a simultaneously disheveled and simplified version of psychoanalytic thought along lines curiously indebted to Hegel, Ricoeur, and Lacan.

rites of the adult, it neglects to ponder the question of how, and in what forms, mytho-symbolic thought proposed to the human being is a virtual code *from the first days of his life*.[305] If, as Juillerat proposes, a specific ritual ("Yangis") rehearses the sequence of the separation of the child from the mother by the father, that scenario would have had to be present—far more precociously—for the child.

In addition, the mythologists leave us in suspense when it comes to knowing *what precisely* the mythic code is expected to "treat." "An anxiety," says Lévi-Strauss. A situation?

My answer, it will have been intuited, is that mytho-symbolic scenarios have as their principal function allowing the child arriving in the (human) world to deal with the enigmatic messages emanating from the adult other. To attain greater clarity, it would still be imperative to work ourselves clear of the two obstacles bequeathed to us by mythology and mythologists: focusing on already elaborated versions of mythical narratives, without dealing with how the myth is transmitted or "passed" to the child; focusing on ethnographic myths (even if they be those of Greece), without raising the question of formations and scenarios that, *in our own time* and *in the West*, embody the mytho-symbolic function. Psychoanalysis has perhaps blinded us on this last point by attempting to impose as sole and unique contemporary myth simplified versions, issuing from Freudian (and later Lacanian) phallocentrism.

I will summarize things in a few formulae: beyond the numerous derivative and secondary hermeneutics, the only *practitioner of fun-*

---

305 From this point of view, Merleau-Ponty's reassessment of the contribution of the culturalists (M. Mead and Kardiner) is quite exciting and deserves to be taken into consideration: "For M. Mead: the Oedipal situation described by Freud is but a particular situation of a universal problem. What is universal is a specific problem posed to all societies by the existence of parents and children. *The universal fact* is that there are children who start out being *weak and small, even as they interact quite closely with adult life*, etc." (*Cours de psychologie de l'enfant*, 1963–1964, in *Bulletin de psychologie*, no. 236 [November 1964]: 120). What is missing, of course, is the notion of the message and translation.

damental hermeneutics is the human being; the primordial hermeneut is the little human being. What is given him to make sense of is not a situation, not even a being in situation as Heidegger would have it; it is sequences that are presented as already having meaning—what I call, in a general way, messages from adults.

The attempts at translation dispatched in order to deal with those messages do not, for their part, start from nothing either.[306] Among the codes that the child finds in his reach is what I call the mytho-symbolic, which is of cultural origin and transmitted by the adult world.

Repression, as I conceive it, is not translation, but, on the contrary, the necessary failures of translation in the face of the intrusion of the sexual-enigmatic in the messages emanating from the adult. It is thus wrong, if one is prepared to follow me, to designate myth as a *formation of the unconscious* on the same basis as a dream or symptom and attempt to derive them from an individual unconscious. Myth, as Freud well said, does not bear the mark of censorship. Even more, for my part, I would situate myth as necessarily on the side of the censor. Far from being sexual, a mythosymbolic formation is what is proposed in order to frame, bind, and ultimately repress the sexual. What, finally, could be less sexual than Sophocles' tragedy?

This brings me back, as a finale, to the question of the unconscious. I have maintained for a very long time the so-called realist conception proposed as far back as 1959 with Serge Leclaire: the unconscious is not a hidden meaning to be deciphered, with more or less difficulty, behind the conscious-preconscious "text" of our words and deeds. The unconscious, in the sense of the repressed, consists in signifiers (which are not primordially verbal) that have been excluded, isolated, and stripped of meaning in the course of repression-translation.

---

306 Gadamer insisted vigorously on this point: there is no hermeneutic that emerges out of nothing, without there being at its disposition preconceptions, expectations of meaning, prejudices, keys. For a summary of this position, see J. Grondin, *L'universalité de l'herméneutique*, Epiméthée (Paris: PUF, 1993), pp. 167–71.

At that time, this conception was pitted against another position—that of Politzer—according to which the latency of the unconscious, an implicit presence, was of the same order as the rules of the game in a tennis match. It should be said that Politzer's conception, far from being abandoned, is one that has flourished almost universally in the psychoanalytic environment. That conception, which can be called "hermeneutical" in a broad sense, is, in fact, the only one that a Lévi-Strauss deemed worthy of consideration.[307]

Here however, I insist on adding that the conception of the individual repressed unconscious, as I maintain, does not at all exclude having to take into consideration, alongside it, the notion of the *implicit*: the very notion that many authors unduly substitute for the Freudian unconscious.

Whatever conception one holds of the superimposition of different codes in a mythic scenario, whether or not one accepts a hierarchy of their levels, it is nonetheless the case that a place should be accorded . . . not to an *other* unconscious, but to another kind of latency, the one that exists notably in collective cultural productions. That latency is on the order of the implicit; reading it entails a movement of clarification or rendering explicit (*Auslegung*), an endeavor that does not demand the overcoming of resistances.

To radically distinguish those two modalities of latency is simultaneously to articulate them in relation to each other: the repressed unconscious is precisely what escapes, what escaped, the encoding whose modalities are proposed to the individual by culture. The implicitly latent, unlike the individual unconscious, has no site— and no id.

But it is here that it would behoove us to distinguish, as I proposed at the beginning, the properly collective level of myth and the derivative level of the "story" (or narrative) of the individual. It

---

307 In point of fact, Lévi-Strauss, when considering Freud's thought, refers solely to texts dating from after the discovery of symbolism.

is with such storytelling that, from the outset, we are confronted in therapy. To render the plot more explicit is one thing; to break its shell, by way of the properly associative method, springs from an inverse movement. To be sure, the analysis of a neurotic subject (as Freud indicates through a comparison with chemistry) is always situated between two or several psychosyntheses, each as ineluctable and spontaneous as the other. Every case finds itself endlessly oscillating between the synthetic dimension—which is, properly speaking, psychotherapeutic—and the dimension of unbinding—which, properly speaking, is analytic. The correct proportion to be attributed to each is certainly a function of the psychopathological assessment of each particular case. But that in turn must be based on a metapsychology of the apparatus of the soul whose ambition, among others, is to account for the story-telling—or casting as narrative—of the human being.

To conclude. I have been intent on opposing two levels of theory and showing how, as part of psychoanalytic thought, it is not for us to endorse the mytho-symbolic assemblages used by the human being in the translations he produces of messages emanating from the other and theorizations he bestows on himself.

Is psychoanalytic theory properly speaking, as a model elaborated at a distance from the facts, amenable to falsification, refutation, and confrontation with analytic and extra-analytic experience? I leave the question open, hoping that it has at least been clarified by the extrication, in relation to mythical thinking, of a metapsychology whose *meta*position is not only affirmed but grounded in the extent to which it gives itself the means of accounting for the function of mythic constructions in the constitution of the human being. In that sense, metapsychology itself ends up being expanded into an indispensable meta-anthropology.

XII
Narrativity and Hermeneutics:
A Few Propositions

I, 1

By "narrativity," we understand an approach to the human being that gives primary importance to the way in which each person formulates his existence for himself in the form of a more or less coherent tale. Narrativity is a category that can be applied to human groups in relation to their history as a group, but narrativity is of interest to psychoanalysis as an account of an individual's history.

The category of narrativity is closely connected to the way in which the human being temporalizes himself as well as to the notion of après-coup. In psychoanalysis and in psychopathology the tendency is to privilege a posteriori accounts: life histories, stories of illness and treatment—this as a function of the clinical situation, which is, as if by definition, retrospective. But narration does not exclude the telling of a life project.

From the theoretical point of view, a large part of Paul Ricoeur's work is devoted to the presuppositions, modalities, and implications of narrativity.[308]

Revue française de psychanalyse, 3 (1998).

308 Specifically: *Temps et récit*, 3 vols. (Paris: Seuil, 1991).

From the point of view of analytic practice, the narrative attitude consists in favoring—in relation to a remembrance or a genuine
reconstruction of the past—the construction of a coherent, satisfying,
and integrated account. The principal authors who have invoked this
point of view (Viderman-Spence-Schafer) stress the importance of
narrativization as the motor of analytic treatment, the joint creation of
the analysand and the analyst.

I, 2

The narrativist point of view clashes from the outset with the critique of relativism (and even of "creationism") it presupposes: the
story would be a creation (ultimately by partners) that would not be
expected to refer to any reality at all.

As with every "relativism," a "strong" and a "weak" version
may be distinguished.

The "strong" version finds one of its clearest formulations in
this sentence of Viderman: "It's not important what Leonardo *saw*
(dream or memory); it's not important what Leonardo *said* (vulture
or kite)—what matters is that the analyst, without consideration for
reality, adjusts and assembles these materials to construct a coherent
whole that does not reproduce a preexisting fantasy in the subject's
unconscious, but makes it exist by saying it."[309]

Comparable formulations may be found in Spence and in
Schafer.

The "weak" version ultimately consists in referring the alleged
creativity of the narrator back to fundamental preexisting structures to
be found as virtualities in the analysand or as theories in the analyst.
For this weak version, Viderman invokes "primal fantasies,"[310] while
Schafer invokes "narrative structures" or organizing "scenarios," such
as the Oedipus complex. These constitute "brilliant narrative strate-

---

309 S. Viderman, *La construction de l'espace analytique* (Paris: Denoël, 1970), p. 164.
310 "La bouteille à la mer," *RFP* 28, nos. 2–3 (1974), specifically, note 354; also p. 330.

gies" sufficient unto themselves and outside any historical reference.

A recent example of the narrativist attitude is furnished by the fate of Margaret Mahler's theory of *symbiosis*. That author, as is known, believed she could infer, on the basis of the clinical observation of psychotic "symbiotic" states, the prior existence of a normal symbiotic phase that every child would have the task of surmounting through a process of "separation-individuation." That theory, which was largely reduced to rubble by the observation of children (Brazelton-Stern-Dornes), found salvation in a narrativist reinterpretation: according to Baumgart,[311] the notion of symbiosis would retain its full value as a "narrative scheme" allowing one to furnish a coherent retrospective account to certain subjects.

One may wonder whether such conceptions do anything other than resuscitate the idea of "retroactive fantasies," which Jung pressed into service against Freud.

I, 3

The theses of the narrativists ran into another critique, which was no less pertinent. Claiming to put the accent on "narrative truth" at the expense of "historical truth," they were led to caricaturize the latter in a way no empiricist would defend. M. Dayan has clearly shown that Viderman remained prisoner of a naive opposition between a pure imaginary, called fantasy, and reality understood as an absolutely objective event in no way revised by memory. The same critique is addressed to Spence by Sass and Woolfolk;[312] Spence compares historical truth to a photograph and assumes, in the manner of Hume, the archaic experience is composed of raw "sensations," a chronologi-

---

311 M. Baumgart, "Die psychoanalytische Metapsychologie im Lichte der Saüglingsforschung: Verwerfen oder überdenken?" in F. Pedrina et al., *Spielraümebegegnungen zwischen Kinder- und Erwachsenenanalyse* (Tübingen: Diskord (1994) pp. 51–82.
312 Louis Sass and Robert L. Woolfolk, "Psychoanalysis and the Hermeneutic Turn: A Critique of Narrative Truth and Historical Truth," *Journal of the American Psychoanalytic Association* 36, no. 2 (1988): 429–53.

cal sequence of atomized facts without any addition of meaning and about which one might therefore give a neutral account. A conception of primal experiences that no philosophers and no psychologists would consider advocating.[313]

II

That last critique, when formulated by supporters of the "hermeneutic turn" in psychoanalysis, allows one to raise the narrativity/hermeneutics question. It is certain that hermeneutics, taken in the broad sense of a theory of interpretation, clarification, or the bestowal of meaning, possesses a number of points in common with narrativism. But, on another score, hermeneutics of a Heideggerian inspiration has taken a decisive step in relation to the narrativists. For Heidegger, interpretation situates itself as secondary, as a rendering explicit (*Auslegung*) in relation to a primal moment of *Verstehen*, which can be understood as a protocomprehension or the way in which being-there (*Dasein*) gives a meaning to its initial situation, to its thrownness (*Geworfenheit*). What is more, certain texts of Heidegger do not contradict the idea that such protocomprehension is the realm of the very small child.[314]

Thus it is that, for psychoanalysts inclined to invoke Heidegger against the relativism of Viderman, Spence, and Schafer, interpretation would be founded, in the last analysis, on a "prereflective" experience that is itself "patterned and full of meaning." "The primal goal of the psychoanalytic dialogue would be to construct a pattern similar to a prior pattern."[315]

---

313 One may find the obsolescence of such theses amusing when one recalls that Maurice Halbwachs's work, *Les cadres sociaux de la mémoire*, dates from 1925 and that one of his major chapters is titled "La reconstruction du passé." Merleau-Ponty's *Phénoménologie de la perception* dates from 1945.
314 *Das frühzeitliche und frühmenschliche Dasein*, in Heidegger, *Gesammelte Ausgabe*, 27: 123. Reference graciously supplied by Professor Jean Greisch.
315 Sass and Woolfolk, "Psychoanalysis and the Hermeneutic Turn," p. 445.

III

Once that decisive advance, as formulated by Heidegger, is accepted, numerous questions remain open to criticism:

- What is it that is to be interpreted, i.e., made into the object of narrativization?
- What are the instruments of such narrativization?
- What are the results of narrativization, particularly in meta-psychological terms?
- What is the function of analytic practice in relation to narrativization?

III, 1

The object of protocomprehension can never be a "natural," unmodified event. Meaning can be bestowed only on what already carries meaning. But here our objection addressed to Spence and Viderman (that they are pitting a narrativity charged with meaning against a raw given) risks leading to an infinite regress. As we see it, that regress can only be blocked if one takes into account the intervention of the other. What is called for is an affirmation that protocomprehension does not bear on a fact but on a *message*. Hermeneutics is thus primarily a hermeneutics of the message. Correlatively, we prefer to describe that process—the transition from a message to its comprehension—with the term that befits it: *translation*. A translation that is not necessarily interlingual, but possibly intersemiotic (Jakobson). Concretely, in the earliest situations encountered by the child, these messages are those addressed to the child by adults.

III, 2

The *instruments* of protocomprehension or of the first translations are the narrative structures, codes, and myths presented to the child by the social world.

In this regard, one may contest the idea that the translational code would be, purely and simply, the verbal language of the adult world. Linguistic structures, as much by their generality (involving a single vernacular language) as by the often considerable structural differences from one to the other, are incapable of accounting for the specificity of the narrative codes presented to the child. On the one hand, those codes are approached by ethnology and, on the other, by psychoanalysis itself, which has compiled a partial inventory under the rubrics of major complexes (so called), "primal fantasies," "infantile sexual theories," "family romances," etc.

The value of such codes as "knowledge" is nonexistent, whereas their potential for binding and endowing with form is undeniable. They belong to the domain of ideology.

III, 3

In order to appreciate the consequences of such prototranslation for *metapsychology*, we should take into account the fact that the first messages emanating from the adult are compromised by sexuality, and, in that sense, enigmatic. And, to that extent, translation has as its necessary counterpart the failure of translation, which is repression. The constitution of the psychical apparatus, ego and id, is to be situated in relation to the misadventures of primal translation.[316]

III, 4

One cannot situate "narrativization" into the framework of analysis without taking into account that its function is, first of all, defensive. In the example of dreams Freud called attention to that function by designating it as "secondary elaboration" or the "considerations of representability." Whether it be a matter of an ultimately "normal" (and in any event inevitable) defense and whether "narrativization"

---

316 See *Nouveaux fondements pour la psychanalyse.*

need be correlated with the psychotherapeutic aspect of all analyses do not in any way modify the metapsychological assessment that sees in it the warrant and seal of repression.

This is tantamount to saying that the properly "analytic" vector, that of "*de*translation," and the calling into question of narrative structures, along with the ideals linked to them, remains opposed in analytic treatment to the vector of reconstruction, synthesis, and narrative.

XIII
Sublimation and/or Inspiration

Is sublimation still a useful and usable concept—one still in use? This is how Pontalis and I concluded our reflections on the subject in 1967: "In the psychoanalytic literature the concept of sublimation is frequently called upon. The idea is indeed the index of a basic need, an exigency, of Freudian doctrine and it is hard to see how it could be dispensed with. The lack of a coherent theory of sublimation remains one of the lacunae in psychoanalytic thought."

Can we still say the same thing? Is there in sublimation a need or an exigency one cannot do without? We may wonder whether the "index," the imperious indication of having to keep the question open, has not become a mere obligatory but vague reference, to which one occasionally pays reverence, but without entailing either a precise use or affirming any metapsychological conception. We know, moreover, Freud himself abandoned or destroyed the essay devoted to sublimation that was slated to be included in his metapsychological writings.

The word has not been abandoned. But the notion, for its part, remains subject to reservations when it is not simply deserted! One may give several illustrations.

Talk given at the University of Athens on January 14, 1999, and at the Soirées de l'APF on January 21, 1999

It is extremely rare for sublimation to play a role in our reflections or debates concerning clinical work. There is a major reason for that, which, following Freud, might be named the "Red Cross reason." In wartime the Red Cross, which was supposed to warn off bombardiers, would instead be taken as a sign that the enemy had taken refuge in the ambulance in order to camouflage himself. "Don't shoot at the ambulance" is not an analytic precept, and properly so. There is no rule that, at the beginning of an analysis, sublimations are to be kept separate, as though respectable and not to be touched. At a practical level, in therapy, when it comes to determining what to analyze, we hardly make a distinction between sublimation and symptom. That decision to analyze everything, without respect or reservation, would be a transposition of Montfort's notorious order: "Kill them all. God will recognize his own," becomes "Analyze everything. Sublimation will recognize its own." As for the end of analysis, if we are occasionally tempted by a Balint-like euphoria of a "new beginning," it is counterbalanced by the rule of refusal that enjoins us to analyze up to the last instant, leaving open, so to speak, the wound of analysis.

Need we then think that sublimation is a concept above all to be consigned to so-called *applied* psychoanalysis? There are good reasons why the most important text dealing with sublimation is Freud's *Leonardo*, with all the elaborations it has received from (among others) Eissler or Maidani-Gérard. But it is precisely the fact that, despite all that the latter did to link the notebooks of Leonardo to the network of associations encountered in treatment, a distance remains. Might it then be said that sublimation would constitute a hindrance when we are engaged in clinical practice, but that the embarrassment or inhibition is diminished when we are alone, without responsibilities, putting a historical personage on the couch?

A third series of questions would be linked to the term *sublime*. Freud, as is known, adopts it in his fashion while defining the alchemy that leads the drive to sublimate itself, as subordination to

254

"socially valued" goals. A definition by way of the "social" that introduces an entire field of reflection, since it cannot be regarded, coming as it does from Freud, as secondary or extrinsic to the process itself. To be sure, that "social adaptation" can be subject to all sorts of restrictions. Thus it is that Lagache, in his text on "Sublimation and Values," shows that the values envisaged by sublimation are not necessarily those of a more or less conformist consensus: they can also be those of a limited or marginal group, a mafia or gang of delinquents. In an adjacent realm of ideas, my attention has frequently been drawn to the somewhat elitist character that is invariably the stamp of our examples of sublimation. Why is it always the painter or the researcher, rather than the lathe operator, the golfer, or the individual who cultivates his garden? And what are we to say of the individual fascinated by surfing the Web?

But the question of the "social" should not be reduced to individual cases. Freud, and along with him some of the dinosaurs of our profession, did not recoil from the ambition of associating sublimation with the genesis of social phenomena in their generality: the genesis of language, following the works of the linguist Sperber; the genesis of social activity, as it emerges from the major meta-anthropological texts of Freud.

As for how the debate crystallized, at a time of the joint (but antagonistic) blossoming of psychoanalytic anthropology and Freudo-Marxism, I cannot resist giving an example, in the form of a brief quotation from Wilhelm Reich recounting a discussion he had with Géza Roheim[317]:

> We talked with Roheim of the interpretation of symbols and, in the same vein, of the psychoanalytic interpreta-

---

317 Wilhelm Reich, "L'effondrement de la morale sexuelle" (1932), quoted in E. Bornemann, *Psychanalyse de l'argent* (Paris: PUF, 1978), p. 65. In English: "Psychoanalysis of Primitive Cultures," in *The Invasion of Compulsory Sex-Morality* (New York: Farrar, Straus and Giroux, 1971), pp. 182–83.

tion of the origin of tools. I maintained that the axe was originally created for rational motives, to split wood more easily, and that, *secondarily*, it might acquire a symbolic value, but it absolutely was not *necessary that it do so*. A tree or a stick *might* signify a phallus in a dream, but it *did not necessarily have this meaning* .... Roheim's position was, on the contrary, that the ax symbolizes the penis and had been invented as a symbol, that the rational function was secondary.

In sum, on Roheim's side, the sexual drive was at the very origin of civilization, so that civilization in its entirety could be listed under the heading of *sublimation*. For Reich, civilization had an autonomous collective origin, which, for purposes of sublimation, the individual reused in a contingent manner by way of symbolization.

Is this debate obsolete? The mere term *Freudo-Marxism* might lead one to think so. After all, sociology and social anthropology have continued to evolve quite remarkably without becoming subservient to either Marxism or psychoanalysis. I shall thus lay aside Freud's deliberately modest term *socially valued* as an open question in the hope of reworking it.

Sublimation is a term bearing the mark of *metapsychology* and, more precisely, of the *theory of drives*. That too is perhaps not quite attuned to the current mood of psychoanalysis.

I mean that frequently we believe we can discuss a case or many other things that are not cases—certain cultural phenomena, for example—without asking ourselves whether we minimally agree as to what fundamentally *moves* human beings. I do not doubt that each of us has forged for himself a rather precise idea of what he calls the death drive—whether it be to accept, refute, or interpret it. But is lack of clarity a matter of politeness, of skepticism regarding all theory, of the "analytic attitude" transposed to a courteous exchange of ideas between colleagues? In these discussions theory seems to be scattered about in barbed remarks

There is a difference, to be sure, with the way things were in Freud's day. In those days, one was assuredly not "postmodern." A scientific "paradigm" was not considered something to be chosen arbitrarily from an entire gamut of possibilities. And yet Freud's almost uncompromising metapsychological rigor needs be articulated with an evolution that may be disconcerting: are you of the first, second, or third drive theory? Of the first or second topographical model? It is there that considerations of structure and evolution need be articulated carefully, unless one is prepared to consider psychoanalysis, as some have done, a tool for asserting everything and its opposite.

Let us take a precise, but central, example: that of relations of "tenderness." At the core of the first drive theory, where the sexual is opposed to the well-defined domain of "self-preservation," it is with the latter that the "tender current" is associated, one that binds the child to the mother and, later on, to other individuals. This tender current is opposed to the sexual or "sensual" current. One might, in a specific way, associate it with Balint's "primary object-love." On the other hand, in the second drive theory, tenderness is derived from sexuality, precisely by way of "aim inhibition" and "sublimation." And yet it would be out of the question to content ourselves with noting a simple contradiction in Freud's thought without asking whether other theoretical elements have not, in the meanwhile, changed place. And specifically whether the "sexual" of the first theory is indeed identical to the Eros of the second one.

The question of the dualism of the drives, of the two dualisms, is thus fundamental. In order to find our bearings in relation to it, let us start out from an apparently polemical point: the accusation of "pansexualism," against which Freud endlessly defended himself. Pansexualism, if asserted in radical fashion, destroys the very idea of sublimation. If "everything is sexual," the only thing at stake in psychoanalysis is tracking down the way in which the sexual manages to camouflage or translate itself under other guises.

But, at the same time, the question undergoes a reversal. If "everything is sexual," the word *sexual* is no more than a faded label, libido becomes the equivalent of more neutral terms, such as *energy, psychical energy,* etc. This is a debate that preoccupied the intellectual world at a time of multiple resistances to the Freudian sexual. The debate was with Jung, but also, in France, with Claparède, Pichon, Laforgue, and many others. The temptation remains constant, even if the narrowly energetic aspect of the discussion has become obsolete. Thus the omnipresence—which at present is accepted virtually without discussion—of the always more or less desexualized notion of "object relations."

Freud always argued against pansexualism, using the following assertion: "In psychoanalysis, the sexual is not everything." This was his way of maintaining the specificity of the sexual, in the strict sense. The problem is that what is *not* sexual takes two quite heterogeneous forms in what is called the "two theories of drives":

- sexuality / self-preservation
- Eros / the death drive

Freud himself frequently described this development, noting, between the two, a transitory monist phase of an "apparent rallying to the views of Jung": A phase in which self-preservation is absorbed into sexuality (under the heading of the sexual investment of the ego, narcissism) at a time when the death drive has not yet appeared.

Beyond this excessively schematic reminder, what is important is that these two dualisms are extremely different in the context of our practice, the one in no way being a substitute for the other.

The first dualism posits, with self-preservation, a genuine exterior, both in relation to sexuality and in relation to the analytic situation.

The second puts on stage a far more inseparable couple, life drives—death drives. Like the two faces of a single coin, the pair advance in step: in life, in therapy, in theory.

In theory Eros and the death drive are presented above all as two great principles of binding/unbinding and are thus correlated. This is confirmed by the fact that Freud always refused to assign an energy specific to the death drive, which suggests that it is indeed *a single and selfsame libido* that is, depending on circumstances, bound or unbound.

I am convinced that the succession of the two dualisms in Freud is in no way the substitution of one system for another less valid one. It has its counterpart in the reality of the human being. The evolution from one to the other corresponds to a genesis, at the point of transition between two successive states or positions, corresponding, perhaps, to what is called the transition from "nature to culture."

How is the life drive/death drive dualism to be assimilated?

First of all, it is a dualism internal to sexuality itself. I have long insisted on this: we should speak of "sexual death drives." The death drive reclaims as its own what Freud initially considered to be the most irreconcilable aspect of sexuality: Lucifer-Amor. It is not by chance that during the same phase of childhood in which Freud places autoerotism Melanie Klein sees sadism at its peak. My hypothesis is that each of them is seeing *one and the same thing* under two different headings: the anarchic and indomitable character of sexuality. The life drive, for its part, corresponds to the most bound aspects of the sexual: bound to the object and bound to the ego-object. Concerning those two forms of the sexual, I have proposed the terms *index drive* and *object drive*—I may come back to this point.

The question might thus be posed as follows: analytic treatment leads us to press considerations of timeliness, material interest, and ultimately survival, to their outer limits, even beyond their frame. If a patient is late, analysis excludes from the field of interpretation train timetables or the strikes of train workers, except insofar as they can be seen to be mediated or invested by the sexual or narcissistic interests of the patient. On the theoretical level, we say that Eros— the Eros of narcissism—adopts the interests of self-preservation for its own ends. Ultimately, the patient is late or on time as a function of his sexual investment, in life or death. Or to put things less paradoxically, he "associates" to these unforeseeable complications only to the extent that he is invested in them. If he is not invested in them, they will remain outside the frame of analysis.

I realize that this brief account is schematic, but at least it helps me raise this question: did the second dualism really come to be substituted for the first, Eros having completely colonized self-preservation? Can this point of view, which is that of analytic practice, be equally well transposed to a general metapsychological consideration of the human being? Has Eros, in man, completely taken over the domain of self-preservation in the same way as may be observed in the evolution of Freud's thought?

And if we admit that this situation, would not the very notion of a genesis, a kind of "pansexualism in the act," oblige us to suppose that this genesis, this colonization, also occurs in the human being? This would imply that, in the reality of human existence, the first dualism would exist before the second and constitute its foundation.

For humans, at the beginning of life and subsisting later on, is there anything on the order of nonsexual tendencies and, to be blunt, of instincts? On this question, I have no certainties, and my thinking continues to waver. I can only give some notes on the trajectory of my thought.

First of all, a complete reevaluation of the term *self-preservation* is in order. It is an abstraction that presupposes an individual faced with an inanimate universe who survives autonomously. This is the system with which Freud's "Project for a Scientific Psychology" starts, a system that is only valid for inferior organisms, only up to and including fish. This sort of homeostatic self-preservation was largely transcended in the evolution of species. The vital subsistence of a large number of species, notably mammals, is integrated into the sphere of communication, notably between mother and child, a sphere that since Bowlby has been called attachment. The current reemergence of that notion is due to observational studies both of animals and of small children, whose precocious capacity for interaction had long been underestimated.

The existence of primal (or at least extremely precocious) relations between the baby and the environment has restored currency to Balint's idea of "primary object-love," concerning which, however, we should emphatically emphasize the fact that is not situated on the sexual level.

From my point of view, to situate clearly the notion of enigmatic message—which is the starting point of the sexual drive—it is necessary to posit a basic nonsexual communication between mother and child, a kind of nonsexual carrier-wave that would be modulated, or more precisely parasitized, by adult sexuality. On the foundation of reciprocal communication, something happens that is vectored from just one side.

So much for the child; but for the adult as well, one must maintain the original self-preservative pole, if only virtually, and even if it is largely covered over and reinvested by narcissism. To give an example that I cannot develop, in a *psychology* of aggressiveness, alongside sadistic destructiveness and narcissistic rivalry, it is hardly possible "to neglect a third factor which, following Denise van Caneghem, can be named "combativeness."

Once again, in man, this "vital order"--or "animal" level in the strict sense of that term--remains a virtual level in exactly the same way as the first drive theory remains a virtual presence within the second.

Having mentioned the uncertainties and questions opened up by the modern renewal of attachment theory, I return to our subject: a possible mutation of the drive—what is called "sublimation." Now, once we consider that in the human being opposition between sexual death drives and sexual life drives, or, more precisely, the opposition between binding and unbinding, comes to cover over the basic animal terrain, we are confronted with a strange paradox.

Under the heading of binding, Eros has, so to speak, taken self-preservation into its own hands. The human being takes sustenance and does combat not in order to survive but, ultimately, out of love for the ego or hatred for the ego of the other. In addition, Thanatos, the sexual drive that has been unchained, has assumed the pole of the irreconcilable, that of the sexual in Freud's original sense of the term.

This sort of reversal, an inversion of polarities and meanings, has a consequence that is more than unexpected from the perspective of sublimation. If indeed it is the ego, the principal agent of Eros, that takes charge of vital interests, and if, as Freud says, the ego's energy is "desexualized and sublimated," then sublimation, the mutation of the drive with regard to its aims and objects, will appear (in truth, just like the transference) as the transposition of the sexual energy of death into the sexual energy of life, as the domestication and binding of a drive that is anarchic and destructive in its origins. This conception (and I will insist on this) entails firmly grasping that in Freud's second vision Eros, the demiurge intent on creating increasingly large units, no longer has anything to do with the fragmentary and fragmenting sexuality of *Three Essays*.

"Wo Es war, soll Ich werden"

Once one fully understands that the core of the id is the sexual death drive, this formula might be transposed as follows: There where the sexual death drive was, Eros, the life drive, must come to be.

The fact that Freud adds that what is at stake is a "cultural endeavor comparable to the draining of the Zuyder Zee" tells us explicitly that the *entirety of the psychical process* that can be called binding can ultimately be assimilated to the domain previously called sublimation. I will clarify my position by indicating several landmarks.

1. Sublimation was classically assimilated (so to speak) to a kind of treatment of pregenital residues of genitalization. I will quote a few lines of Freud from "On the Transformations of Instinct as Exemplified in Anal Erotism": "From that moment we had to face the problem of

the later history of the anal-erotic instinctual impulses. What becomes of them when, owing to the establishment of a definitive genital organization, they have lost their importance in sexual life?"[318] We know that Freud consistently asserted that sublimation as a vicissitude was first of all that of the unintegrated residues of pregenital drives.

But as soon as we subsume that "genitalization" under the general heading of processes of binding, it loses its privilege, its uniqueness in relation to the general movement of acculturation and, need we say, of desexualization. I risk shocking my reader by continuing to assert that the Oedipus complex is profoundly nonsexual and an agent of desexualization. The "legend of the conqueror," with its elimination of the father and marriage with the mother, relegates to recesses barely visible an orgasmic sexuality one can do little more than suspect in the intercourse with Jocasta, the mother, and the ecstatic murder of Laius, the father.

As for matters of daily life, let us approach the "genital relation," and do so in all its forms—from "mad love" to the marriage "for love," which becomes a "sensible" marriage—from ephemeral unions to commitment to a shared creative existence—from childless union to family destiny. The forms are rich and innumerable, but how are we to assert that we are dealing solely, or even principally, with forms of "sexual life?" The sexual aspects of these forms, sexuality properly speaking in the sense of the *Three Essays*, whether genital or paragenital, quantitatively represent no more than a small part of each form, and these sexual aspects are invariably qualitatively integrated into a relation that exceeds them, whether social or asocial matters little. One could rightly refer to all these forms of genitality as *modes of sublimation* of sexuality. "Tenderness," about which we spoke earlier, is but one aspect among others.

2. A second point is that in all these forms of *life* (taking the word in the sense of life drives, Eros), what again and again come to be

---

318 *SE* 17:127.

bound are the multiple components of the sexual death drive, sadism and masochism. I will return in a moment to the central meaning of anality from this point of view. It is, in any event, no accident that most examples of sublimation, notably the professions, refer to the integration of aggressiveness. The paradigm of the surgeon remains central: handling of the scalpel is mastered, bound, integrated into a scenario or rather into a multitude of short stories in which technique combines with the medical and even with "solicitude" for the human case.

3. Finally, my third point is to note how much the element Freud calls "social valuing" changes. While initially it had been a factor added on, with the idea of a *cultural process* it becomes something intrinsic to the very process of binding.

We should emphasize that this does not mean placing ourselves in a position of approbation with regard to a specific culture, nor (inversely) are we rallying to cultural relativism. But that reservation deserves an explanation, which I will give using a brief review of modes of binding by the ego. We can categorize the synthetic action of the ego into two rather different types. According to a first mode, which might be called *Gestaltist*, the ego imposes unity on what is diverse and anarchic in the drive by way of the ego's unitary and specular form. This type of binding is eminently narcissistic and, as such, rather crude. The ego unifies what is diverse either directly or through simple term-to-term opposition. We rediscover here the character traits (stubbornness, orderliness, thriftiness) Freud invokes and privileges in the case of anal eroticism. The character trait of stubbornness is the direct descendant of anal aggression, through blockage, steadfastness, and generalization. The traits of cleanliness and orderliness are presented as reaction formations, that is, as the reverse image, as in a mirror, of an interest in excrement. As for thriftiness, its derivation touches on the complex problem of exchange, which will be taken up again by Freud in "On Transpositions of Instinct as Exemplified in Anal-Erotism." Here what I want to emphasize is that character formations activate a simple (and even simplistic) type of binding, one that is narcissistic and only minimally inserted into networks of meanings.

The other mode of binding, however, is accomplished by way of symbolic connections. I have proposed the idea that the binding of the enigmatic message coming from the other is accomplished on the model of a translation, thanks to elaborate or elementary codes furnished to the child by his surroundings. That translation is not only a matter of first messages and primal acts of repression. Throughout childhood (and, we should add, throughout a psychoanalysis), there are episodes of detranslation and retranslation, governed by après-coup. In contrast with the stupidity of the narcissistic-Gestaltist type of binding, in which a unifying totality is imposed without mediation, there is the complexity of symbolizing links and symbolic systems in which—if one needs philosophical point of reference—object and concept are necessarily correlated with scenarios, propositions, and judgments. I lack the time to demonstrate—I shall merely assert—that the ego's two modes of binding are nonetheless complementary and associated. Thus mytho-symbolic codes can be invested like narcissistic objects and, inversely, the narcissistic investment of distinct forms causes objects to clump together, so to speak, in the course of scenarios proposed to the subject. To illustrate this with a famous example, there is no Hannibal or identification with Hannibal without the legend of Hannibal. But there is no legend of Hannibal without the ego, in specular fashion, splitting off and annexing the character into the ego's own story.

"On Transpositions in Instinct as Exemplified in Anal Erotism,"[319] a text I have already mentioned, proposes an intersection between symbolization and sublimation. In this article we see mutations of the drive, its object and—necessarily--its aim, under the sign of the *part object*. Let us say immediately that if one were

---

319 *SE* 17:126.

to characterize this moment of binding of the drive, one would have to speak of *exchange*, an exchange in which the anal object remains a special, if essential, case. (The error would be to consider anality as a stage, whereas it is present from the very first days.)[320] Let us recall that extraordinary quadrilateral or pentagon Freud sketches in his article, with its paths of internal communication and also of escape. Its four poles are excrement, the penis, the child, and the gift, to which is added the man-object, which indicates to us that on this occasion Freud is centering his reflection on the drive in women. There is thus a polygon of exchanges on the basis of equivalence. Freud has a great deal of difficulty founding this exchange value at the empirical level, searching for what he calls the *tertium comparationis*. Thus it is that the element characterized as "the little one" barely holds up as soon as one wonders (as has been done since the Socratics): "little in relation to what?" All this to allow the intuition that the exchange cannot easily be deduced empirically, not even the exchange of the excrement-gift for a parental recompense.

In point of fact, after Mauss and Lévi-Strauss, we might be led to consider exchange as the symbolic system that *holds* the quadrilateral *together*. But with Marcel Mauss in particular, the idea emerges as well that the generalized, reciprocal, abstract exchange that Freud seems to take as his point of reference is only one among other possible codes. Mauss, for example, draws our attention to systems in which the object exchanged nonetheless remains attached to the giver, and possibly to the creator. This clock remains forever the one given by a specific friend, Pierre's clock; this painting, were it to change hands and owners a hundred times, remains a painting by Picasso. Freud, it is true, seems to reject the link of the work to the author, of speech to the person uttering it, even of the penis to the man bearing it. We are aware of a particularly violent sentence in the text: "We can

---

320 But not, during the earliest days, in the form of the fecal mass. [Here the French is *bâton fécal*—*bâton* literally means "stick," "club," "cudgel," or the like.]

say what the ultimate outcome of the infantile wish for a penis is . . . it changes into the wish for a man, and thus puts up with the man as an appendage to the penis." The man is the "little thing" of the penis, as the penis is the "little thing" of the man. One could not go any further in the direction of an "exchangist" system—whether the term be understood in an economic or a sexual sense.

These several reflections cannot convey the richness of this text and the veritable intersection that it represents. Its subject is the birth of the part object.[321]

A further remarkable feature of this pentagon: aggressiveness is absent from it, or at least carefully controlled. On the subject of the transitions and mutations between death drive and life drive, Green has formulated the notion of an "objectalizing function—deobjectalizing function." It is an idea that demands to be reworked: the term *function* seems to me quite unjustified in its functionalist connotation. On the other hand, nothing forbids us from recognizing an objectalizing impulse (aimed at the part object) and its deobjectalizing inverse (aimed at the unconscious sign or pure *designified signifier*). This on the condition that it be clearly indicated that "deobjectalization" *is in no way a disinvestment or decathexis*, but a *different* investment, the investments of signs as sources of the drive; essentially sources of the death drive, which, precisely, reduces the object to a pure sign.

At this point I will quote a brief anecdote. A small boy, at the age when he is losing his baby teeth, is accustomed to placing his tooth in a little box beneath his pillow. During the night the tooth fairy comes to exchange the tooth for a gift. Upon awakening, then, there he is sliding his hand beneath the pillow, feeling around . . . he encounters a small piece of paper. Convinced that it is a letter informing him that he has been too naughty to receive a present, he bursts into tears. He will be only partially consoled by his mother, who shows him that the little paper is paper money (*un billet*).

---

321 With one absent element: the breast—concerning which a number of hypotheses might be formulated.

Why this change from good to bad, from gift to punishment? I will risk a hypothesis, suggested by the very word *billet*, which in French can mean both a note of reprimand and a bank note. At both extremities that frame the partial or part object of the gift, we encounter the pure signifier: on one side, the unconscious signifier, still linked to a certain internal attack (and we know that, when confronting the unconscious, no one is innocent), but on the other side, beyond the personal gift from the tooth fairy, we rediscover the pure signifier, as monetary sign the object-money, which becomes a nonobject (Marx used to say that money as a commodity is a noncommodity). I am, in this way, emphasizing this passage from sign to part object and also, with Freud, emphasizing the circulation of part objects as determinants in the movement of symbolization. The fact that sublimation has the most intimate relations with the part object, that the very movement of symbolization by way of the death drive occurs through a system of which Freud's pentagon is one of the paradigms, is something attested to as well by a certain terminological discrepancy whose result is, since Melanie Klein, that there has been a tendency to speak of creativity in preference to sublimation. The notion of "creativity" presupposes, at the start of the "creative" process, that the part object is experienced as part of the person who is its donor, author, or transmitter. It is opposed to the rather simplistic idea of a transition from part object to whole object through an undefined "totalization." For the "total" other, assuming the word *total* can be retained, is present from the outset, or at least from very early on, as an aspect of the foundation of the psychical apparatus, both as other of the message and as specular other.

I return yet again to the schema of production, gift, and exchange, the text on "transpositions of drives," which is a veritable lynchpin for sublimation. The connection with feces is central, as they are a human being's first production. On the other hand, it should be noted that the sexual, considered as pleasure, has been demoted to a matter of secondary importance. If one opts to take up, following Hans Blüher and Lou Andreas Salomé, the distinction between the anal and the fecal,[322] *anal* erotism emerges as one of the principal repressed matters of this system.

The transition from the unbound sexual drive to a binding under the sign of the part object is the work of the ego, activating this specific symbolico-ideological system. Here, we are dealing with quite primordial systems, administering an exchange at the anthropological level. Nothing allows us to conclude that one or another system has exclusive dominion. A moment ago I mentioned Mauss, who pits the abstract universal exchange of our modern economy, in which everything has an abstract price (even time or a Van Gogh painting or the cost of the social investments necessary to "produce" an airline pilot), against more restricted modes of exchange, in which, to cite Mauss, "things sold still have a soul and are still followed about by their former owner, whom they follow."[323] There can be no question of opting for one mythology against another. But one cannot fail to notice that with abstract and generalized exchange there occurs a sort of *regression of the part object toward the sign*, of the life drive toward the death drive, and with it a desublimation. Moreover, it is true that the part object, by virtue of being a part of something, already conceals a signification of weapon or fatal projectile, a signification to which Melanie Klein never stopped drawing our attention. Already, in an article dating from 1921, Mauss insisted on the two meanings of the Germanic word *Gift*: present and poison: "The thing received . . . coming from one, fabricated and appropriated by him, being *his*, confers power on him over the other who accepts it."[324]

Let us regroup things. Sublimation, as we have been led to conceive it, is in no way a separate process. It is, we should say, the normal process of acculturation by which the ego attempts to drain

---

322 Hans Blüher, quoted by Lou Andreas-Salome in "Anal et sexuel," in *Amour du narcissisme* (Paris: Gallimard, 1980), p. 109.

323 Marcel Mauss, "Essai sur le don," in *Sociologie et anthropologie* (Paris: PUF, 1960), p. 259.

324 *Le Monde*, March 30, 1968, supplement, p. v.

the Zuyderzee of the id, partly transposing death drives into life drives. A process in which we have put the accent in this context on the function of the part object, an object of production that is maintained as such. In that sense, we can confront it with the pure "object" of consumption, the indication [*index*] of an ecstasy in which all specificity and all origin disappear. Perhaps that movement—which Freud attributes to the anal stage, but which considerably exceeds its temporal limits, and whose significance for creativity is quite important—comes in the après-coup of primal repressions and their link with the indications of orality.[325]

Finally, I would not like to leave this argument, which deals with ordinary sublimation, in the broadest sense possible, without taking some distance from the privilege attributed by Freud to the conquering advance of the life drive. However necessary the process of binding might be, it must not be forgotten that it is accomplished by the ego, and accomplished according to two principal modalities: binding through the narcissistic image, on the one hand, binding through mytho-symbolic systems, on the other. With regard to the latter, we have learned to be distrustful, and an analysis cannot be undertaken without accepting that they be called into question—in their contingency, their historicity, and even their contradictions and absurdities. The diatribes of a Bourdieu against the dominant "symbolic systems" ought not to inhibit us, *a contrario*, in what should be an analytic attitude regarding them.

We will also note, differing here from what is postulated by a certain Lacanianism, that the "symbolic," like the "imaginary," are both in the service of the ego. In the service of the ego, and, as a result, caught in the all but ineluctable perspective of "Ptolemaic" closure.

In each individual existence, this progression of Eros, principally by way of symbolization, is hard to distinguish from sublimation. It is sublimation itself: the integration of anarchic sexual aims into a "socially valued" perspective.

---

325 See the absence of oral sexuality in the Freudian pentagon discussed just above.

This movement of sublimation might be situated between two poles: that of the *symptom* and that which I call *inspiration*.

Concerning the former, I will merely recall that it too marks a modification and partial desexualization of aims. But the latter takes place principally on the mode of compromise, from which, to be sure, a certain symbolization is not absent, but is always unstable in relation to the ego as a whole. In many existences a neurotic sexualization—in which the sexual often returns in the crudest forms—comes to be juxtaposed with a sublimation that effectively exists in every human being, and does so either through infiltration into the performance of daily material tasks, subject to obsessiveness and even overt anality, or by insinuating itself into interpersonal relations, which are often characterized by sadomasochism if not hatred.

It is here that so-called pregenital sexuality (but also infantile genital sexuality) takes on its preeminence. It has perhaps not been sufficiently noted that, unlike adult genital sexuality, its aims are essentially fantasmatic. Thus the actions described by Klein concerning the paranoid position (attacking the interior of the other, chopping it into pieces, burning it, etc.), which are largely borrowed from the customs of daily life, quite naturally find their point of insertion there in more or less disguised forms.

Dare I add that such almost overt sexualization helps a part of humanity—and perhaps the larger part—quite simply to live, that part which, to be sure, we barely or never see unless in the media.

I regard it as indispensable to mention this essential point, since we are dealing with a subject of psychoanalytic anthropology—sublimation—which is itself in need of being viewed in anthropological perspective. Let us not simply forget that analysis effectively has in its realm of experience only 0.000 . . . percent of the individuals whose existence we scarcely know other than from our television screens: perpetrators and victims of massacres, killers, rapists and rape victims, deportees, jailers and prisoners, slaves from modern times and from all time. The primary benefit (and above all the secondary benefit) yielded by a non-sublimated sexualization should not be underestimated. A sexualization under the heading, above all, of the sexual sadistic (but especially masochistic) death drive, which does not at all imply that the tendency to binding and symbolization does not continue its work elsewhere.

But it is not one of the lesser results of the analytic approach when, exceptionally, one follows a case close to those I am evoking, to see the tasks themselves diversify, become unbound, open up. There are occasionally, as is said, cases of social ascension, but not necessarily. What happens is, rather, a kind of mutation. Sexualization persists, but becomes less rigid, less crude, less extrinsic, less in the grips, as well, of a social confrontation without mediation. The path of symbolization appears to beckon.

With my other pole, that of *inspiration*, I come to waters that seem calmer. But only seemingly. To state things in anticipation, if successful sublimation always emerges under the aegis of the ego and Ptolemaic closure—or with the blessings of a "philosophy of the subject"—are we not obliged to recall what we situate at the origin of the drive: a relation to the enigmatic message of the other? To retain some reminiscence of it, and from a twofold point of view: in theory and at the very core of the human being, since the reminiscences of one are also those of the other.

Yet again, it is in Freud that I intend to locate that reminiscence, by way of his very difficulties in structuring the notion of sublimation. It is in that precise sense that two theoretical attitudes can be opposed: "situating" sublimation and setting it "adrift."[326]

---

326 [Editor's note: The word here is *dérive*, which both means "to drift" (as a boat can be "adrift") and is the basis of the word *dérivation* (directly translatable into its English cognate 'derivation'). Many of Laplanche's Francophone readers would also be familiar with Lacan's bilingual playing with the word; Lacan added to the word's usual meanings in French the meaning of the English word *drive* which, with a French accent, sounds like *dérive*. On the more general point, Anglophone readers may wish to consult Laplanche's article "The Derivation of Psychoanalytic Entities," which is the appendix of his *Life and Death in Psychoanalysis* (Flammarion, 1970; trans. Jeffrey Mehlman, The Johns Hopkins University Press, 1976).]

To situate sublimation is to grow attached to the play of drive-transpositions, as we have sketched them, considering the process of symbolization to occur on the basis of drives already constituted by repression. To "derive sublimation" (but also to set it "adrift") is to attempt to follow the trail of a genesis situated in the primordial movement of the drive itself: in primal repression.

Now the period in which the question of pansexualism was to take on urgency, with the absorption of self-preservation into Eros, also saw the advent of the great text of Freud on scientific and artistic creativity: the *Leonardo* of 1910. And it is striking, for our purposes, to note that the major (or, in any event, most inspired) text on sublimation constitutes, at the same time, one of the major resurgences of precocious infantile seduction.

What would be most simple for our purposes is to take the pages on the genesis of the "drive to know": *Wisstrieb* or *Forschertrieb*. A genesis that Freud situates in Leonardo, and perhaps in general, as far more primordial than other sublimations, even those of an artistic order.

At the start, Freud locates two "drives" (we will say two "functions") partaking of self-preservation: one, the pleasure-desire of seeing, *Schaulust*, and the other the drive to mastery. Those two functions, which are thus initially nonsexual, two pieces of psycho-physiological equipment, we might say, of which nothing forbids us from supposing them to have more or less constitutional strength, are, very early on, perhaps from the outset, caught in the sexual process in which the adult has the initiative. To state things differently, those functions constitute the locus, the very site of seduction. Let us follow Freud once again. The investigation, which will henceforth be sexual, may know three "fates." All three are preceded by (and linked with) a repression that is even said to be "energetic."

(1) Intellectual inhibition. A victory of repression (which is often bolstered by religion).

(2) Thought tending toward the obsessional. The sexual

invades defense by reaction formation. "Conducting research in this case becomes a sexual activity, an often exclusive activity . . . but the character without possible conclusion of infantile investigation is also repeated in the fact that such rumination never finds an end."

(3) *But,* before moving on to the third type, *it must be emphasized* that these three modes are not exclusive of each other. The "rarest and most perfect" case (which is the third one) can coexist or alternate with moments of inhibition and rumination. Such is the case for Giacometti, whose case I am evoking here for the first time.

In point of fact, in Freud's text, this third type gives us vistas onto the sublime—and also a certain dissatisfaction. There is indeed repression, but not of a certain component, which is the one linked to sexual *investigation.* Yet there is repression all the same . . . since the investigation would avoid so-called sexual themes. Which is false, in a way, precisely with regard to Leonardo.

Freud's most evocative words are those expressing the idea of a sublimation "from the beginning (*vom Anfang an*)":

> the libido evades the fate of repression by being sublimated from the very beginning into curiosity and by becoming attached to the powerful instinct for research as a reinforcement.[327]

This is not the only passage:

> The original sublimation for which they had been prepared on the occasion of the first repression.[328]

This emboldens us to move from the level of secondary repression (with its already constituted drives) to that of *primal repression.* In other words, *this beginning of sublimation* takes us back to the *beginning of the sexual drive.*

---

327 *Leonardo da Vinci and a Memory of His Childhood,* in *SE* 11:80.
328 Ibid. p. 133.

We cannot neglect at this juncture the fact that, in Freud, the Leonardo study marks the temporary *resurgence* of *seduction*—in the form of details of a maternal seduction. To be sure, the theory of seduction, as theory, does not have a resurgence. It is up to us to summon it. More precisely, behind the secondary vectorization of the drive, it is for us to seek a more primal vectorization, which is played out, perhaps not between intrapsychical forces, but in the interpersonal relation; on the basis of a primitive reciprocal relation, something is played out that is no less primordial: the unilateral character of what is sexual—and compromised in its sexuality—in adult communication.

The enigmatic message is what marks the irreducible dimension of alterity. Not by virtue of an undefined alchemy or metaphysics, but because that message carries within it the irreducible and unreadable trace of the sexual unconscious of the other, the adult other. The vectorization of the enigmatic message is "Copernican." It is inscribed against a ground of interpersonal vectorization, that of nonsexual attachment.

The enigmatic message is registered in the child as a message. As "signifying for" and not as trace or representation; a metapsychology of the trace or representation remains irreducibly solipsistic.

That being the case, what can the child do with the message. Its *vicissitudes* are multiple.

1. The message can be left untranslated, foreclosed. Thus the persecutory message and its cousin, the message from the superego.

2. The message can be treated—i.e., translated. Apparently without residue. "Apparently," since the untranslated residue is repressed. It is thus akin to nothing for the ego.

The ego is always the one who says (to paraphrase O. Mannoni): "I am quite aware of that." That is: I can encompass it in a translation. And of the residue: "I don't want to know anything about it."

This is the repression that Freud regularly defines as a not-wanting-to-know.

3. Can we now imagine the third "treatment" discussed by

Freud in this passage about sublimation from the beginning? *A repression, but while maintaining the sting of the enigma?* Something like:

"I'm well aware, and what I am not aware of, I don't want to know about insofar as the content is concerned; but all the same, I have the intuition—that never ends—that I don't really know."

This retention of the dimension of the enigma despite the avatars of repression is what I believe Freud is attempting to show in *Leonardo.* He consistently contrasts two distinct sublimations: a pictorial variant, which comes later and is linked to *joie de vivre;* an original intellectual variant, which serves to enliven but also to paralyze artistic creation.

This is the place in which to evoke again that true brother of Leonardo, Giacometti.

And alongside the Leonardo of Freud, the Giacometti of Yves Bonnefoy, on whom we spent a year participating in a collective endeavor.

The difference, in the case of Giacometti, would be that research—investigation—*directly animates* the painting or sculpture. But it is barely a difference once one looks at things up close. I am evoking Freud's celebrated pages in which he takes up the great opposition between knowing, on the one hand, and loving or hating, on the other. Loving and hating being situated on the side of painting; "knowing" being posited at the outset as the indispensable auxiliary of art, but occasionally also becoming its enemy:

> "Nothing can be loved or hated if it is not first known.
> But finally, it is investigation that has the upper hand,
> at the risk of paralyzing creation."[329]
> "The artist had once taken the investigator into his service to assist him, but now the servant had become the stronger of the two, and had suppressed his master."[330]

---

329 Ibid., p. 73.
330 Ibid. p. 77.

And in *Giacometti*:

"Art interests me a lot, but truth interests me infinitely more."[331] "Neither making beautiful sculpture nor expressing myself, it's the subject that counts." To the point of often asserting that he would throw the sculpture out, like an empty shell, once he would triumph: "in a certain sense, I haven't begun yet."

"I do sculpture in order to get rid of it."

"It's in order to get rid of it." (Interview in the French television broadcast *Les heures chaudes de Montparnasse*).

In Giacometti the aspect of *sexualization* I have called secondary is certainly not absent; in Leonardo Freud also notes that meshing of different levels: "In this manner the repression, fixation, and sublimation participated in disposing of the contributions which the sexual impulse furnished to Leonardo's psychical life."[332]

In the case of Giacometti, there is the participation of elements—and notably anal-sadistic elements—extremely close to those of Leonardo. Anal, by which I mean from the precocious daubing with excrement of a canvas of his father to those painted plaster sculptures that were also covered with a quasi-sacrilegious daubing.

And in the case of Leonardo all the exercises in scatological clowning that are known.

The practice of sculpture, in a manner more immediate than painting—I mean the modeling—is plainly in direct contact with anality, and Giacometti (who knew Freud) is well aware of it:

"It is a mania like any other to grope the earth under the pretext of working the land."

---

331 Alberto Giacometti, *Écrits* (Paris: Hermann, 1900), p. 267.
332 *SE* 11:132.

As for sadism and death . . .

But before uttering a word about the subject in regard to Giacometti and in Leonardo, I want to assemble a few points.

• Creation, in Leonardo and above all in Giacometti, seems to be *transfixed by the vector of "investigation"* or, better put, of the "quest." But in what direction is that vector oriented? No doubt investigation, as creation, comes from the individual and is in that sense centrifugal. But what calls and orients it is a vector emanating from the other. For *Leonardo* "the eye is the window of the soul," which indicates an opening and even an exposure of the soul to the trauma of the other.

• In the case of *Giacometti,* it is the gaze of the other that needs be restored. The subject is not random, but the human face, and above all its gaze. Not a specific individual gaze, and not an abstract gaze either, but what makes the gaze of the other an enigma. According to Yves Bonnefoy: "To create a semblance, for Giacometti, was to understand and express the tension causing that inner being, that "soul" (we can risk the word), to take control of the eyes, mouth, and forehead, and withdraw them from space."[333]

This circumstance, which is so manifest in Giacometti, is also found in Leonardo with the smile—a smile that is also a form of communication or address—said to be forever indecipherable. And such is the case despite all the derision with which a Dali may have bespattered the *Mona Lisa.*

I have used the word *transfix* to characterize the vector of the investigation. But it should be emphasized that this is not a centrifugal vector carrying, so to speak, the subject toward its object. It is a centripetal vector, emanating from the other. And the only thing the subject can do is remain open to the trauma and by the trauma.

This trauma of the enigma is not acquired or opened once and for all: it exists in flashes and eclipses. The opening is precisely being available to the other who will come surprise me.

---

333 Yves Bonnefoy, *Giacometti* (Paris: Flammarion, 1991), p. 37.

I seem to be using a somewhat mystical tone. And yet that is precisely how, in a manner of wonderment, Freud speaks of the aging Leonardo and of his encounter with the Gioconda:

> At the summit of his life, in the age of the first fifties . . . a new transformation came over him. Still deeper layers of the contents of his mind became active once more, but this further regression was to the benefit of his art, which was in the process of becoming stunted. He met the woman who awakened his memory of his mother's happy smile of sensual rapture. . . . He painted the Mona Lisa, the "Saint Anne with two others," and a number of mysterious pictures which are characterized by the enigmatic smile.[334]

We do not, to be sure, have any photos of Leonardo as a child! But, in the case of Giacometti, we have an extraordinary family portrait, with an exchange of gazes that exceeds any description: a confrontation of the genuinely Leonardesque smile of the mother and the inquisitive eye, as hard as stone, of Alberto.[335]

An inquisitive gaze one imagines also as that of Leonardo, accompanying prisoners sentenced to death to the gallows, in quest of the final enigma.

I have little sympathy for the idea that, as Levinas would have it, the enigma of the other is always mediated, vectorized by the gaze.

But, on the other hand, I am convinced that it is *the enigma of the other—of the adult human other—that is the vehicle of other enigmas said to be primordial.*

With Giacometti, encounters with the face, with the stare of the other, come to punctuate, to reignite the quest. He has several privileged models that he feels called upon literally to exhaust.

---

334 *Leonardo da Vinci and a Memory of His Childhood*, in *SE* 11:133–34.
335 Bonnefoy, *Giacometti*, p. 37.

There is the stare of the dying other, in two celebrated and frequently recounted episodes (*The Death of Van M. — Death of T*). Shall I rehearse here the profound meditation of Freud: the enigma of one's own death, our own death, is mediated by the death of someone to whom we are close; "man could no longer keep death at a distance, for he had tasted it in his pain about the dead."[336]

Such is also the case, in my view, concerning what I have designated (not without reticence) the enigma of being, for which I was inclined to generalize Bonnefoy's formula concerning Giacometti: "There is meditation on being only in the encounter with beings."[337]

It is consequently at this juncture that I attempt to reintroduce the old term *inspiration*, given currency in times past by the Romantics, but concerning which one is obliged to admit that clarification, even in the German Romantics, does not take us very far.

Why advance this term as an alternative to (or perhaps as more adequate than) the *primal sublimation* about which Freud spoke?

It is because it is not in fact a matter of substituting one mechanism for another. A mechanism is always conjugated in the first person—or in the subject. But inspiration is conjugated in the other. Its subject is not "the" subject, but the other: exactly as in the cases of seduction, persecution, and revelation. In resonance with the primal adult other, the other, at privileged moments, comes to reopen the wound of the unexpected—the enigma.

Without referring to any specific content, available to numerous translations, the equivocal smile of *Saint John the Baptist* is endlessly provocative:

> These pictures breathe a mystical air into the secret of which one dares not penetrate. . . . The figures are still androgynous but no longer in the sense of the vulture phantasy, they are pretty boys of feminine tenderness

---

336 "Thoughts for the Times on War and Death," in *SE* 14:294.
337 Bonnefoy, *Giacometti*, p. 365.

with effeminate forms; they do not cast their eyes down but gaze in mysterious triumph, as if they knew of a great achievement of happiness, about which silence must be kept. The familiar smile of fascination leads us to infer that it is a secret of love.[338]

Freud's very terms serve to say that an explanation in the first person is, no doubt, possible, but insufficient: "a mystical air into the secret of which one dares not penetrate"; "a great achievement of happiness about which silence must be kept"; "a secret of love"; "the boy, infatuated with his mother." These are words impregnated with respect on the part of a man as disrespectful as the inventor of psychoanalysis.

No doubt inspiration is never pure, nor ever completely dissolved in the analytic gaze. The interference with neurotic—and, even more, with psychotic—elements is frequently overt. But is not psychosis itself a reminiscence of the primacy of the other?

Before leaving the individual we call the creator, let us attend to one last paradox and stake out another reversal. Beyond the other, whose traumatic action we have attempted to uncover (the other of the encounter and also, mediated by the other of the encounter, the other of Death and even of Nature), the poet, and creative artists in general, is exposed to an additional appeal, by which I mean the one issuing from his *audience*.

There is, to be sure, the chosen audience on whom it is a matter of producing a certain effect, through adjusted and calculated means. That audience can be defined as being the object of a *pragmatics*, and even of a technique, in a movement whose objective is always Ptolemaic. But, beyond that, there is the indeterminate other to whom an infinite message, without recourse, is addressed, to paraphrase Stendhal, the other of the century to come.

I don't think that one can reduce this moment of "address"

---

338 *Leonardo da Vinci and a Memory of His Childhood*, in *SE* 11:117.

to its narcissistic aspects, as Freud appears to be doing in "Creative Writers and Day-Dreaming"—a movement going from the creator "expressing himself" to a "receptive" audience, from which a certain benefit is expected in return. The Ptolemaic-narcissistic movement of creation is undeniable. But beyond it, and conjointly with it, an inversion occurs: it is the audience's expectation, which is in itself enigmatic, that then becomes the *agent provocateur* of the effort of the work.

There would thus be an opening in the double sense of *being opened by* and *being open to*: an opening by way of an encounter that renews the trauma of the primal enigmas; an opening to and by the undetermined audience, scattered in the future.

"Psychoanalysis as Sublimation." From Daniel Lagache's article I will retain the questioning linked to its title.[339] And, to increase the burden, I will say: "Psychoanalysis as sublimation and/or inspiration."

For we can continue to sustain ourselves in this practice—unless we consider it to be a professional instrument among others—only if we are intimately convinced that it has something to do with what is primordial in the human being. The analytic situation reiterates the questioning in the face of the enigma emanating from the other. It restores and firmly maintains that opening. Its ineluctable and indispensable opposite is the psychotherapeutic motion intrinsic to analysis itself, but that constitutes, quite simply, the ego-centric pole corresponding to the incessant tendency toward closure.

In the situation created for the analysand by the presence of the analyst are to be found the *two alterities* that characterize what I have called inspiration. On the one hand, what does this analyst want for me, this enigmatic emitter charged with a desire unknown even to himself. And, also, what does he want *from me*, a kind of "audience" or recipient whose expectation is perennially suspended, made in order not to be fulfilled.

---

339 Daniel Lagache, "La psychanalyse comme sublimation," in *Oeuvres*, vol. 5 (Paris: PUF, 1984)

Freud sometimes compared analysis to a surgical operation. You are not, he says to the patient, going to leave things as they are and jump off the operating table with your belly open! The comparison is pertinent, since analysis is primarily a labor of unbinding. One might say that it is a masterly practice of debridement—and even of the sexual death drive.

Analyses that close wounds: what could be more legitimate? Analyses that close themselves up, sometimes, over wounds. Let us not press the comparison too far. Moreover, quite often the decision to "close up" does not come from us.

But what I believe I know is that there is a kind of opening that analysis on occasion maintains: one that is its stamp of origin, its stamp *by* its origin. And that that opening can be maintained, transported outside itself toward other fields of alterity and inspiration. A transference of the "hollowed out" transference, clearly, that is a transference of the relation to the enigma as such.

To be sure, one thinks first of all of the transition to analytic practice, which implies not some undefined lack in being, but the possibility of being surprised, gripped, traversed by the bottomless questioning of whoever comes to our encounter. But there are many other fields of inspiration onto which that expropriation, the mourning marked by the end of an analysis, may open. I have formulated the hypothesis that the essence of that divestment was not the loss of an object, but the irreparable realization that the discourse of the other—of the deceased—would remain forever incomplete.

It is the same incompleteness that characterizes the words of the analyst during the last minutes and during the entire course of an analysis. An incompleteness that it falls to the analysand to transport elsewhere. And, that being the case, the frequently formulated fear that analysis runs the risk of drying up inspiration turns out to be utterly unjustified.

BIBLIOGRAPHY

André, Jacques: *Aux origines féminines de la* sexualité. Paris: PUF, 1995.

———. La révolution fratricide. Paris: PUF, 1993.

Anzieu, Didier: *Freud's Self-Analysis*. Connecticut: IUP, 1986.

Barande, Ilse and Robert Barande: *Histoire de la psychanalyse en France*. Toulouse: Privat, 1975.

Baumgart, Matthias: "Die psychoanalytische Metapsychologie im Lichte der Säuglingsforschung: Verwerfen oder überdenken?" in Pedrina, F. et al., *Spiel-raümebegegnungen zwischen Kinder- und Erwachsenenanalyse*. Tübingen: Diskord, 1994, pp. 51–82.

Benveniste, Émile: "Catégories de langue, catégories de pensée," in *Problèmes de linguistique générale*. Paris: Gallimard, 1966.

Berman, Antoine: *L'Epreuve de l'étranger*. Paris: Gallimard, 1984.

Blüher, Hans, quoted by Lou Andreas-Salome in "Anal et sexuel," in *Amour du narcissisme*. Paris: Gallimard, 1980, p. 109.

Bonnefoy, Yves: *Giacometti*. Paris: Flammarion, 1991.

Cahiers de l'École des Sciences religieuses et philosophiques, no. 16. Brussels, 1994.

van Caneighem, Denise: *Agressivité et combativité*. Paris: PUF, 1978.

Caruth, Cathy: *Empirical Truths and Critical Fictions: Locke, Wordsworth, Kant, Freud*. Baltimore: Johns Hopkins University Press, 2009.

Cassin, Barbara: *Vocabulaire européen des philosophies: Dictionnaire des intraduisibles* (Paris: Seuil and Dictionnaires Robert, 2004). In English: *Dictionary of Untranslatables: A Philosophical Lexicon*, trans. Steven Rendall, Christian Hubert, Jeffrey Mehlman, Nathanael Stein, Michael Syrotinski. Princeton: Princeton University Press, 2014.

Fichte, Johann Gottlieb: *Attempt at a Critique of All Revelation*. Trans. G. Green. Cambridge: Cambridge University Press, 2010.

Freud, Sigmund: *Traumdeutung*, in *Gesammelte Werke* Vol. 2–3.
———. *Studies in Hysteria*, in *SE* 2.

———. *The Psychopathology of Everyday Life*, in *SE* 6.
———. "On the Sexual Theories of Children," in *SE* 9.
———. *Leonardo da Vinci and a Memory of His Childhood*, in *SE* 11.
———. "The Psychoanalytic View of Psychogenetic Disturbance of Vision," in *SE* 11.
———. "The Case of Schreber," in *SE* 12.
———. "Psychoanalytic Notes on an Autobiographical Account of a Case of Paranoia (Dementia Paranoides)," in *SE* 12.
———. *Totem and Taboo*, in *SE* 13.
———. "The Unconscious," in *SE* 14.
———."A Metapsychological Supplement to the Theory of Dreams," in *SE* 14.
———. "Thoughts for the Times on War and Death," in *SE* 14.
———. "A Difficulty in the Path of Psychoanalysis," in *SE* 17.
———. "From the History of an Infantile Neurosis," in *SE* 17.
———. "Some Neurotic Mechanisms in Jealousy, Paranoia, and Homosexuality," in *SE* 18.
———. "The Loss of Reality in Neurosis and Psychosis," in *SE* 19.
———. "Neurosis and Psychosis," in *SE* 19.
———. "Some Additional Notes on Dream Interpretation as a Whole," in *SE* 19.
———. *Inhibitions, Symptoms and Anxiety*, in *SE* 20.
———. "The Question of Lay Analysis," in *SE* 20.
———. *Civilization and Its Discontents*, in *SE* 21.
———. *New Introductory Lectures*, in *SE* 22.
———. *The Subtleties of a Faulty Action* 1935, in *SE* 22.

Freud, Sigmund and Wilhelm Fliess: *The Complete Letters of Sigmund Freud to Wilhelm Fliess: 1887–1904*, trans. Jeffrey Moussaieff Masson. Cambridge: Harvard University Press, 1985.

Giacometti, Alberto: *Écrits* (Paris: Hermann, 1900), p. 267.

Goldberg, Jacques: *La culpabilité, axiome de la psychanalyse* (Paris: PUF, 1985).

Gopnik, Adam: "Word Magic" in The New Yorker, May 26, 2014.

Green, Andre: Le Temps de la réflexion, 1. Paris: Gallimard, 1980.

Grondin, Jean: *L'universalité de l'herméneutique*. Paris: PUF, 1993.

Grünbaum, Adolf: "Précis of the Foundations of Psycho¬analysis," in *The Behavioral and Brain Sciences* no. 9, 1986.

Halbwachs, Maurice: *Les cadres sociaux de la mémoire*. Paris: PUF, 1952, originally published in *Les Travaux de L'Année Sociologique*, Paris: F. Alcan, 1925.

Heimann, Paula: "Notes on the Theory of Life and Death Instincts," in *Developments in Psychoanalysis*. London: Hogarth, 1952.

Imbert, Claude: "For a Structure of Belief: Anselm's Argument," in *Nouvelle Revue de psychanalyse*, no. 18, 1978.

Jones, Ernest: *On the Nightmare*. London: Hogarth, 1931.
———. *The Life and Work of Sigmund Freud*. New York: Basic Books, 1974.

Juillerat, Bernard: *Oedipe chasseur*. Paris: PUF, 1991.

Kant, Immanuel: *Critique of Pure Reason*. London: Dent, 1934 [1781].

Kardiner, Abram: *My Analysis with Freud*. New York: Norton, 1977.

Kris, Ernst: "The Personal Myth—a Problem in Psychoanalytic Technique." *Journal of the American Psychoanalytic Association*, no. 4.

Lacan, Jacques: *Function and Field of Speech and Language in Psychoanalysis*, trans. Alan Sheridan, in *Écrits*. London: Tavistock, 1977.

Lagache, Daniel: "La psychanalyse comme sublimation," in *Oeuvres*, vol. 5. Paris: PUF, 1984.
———. "Psychocriminogenesis," in *The Work of Daniel Lagache: Selected Writings*. London: Karnac 1993.

"La bouteille à la mer," *RFP* 28, nos. 2–3, 1974.

Levinas, Emmanuel: *Éthique et infini*, Paris: Fayard, 1985.

Laplanche, Jean: *Vie et mort en psychanalyse*. Paris: Flammarion, 1970. Trans. Jeffrey Mehlman: *Life and Death in Psychoanalysis*. Baltimore: Johns Hopkins University Press, 1976.
———. *Problématiques I: L'angoisse*. Paris: PUF, 1980.
———. *Problématiques II: Castration. Symbolisations*. Paris: PUF, 1980.
———. *Problématiques IV: L'Inconscient et le ça*. Paris: PUF, 1981.
———. *Problématiques V: Le baquet. Transcendance du transfert*. Paris: PUF, 1987.
———. *Nouveaux fondements pour la psychanalyse*. Paris: P.U.F., 1987. Trans. David Macey, *New Foundations for Psychoanalysis*. London: Blackwell, 1989.
———. "Une révolution sans cesse occultée," in *Revue internationale d'histoire de la psychanalyse*, no. 2, 1989.
———. *La Révolution copernicienne inachevée*. Paris: Aubier, 1992.
———. "Séduction, persécution, révélation," in *Psychanalyse à l'université*, no. 18, 1993.
———. *Le fourvoiement biologisant de la sexualité chez Freud*. Paris: Synthélabo, "Les empêcheurs de penser en rond," 1993. Trans. Donald Nicholson-Smith: *The*

Temptation of Biology: Freud's Theories of Sexuality. New York, The Unconscious in Translation, 2015.

———. *Seduction, Translation, and the Drives*. Ed. John Fletcher and Martin Stanton. London: ICA, 1992.

———. *Essays on Otherness*. London: Routledge, 1999.

———. *Freud and the Sexual*. New York: The Unconscious in Translation, 2011.

Laplanche, Jean, and J.-B. Pontalis: *Vocabulaire de la psychanalyse*. Paris: P.U.F., 1967. Trans. Donald Nicholson-Smith, *The Language of Psychoanalysis*. New York: Norton, 1974.

———. *Fantasme originaire, fantasmes des origines, origines du fantasme*. Paris: Hachette, 1985. Trans. Jonathan House, in Dominique Scarfone: *Laplanche: an Introduction*. New York: The Unconscious in Translation, 2015.

Lévi-Strauss, Claude: *La pensée sauvage*. Paris: Plon, 1962.

———. *La Potière jalouse*. Paris: Plon, 1985. Trans. Bénédicte Chorier: *The Jealous Potter*. Chicago: University of Chicago Press, 1988.

Lothane, Zvi: *In Defense of Schreber: Soul Murder and Psychiatry*. Hillsdale, NJ: Analytic, 1992.

Maïdani-Gérard, Jean-Pierre: *Léonard de Vinci: mythologie ou théologie?* Paris: PUF, 1993.

Mehlman, Jeffrey: "*Poe pourri*: Lacan's Seminar on 'The Purloined Letter'" in *Aesthetics Today*, ed. M. Philipson and P. Gudel. New York: Meridian, 1980.

———. (Ed.) *French Freud: Structural Readings in Psychoanalysis, Yale French Studies*, 1972.

———. "Writing and Deference: The Politics of Literary Adulation," in *Genealogies of the Text: Literature, Psychoanalysis, and Politics in Modern France*. Cambridge: Cambridge University Press, 1995.

Moscovici, Marie: *Il est arrivé quelque chose* (Paris: Ramsay, 1989), p. 205

Nietzsche, Friedrich: "Dream and Responsibility," in *The Dawn of Day*. Trans. John McFarland Kennedy, New York: The MacMillan Company, 1911.

Ortigues, Edmond: "Schreber revisité," in *Psychanalystes*, no. 48, 1993–1994.

Poncela, Pierrette: "Se défendre de l'expertise psychiatrique," in *Psychanalystes*, no. 37, 1990.

Pontalis, Jean-Bertrand: Introduction, *La Nouvelle Revue de psychanalyse*, no. 18, 1978.

Popper, Karl: *Conjectures and Refutations*. New York: Harper and Row, 1968.

288

Program of the XII Journées occitanes de psychanalyse, November 1993.

Reich, Wilhelm: "L'effondrement de la morale sexuelle," quoted in E. Bornemann: *Psychanalyse de l'argent*. Paris: PUF, 1978. Trans. Werner and Doreen Grossman, "Psychoanalysis of Primitive Cultures," in *The Invasion of Compulsory Sex-Morality*. New York: Farrar, Straus and Giroux, 1971.

Ricoeur, Paul: *Temps et récit*, 3 vols. Paris: Seuil, 1991.

Rosolato, Guy: *Le Sacrifice*. Paris: PUF, 1991.
———. "Paranoia et scène primitive," in *Essais sur le symbolique*. Paris: Gallimard, 1969.

Sass, Louis and Robert L. Woolfolk: "Psychoanalysis and the Hermeneutic Turn: A Critique of Narrative Truth and Historical Truth," in *Journal of the American Psychoanalytic Association* 36, no. 2, 1988, pp. 429–53.

Scarfone, Dominique: *Adventures in the French Trade: Fragments Toward a Life*. Stanford: Stanford University Press, 2010.
———. "La réalité dans la névrose et la psy¬chose." Paris: Société française de psychanalyse, 1961.
———. *Legacies of Anti-Semitism in France*. Minneapolis: University of Minnesota Press, 1983.

Schafer, Roy: *A New Language for Psychoanalysis*. New Haven: Yale University Press, 1976.

Schiff, Stacy: *Saint- Exupéry: A Biography*. New York: Knopf, 1994.

Thomä, Helmut and Neil Cheshire: "Freud's *Nachträglichkeit* and Strachey's 'Deferred Action': Trauma Constructions and the Direction of Causality," in *International Review of Psychoanalysis*, no. 18, 1991, pp. 407–27.

Viderman, Serge: *La construction de l'espace analytique*. Paris: Denoël, 1970.

Widlocher, Daniel: "Temps pour entendre, temps pour interpréter, temps pour com¬prendre," in *Bulletin de la Fédération européenne de psychanalyse*, no. 40, 1993.

Index

abandonment of the theory of seduction, x, 4, 9, 51, 75, 150, 161, 163, 190, 212, 221
aberration, 28, 156, 162
abolished, 23-24
absence of negation, 75, 81, 172
absorption, 74, 169, 236, 273
abstraction, 22, 25, 27, 90, 92-93, 110, 114-115, 150, 166, 176, 194, 221, 239, 260, 266, 269, 278
academia, 145, 155-156
acculturation, 263, 269
accusation, 152, 222, 257
activity, xx, 7, 47, 66, 112, 124, 168, 190-191, 213, 229, 255, 274
adaptation, 109-110, 113, 255
adult-child relationship, 5, 66-67, 120, 180, 192, 197
afterwardsness, xx, 53; *see also après-coup; Nachträglichkeit*
aggression, 118-119, 160, 165-166, 169, 177-181, 191, 225, 261, 264, 267
Akhenaton, 37, 39-40
alchemy, 121, 254, 275
alienation, 16-17, 90-92; *see also Entfremdung*
alterity, 7-8, 16, 25, 44, 84, 86, 88, 174-175, 179, 194-195, 197-199, 275, 282-283
ambivalence, 34, 138, 210, 228, *see also Gleichgültigkeit; Indifferenz*
anaclisis, xx
anality, 13, 264, 266, 270-271, 277
    anal object, 41, 151, 266
    anal-eroticism, 262, 264-265, 269
    anal-sadism, 25, 27, 138, 277
analytic situation, 5, 9, 88, 144, 150, 189, 197, 214, 224, 258, 282
Andere
    das Andere, 86, 194, 217
    der Andere, 86, 194, 217
Anlehnung, x, xx; *see also étayage*; leaning-on
Anna O., 85
anthropomorphism, 93, 95
antihermeneutics, 90, 199, 203-207, 209, 211, 213, 215, 217; *see also* hermeneutics
antinomy of pure reason, 32-33
Anzieu, Didier, 223
apperception, 91
après-coup, xx, 4, 49-56, 71-72, 76-77, 115, 166, 245, 265, 270
Aristophanes, 60, 163, 167-168
Aristotle, 183
Artemidorus, 216
Association Psychanalytique de France (APF), 7, 97, 102-105, 157, 219, 253
atemporallity, 40, 75, 77-78
attachment theory, 110, 181, 191, 260-261, 275
Augustine of Hippo (Saint Augustine), 180
Auslegung, 205, 232, 242, 248; *see also Deutung*; interpretation

autoerotism, 163, 168-169, 259

Balint, Michael, 254, 257, 261
Baudelaire, Charles, xi, 94
Bekanntmachung, xiii-xvii, 31-32, 46, 48
binary logic, 82, 210
binding, 82-84, 116-121, 160, 163, 172, 175, 193-196, 200, 207, 235, 250, 259, 261-266, 269-270, 272
biology, 3, 37, 59, 114, 139, 159, 166, 178
Boileau (Nicolas Boileau-Despréaux), 126
Bonnefoy, Yves, 276, 278-280
Bonneval, 57, 60, 67, 75, 88
breast, x, 12, 54-55, 110, 191, 237-238, 267

cannibalism, 141, 180
castration, 9-10, 12-13, 15-16, 20, 47, 67, 82, 84, 89, 113, 119-121, 146, 151-152, 157, 172, 175, 198, 207-210, 215, 224, 226, 228, 233, 235-237
causality, 14, 32, 52, 94
Charcot, Jean-Martin, 129
childhood, 3, 34-35, 69-71, 88, 136-137, 142, 162-163, 208, 259, 265, 274, 279, 281
circumcision, 67, 228
Claparède, Édouard, 258
Comité national des écrivains (CNE), xvi
complementarity, 82, 232-233, *see also Ergänzung*
compulsion to synthesize, 198
Comte, Auguste, 92-95, 220
condensation, 61-62, 82-83, 87, 117, 195
Condillac (Étienne Bonnot de Condillac), 21, 92
contingency, 14, 162, 184, 210, 256, 270
Copernicus, viii, 42, 44, 86, 92, 130-131, 135-136, 138, 193-194, 197, 201, 275
countertransference, 197
criticism, 34, 115, 150, 190, 249

Dasein, 136, 190, 204, 214, 248
decentering, 8, 31, 44, 130-131, 135-136
Deckerinnerung, 71; *see also* screen-memory
deconstruction, xv, 198, 211
deferred action, 49, 52-54
Deleuze, Gilles, xiv
delusion
    delusion of persecution, 7, 20, 47
    delusional idealism, xii, 16, 143
Derrida, Jacques, xv
Descartes, René, 33, 43, 135, 149, 214
desexualization, 27, 47, 210, 258, 262-263, 271

feces, 266, 268-269
Ferenczi, Sándor, 99, 102, 200
Feuerbach, Ludwig, 34
Fichte, Johann Gottlieb, xii-xiv, 16, 30-32, 42, 46, 48
filiation, 146-147; *see also* transmission; *Übermittlung*
Fliess, Wilhelm, x, 50-51, 53, 149, 172, 238
folklore, 227-229, 232
fundamental anthropological situation, 3-4

Gadamer, Hans-Georg, 203, 241
gender, 151, 209-210, 213, 215
General Theory of Seduction, xxi, 46, 137, 204, 211-213
genitality, 162, 262-263
Giacometti, Alberto, 274, 276-280
Gleichgültigkeit, 187, *see also* ambivalence; *Indifferenz*
God, 18, 27, 39-40, 42-43, 93, 138, 254, *see also* religion
Gopnik, Adam, vii
Groddeck, Georg, 59, 228
Grondin, Jean, 203, 241
Guattari, Félix, xiv

hallucination, 24, 78, 133-134; *see also* delusion
Hegel, Georg Wilhelm Friedrich, 16, 77, 93, 142, 171, 174, 180, 239
Heidegger, Martin, 135-136, 171, 190, 213-214, 220, 241, 248-249
Heisenberg, Werner, 33
helplessness, 34
hermeneutics, xviii, 3-4, 29, 51-56, 61-62, 67, 81, 89-90, 93, 190-192, 199, 203-205, 207,
    211-216, 218, 223, 232, 234, 240-242, 245, 247-249, 251
heterosexuality, 162
historiography, 69-70
Hobbes, Thomas, 139, 177-178
Hölderlin, Friedrich, 214
hollowed-out transference, 90, 197
holocaust, 140, 178
homosexuality, 20-21, 25-28, 46, 176, 184-185
Hume, David, 247
Husserl, Edmund, 135-136
hypnosis, 78, 188
hysteria, xxi, 38, 53, 113, 129-130, 149, 151, 187, 189, 206

idealism, xii, 16, 74, 101, 188, 196
imaginary, xii, 9-10, 45, 54, 65, 101, 133, 141, 161, 180, 235, 247, 270, 279; *see also* fantasy
incest, 127, 237
Indifferenz, 21, 109, 187; *see also* ambivalence; *Gleichgültigkeit*
Infans, xi, 4, 55, 72, 110-111, 137, 177, 181, 191, 214-215

infantile sexual theories, 150, 152, 174, 216, 228, 250
instinct, ix-x, xx, 3, 8, 19, 27, 59-60, 80, 89, 109-110, 114, 139-141, 161-168, 175-177, 180, 184, 188, 192, 207, 235, 260, 262, 264-265, 274; *see also* drive
interdiction, 113, 120, 222
intromission
    Nahrungseinfuhr, 192
    Nahrungszufuhr, 192
investment, xiv, xvii, 44, 82, 109, 112, 116, 258, 260, 265, 267, 269; *see also* disinvestment
International Psychoanalytic Association (IPA), 97, 99-100, 105

Jakobson, Roman, 249
Jealousy, 25, 46, 181, 217, 219
Jocasta, 263; *see also* Laius; null
Judaism, xvii, 37-38, 67, *see also* religion
Jung, Carl
    Jung's instinctual monism, 19

Kant, Immanuel, x, xiv, 31-32, 42-43, 135-136
Klein, Melanie, 13, 120, 128-129, 165-166, 171, 175-176, 201, 207, 216, 222, 235, 259, 268-269, 271

Lacan, Jacques, xi, xiii-xiv, xx, 5, 9, 15-16, 24-25, 29, 49, 60, 65-66, 68, 84, 93, 97-99, 101-103, 115, 128, 137, 142, 147-148, 161, 180-181, 188, 207, 210, 216, 222, 228, 235, 239-240, 270, 272
Laforgue, Jules, 258
Lagache, Lagache, 98, 109-110, 255, 282
Laius, 263; *see also* Jocasta; Oedipus complex
latency, 34, 36, 99, 164, 166, 174, 197, 231-232, 242
leaning-on, x, xx; *see also* étayage
Leclaire, Serge, 57, 60, 203, 241
Lehrsatz, 39, 43; *see also* dogma
Leonardo, 27, 35, 55, 69, 71-73, 76, 85, 234, 246, 254, 273-279, 281
Lévi-Strauss, Claude, 152, 154, 217, 219, 236, 238-240, 242, 266
Levinas, Emmanuel, 135-136, 279
liberalism, 103
libido, ix, xvii, 23, 26-27, 116-117, 121-122, 167, 170-171, 237, 258-259, 274
Little Hans, 40, 50, 52, 152, 209, 228
Lothane, Zvi, 234
love, xvii, 26, 168, 276
Lucifer, 259
lupus, 139, 177-179; *see also* Hobbes, Thomas
Lyotard, Jean-François, 38

Machiavelli, Niccolò, 24
Maïdani-Gérard, Jean-Pierre, 7, 72, 234

Mallarmé, Stéphane, 201
Manichaeism, 176
marriage, 101, 184-185, 263
Marxism, 220, 255-256
masculinity, 210
masochism, 27-28, 166, 264, 272; *see also* sadism; sadomasochism
masturbation, 10
Mauss, Marcel, 266, 269
Mehlman, Jeffrey, vii-viii, xiii, xv, xviii, xx, 272
mental, xix, 58, 72, 88, 107, 149
Merleau-Ponty, Maurice, 240, 248
metabiology, 58, 138, 163, 166
metacosmology, 58, 139, 163
metaphor, 29, 81, 129, 196, 216, 238
metaphysics, 60, 64-65, 90, 92-95, 152-153, 166, 171, 175, 182, 203, 210, 220-221, 228, 275
metapsychology, xv, 26, 90-91, 93-94, 113-114, 127, 148-150, 152-154, 156, 159, 171-172, 176, 186, 188-189, 217, 221, 237, 243, 247, 249-251, 253, 256-257, 260, 275
metonymy, 81, 129
Mnemosyne, 214
monotheism, 34, 37-39, 114, 193
morality, 32, 124-125, 127-128, 143, 255
morphology, 3
Moscovici, Marie, 37, 219
mytho-symbology, 223, 231, 234-235, 237, 240-241, 243, 265, 270
mythology, 139, 163-164, 167, 179, 181, 196-197, 207, 217, 220-223, 225-228, 231-232, 237-240, 242-243, 269

Nachträglichkeit, xx, 4, 49-54, 223; *see also* afterwardsness; *après-coup*
narcissism, ix, 19, 27, 86-87, 115-116, 118-120, 128, 167, 169-170, 176, 178-181, 200, 223, 258-259, 261, 264-265, 270, 282
    narcissistic identification, 27, 116
narrativity, xviii, 4, 77, 119, 206-208, 222-223, 228, 240, 242-243, 245-251
Nazism, xiii, xvii, 140
negation, 25-26, 75, 78-79, 81-82, 84, 94, 172, 188; *see also Verneinung*
neurophysiology, 237
neuroses of defense, xxi, 195-196, 230, 274; *see also* hysteria; null
Newton, Isaac, 75
Nietzsche, Friedrich, 124-127, 129, 141
Nirvana, 60, 171; *see also* death drive
normativity, 104, 152
nourishment, ix, 54, 109-110, 113, 178, 191
Nüchternheit, 124-126, 129, 143
nursling, 175, 192, 214; *see also* Infans

object of belief, 39
objectivity, 13, 16, 45, 127, 136
obsessiveness, 33, 134, 271, 273
occultism, 131-132, 134
oceanic feeling, 44
Oedipus complex, xi, xiv, 34-35, 40, 82, 89, 119-121, 123, 151-152, 162, 175, 198, 207, 220, 223-224, 227-228, 230-231, 235-236, 240, 246, 263
ontogenesis, 52
ontology, x, 136
Oppenheim, David Ernst, 227-228, 230; *see also* folklore
orgasm, 59, 263
orthodoxy, 25, 67, 99, 102
Otherness, xii-xiii, xviii, 67, 76, 87, 89, 92-93, 115, 122, 194-195, 197
overdetermination, 83

pansexualism, 112, 114, 116, 257-258, 260, 273
paradox, 8, 21, 68, 88, 110, 120, 203, 208, 226, 260-261, 281
paranoia, 17, 19-23, 27-28, 38, 46-48, 171, 221, 271
parapraxis, 11, 61, 81, 215; *see also* slip of the tongue
parent, xi, 4, 13, 82, 119-120, 123, 142, 151, 173-174, 184, 191, 208, 222, 225, 240, 266
parental intercourse, 13, 151, 208, 225
paternity, 34, 146
Paulhan, Jean, xv-xvi
penetration, 12, 16, 73, 77, 280-281
penis, 10, 151, 209, 256, 266-267
perception, 3, 23, 37, 44, 63, 76-78, 92, 108, 133-135, 151, 248
perceptual indices, 72, *see also Wahrnehmungszeichen*
percipiens, 24, 45
persecution, xii-xiv, xvii-xviii, 7, 9, 11, 13, 15-21, 23, 25-27, 29, 31, 33, 35, 37, 39, 41, 43-47, 67, 134, 137-138, 175, 275, 280
perversion, xi, 72, 113, 127, 140, 150, 162-163, 165, 184, 188, 192
phallus
    phallic logic, 210, 228
    phallocentrism, 240
Phantasien, 53; *see also* fantasy
phantasmagoria, 210, 217
phantasy, 280; *see also* fantasy
phenomenology, 90-92, 203
phobia, 179, 195-196, 227
phylogenesis, 8, 36, 52, 58, 80, 109, 151, 163, 235
Picasso, Pablo, 266
Pichon, Eduard, 258
pineal gland, 33
Plato, 183-184, 187
Plato's Symposium, 168

Plautus, 177
pleasure principle, ix, 79, 83, 164, 166-168
Poincaré, Henri, 92
Politzer, Georges, 90-91, 94, 242
polysemy, 41, 61, 81, 111
Pontalis, J.-B., vii, xx, 13, 21, 43, 50, 103, 253
Popper, Karl, 75, 148, 150, 152, 220-221
Positivism, 221-222, 236
pragmatism, 88, 185, 189, 281
primal scene, 9-10, 12-14, 16, 47, 52, 225
primal situation of seduction, 119, 122, 195, 214
primary process, 82-86, 116, 160, 170, 194
principle of counteridentity, xv-xvi
propping, x, xx; *see also* leaning-on; *étayage*
Proust, Marcel, 176
pseudoscience, 220-221
psychogenesis, 3, 27, 113
psychopathology, xxi, 22, 93, 111, 243, 245
psychosis, 7, 10, 17, 19-20, 22-24, 29, 38, 107, 120, 184, 247, 281
psychotherapy, 185, 198, 243, 251, 282
Ptolemy, viii, 16, 30-31, 42, 86, 90, 122, 135, 141, 193, 195-196, 200-201, 214, 238, 270, 272, 281-282
puberty, 162-163

race, 211, 228
rape, 141, 211, 271
realism of the unconscious, 60, 62, 65-66, 91, 111
recentering, 8-9, 47, 135
reciprocity, 46, 57, 82, 110-112, 137, 191-192, 226, 232-233, 261, 266, 275
reductionism, 45
regression, 28, 249, 269, 279
reification, 62, 195
reinforcement, 145, 176, 185, 274
relativism, 246, 248, 264
religion, xii, xix, 7, 18, 30-31, 33-42, 45-48, 56, 93, 140, 152-153, 273
renunciation, 99, 121, 125, 188
repetition compulsion, 83, 91, 166, 196
residues, xi, 18, 29, 44, 63, 68-69, 77, 80, 83, 86, 92, 117, 133, 141-142, 173-174, 179, 185, 193, 195, 199, 216, 262-263, 275
resistance, vii, xi, xvi, 5, 83, 91, 110, 242, 255, 258
retranslation, xiv, 55-56, 151, 199, 206, 265
retroactivity
    retroactive fantasy, 52, 54
    retrogression, 51, 56
    retrospectivity, 51, 53-54, 60, 245, 247

return of the repressed, 20-21, 36, 62
Ricoeur, Paul, 203-204, 223, 239, 245
Rimbaud, Arthur, 236
ritual, 33, 58, 178, 228, 230, 240
Roheim, Géza, 210, 228, 255-256
Rückbildung, xv, 211; *see also* deconstruction

Sachvorstellung, 63-64, 195, 238, *see also* thing-presentation
sadism, 27, 127-128, 138, 140-141, 151, 166, 178-179, 259, 261, 264, 272, 277-278; *see also* anal-sadism; masochism; sadomasochism
sadomasochism, 129, 140, 143, 174, 180-181, 271; *see also* masochism; sadism
Saint Augustine, 180
Saint Thomas, 43
Saint-Exupéry, Antoine de, vii
Salomé, Lou Andreas, 268-269
Saussure, Ferdinand de, 66
schizophrenia, 93
Schleiermacher, Friedrich, 213
Schopenhauer, Arthur, 58
Schreber case, xii, xiv, 17-22, 25-29, 38, 40-41, 47, 59, 176, 234
Schwärmerei, 143
scotomization, 126
screen-memory, 71-72; *see also* Deckerinnerung
self-preservative instinct, 18-19, 22, 44, 61, 108-114, 118, 164, 170, 174, 177, 180-181, 191-192, 257-260, 273
semiology, 79, 111, 212
sexes, 3, 209, 228; *see also* gender
sexuality
    genital sexuality, 10, 15, 20, 151, 263, 271
    sexual-presexual, 30
    sexualization, 113, 141, 271-272, 277
signified, 66, 72, 85, 111, 117, 226
signifier, xiii, 40, 64-69, 72-73, 79-82, 85, 89, 92, 94, 111, 115, 117, 137, 141-142, 210, 215-216, 226, 241, 267-268
Sittlichkeit, 127; *see also* normativity
Slotkin, Philip, xiii, xviii, 67, 89
sociology, 37, 61, 95, 256, 269
sodomy, 25; *see also* anality
solipsism, xii, 275
sophism, 135-136
Sophocles, xi, 227, 241
Spinoza, Baruch, 221
Stekel, Wilhelm, 224
Stendhal, 176, 281
Strachey, James, 8, 50, 52-53, 231

strangerness, xxi, 116-118, 134, 137, 142, 144; *see also* étrangèreté
structural model, 107, 116, 126
structuralism, viii, 25, 66, 115
subjectivity, 9, 12, 42-43, 65, 109, 125, 161, 180, 185
sublimation, xviii, 140-141, 201, 220, 253-257, 259, 261-265, 267-277, 279-283
sublime, 254, 274
suckling, 54, 72; *see also* Infans
superego, 17, 84, 107, 115, 120, 125, 127-128, 220, 222, 237, 275
surrealism, xiii, 31
symbiosis, 247
symbolic, 24, 65-66, 93, 118, 186, 207, 224, 226-228, 230, 232-233, 235, 237, 256, 265-266, 270
symbolism, 15, 93, 118-119, 141, 190, 206-212, 224, 226-231, 233-234, 242, 256, 265, 268, 270-273

telepathy, 131-134
temporality, x, 40, 50, 52, 54-56, 76-78, 137, 172, 174, 223, 245, 270
tenderness, 110, 174, 177, 181, 257, 263, 280; *see also* attachment theory
tertium comparationis, 266
Thanatos, 182, 262
theology, xiii, 7, 20, 27, 30, 33, 40-41, 52, 66, 92-93, 95, 99, 112, 141, 230, 235, 245, 257, 259, 272; *see also* God; religion
thing-presentation, 63-64, 66-67, 78, 83, 85-86, *see also* Sachvorstellung
torture, 142, 177
totalization, 268
totemism, 61, 239
Training Analysis, 97, 99-101, 103, 105, 146-147, 155, 157, 186
transference, xvii, 17-18, 36, 43, 45, 73, 87-88, 90, 100, 122, 132-133, 146, 150, 189, 197-198, 200-201, 214, 216, 262, 283; *see also* countertransference
Traum, 53, 127, 233; *see also* dream
trauma, x, 12, 52-53, 71, 192, 200, 278, 281-282
Traumdeutung, 111, 126, 131, 151, 207, 224-227, 229

Übermittlung, 146, *see also* filiation
universality, 20-21, 45, 90, 133, 151, 155, 170, 185, 207, 209-211, 228, 240-241, 269
untranslatable, vii, x, 38, 43, 77
utopia, 33, 196
utterance, 9, 88

Vattimo, Gianni, 203
victim, 165, 271
Viderman, Serge, 223, 246-249

Wahrnehmungszeichen, 72; *see also* perceptual indices
Weltanschauung, 153

werewolf, 179
Winnicott, Donald, 21
Wittgenstein, Ludwig, 220
Wolf Man, 12, 34, 40, 49-50, 52, 179
womb, 9
word-presentation, 63-64, 66, 78; *see also Wortvorstellung*
Wortvorstellung, 63; *see also* word-presentation
wound, 200, 283

Zurückphantasieren, 52, 54; *see also* Jung, Carl; retroactivity

Jeffrey Mehlman (*translator*) is Professor of French Literature and University Professor at Boston University, as well as a literary critic and intellectual historian. He is the author of such books as *A Structural Study of Autobiography; Revolution and Repetition; Legacies: Of Anti-Semitism in France; Walter Benjamin for Children: An Essay on His Radio Years; Emigré New York: French Intellectuals in Wartime Manhattan*; and, most recently, a memoir: *Adventures in the French Trade: Fragments Toward a Life*. Mehlman is also a celebrated translator, with his remarkable 1976 translation of Laplanche's *Life and Death in Psychoanalysis*, and the collection *French Freud: Structural Studies in Psychoanalysis*, playing an important role in the naturalization of recent French thought in English and American discourse. In this volume he returns to the translation of Laplanche, with whom he maintained a friendship until the latter's death in 2012.

Co-editors:

Jonathan House teaches courses on Freud and Laplanche in the Psychoanalytic Studies Program of Columbia University's Institute for Comparative Literature and Society. At Columbia he is also on the faculty of the Department of Psychiatry and of the Center for Psychoanalytic training and Research, where he is a Training and Supervising Analyst. At Laplanche's invitation, he agreed to serve on the Conseil Scientifique of the Fondation Laplanche. In 2010 he founded a publishing house, The Unconscious in Translation, dedicated to translating and promoting the work of Jean Laplanche and other notable French psychoanalysts. He has been Secretary of the American Psychoanalytic Association and remains on its Board of Directors. He currently serves on the Free Association Work Group of the Committee on Conceptual Integration for the International Psychoanalytic Association. He practices psychiatry and psychoanalysis in New York City.

Julie Slotnick studied comparative literature at Columbia University and the Freie Universität Berlin. She is co-editor of The Unconscious in Translation and works as a freelance translator and editor. She lives in New York City.

Book design, Bill Schultz
Copy-editor, Susan Pensak